MW01030296

The Psychology of Death Investigations

Behavioral Analysis for Psychological Autopsy
and Criminal Profiling

The Psychology of Death Investigations

Behavioral Analysis for Psychological Autopsy and Criminal Profiling

Katherine Ramsland, PhD

CRC Press
Taylor & Francis Group
Boca Raton London New York

CRC Press is an imprint of the
Taylor & Francis Group, an **informa** business

CRC Press
Taylor & Francis Group
6000 Broken Sound Parkway NW, Suite 300
Boca Raton, FL 33487-2742

© 2018 by Taylor & Francis Group, LLC
CRC Press is an imprint of Taylor & Francis Group, an Informa business

No claim to original U.S. Government works

Printed on acid-free paper

International Standard Book Number-13: 978-1-138-73529-3 (Hardback)

This book contains information obtained from authentic and highly regarded sources. Reasonable efforts have been made to publish reliable data and information, but the author and publisher cannot assume responsibility for the validity of all materials or the consequences of their use. The authors and publishers have attempted to trace the copyright holders of all material reproduced in this publication and apologize to copyright holders if permission to publish in this form has not been obtained. If any copyright material has not been acknowledged please write and let us know so we may rectify in any future reprint.

Except as permitted under U.S. Copyright Law, no part of this book may be reprinted, reproduced, transmitted, or utilized in any form by any electronic, mechanical, or other means, now known or hereafter invented, including photocopying, microfilming, and recording, or in any information storage or retrieval system, without written permission from the publishers.

For permission to photocopy or use material electronically from this work, please access www.copyright.com (http://www.copyright.com/) or contact the Copyright Clearance Center, Inc. (CCC), 222 Rosewood Drive, Danvers, MA 01923, 978-750-8400. CCC is a not-for-profit organization that provides licenses and registration for a variety of users. For organizations that have been granted a photocopy license by the CCC, a separate system of payment has been arranged.

Trademark Notice: Product or corporate names may be trademarks or registered trademarks, and are used only for identification and explanation without intent to infringe.

Library of Congress Cataloging-in-Publication Data

Names: Ramsland, Katherine M., 1953- author.
Title: The psychology of death investigations : behavioral analysis for psychological autopsy and criminal profiling / by Katherine Ramsland, Ph.D.
Description: Boca Raton : CRC Press, [2018] | Includes bibliographical references and index.
Identifiers: LCCN 2017027689| ISBN 9781138735293 (hardback : alk. paper) | ISBN 9781315186597 (ebook)
Subjects: LCSH: Psychological autopsy. | Criminal investigation. | Criminal behavior, Prediction of. | Forensic psychology.
Classification: LCC RA1137 .R36 2018 | DDC 614/.15--dc23
LC record available at https://lccn.loc.gov/2017027689

Visit the Taylor & Francis Web site at
http://www.taylorandfrancis.com

and the CRC Press Web site at
http://www.crcpress.com

Contents

List of Tables

Acknowledgments

I've written a lot about death and death investigation, and for many years, I've taught a course on the psychology of death investigation. I've consulted on death investigations, been on exhumation teams, and provided expert commentary for TV series and documentaries. I have a number of people to thank for giving me opportunities, teaching me, and supporting me. Among them are Marilyn Bardsley, Traci Brasse, Dana DeVito, John Douglas, Vernon Geberth, Roy Hazelwood, Donna Johnston, Sally Keglovits, Henry Lee, Kim Lionetti, Lee Lofland, Susan Lysek, Zachary Lysek, Carol Nesbitt, Mark Nesbitt, Gregg McCrary, Laura Pettler, Robert Ressler, M. Fredric Rieders, Mark Safarik, Louis Schlesinger, James Starrs, Cyril Wecht, and the suicide researchers who have provided so much material about this difficult subject.

This book grew out of a chance encounter with Mark Listewnik at the CRC book display. I'm grateful for his interest in this subject and his encouragement to write a book. I've wanted to write this one for years.

I wish also (and especially) to thank my agent John Silbersack of Trident Media Group for guiding me through my writing career for decades, with plenty of insight for my forensics work.

Author

Dr. Katherine Ramsland manages and teaches the forensic psychology track at DeSales University, USA. Among her courses at the graduate and undergraduate level is a course on the psychology of death investigation. She is a member of several professional organizations, including the American Academy of Forensic Sciences and the American Association of Suicidology. She has published over 1,000 articles, stories, and reviews, and 60 books, including *The Mind of a Murderer, The Forensic Psychology of Criminal Minds, The Forensic Science of CSI, Inside the Minds of Serial Killers, The Human Predator: A Historical Chronicle of Serial Murder and Forensic Investigation, The Criminal Mind, The Ivy League Killer*, and *The Murder Game*. Her book, *Psychopath*, was a #1 bestseller on the *Wall Street Journal*'s list. With former FBI profiler Gregg McCrary, she has co-authored a book on his cases, *The Unknown Darkness: Profiling the Predators among Us*, with Dr. Henry C. Lee, *The Real Life of a Forensic Scientist*, and with Professor James E. Starrs, *A Voice for the Dead*. She assisted former FBI profiler John Douglas with research on *The Cases That Haunt Us*. Ramsland presents workshops to law enforcement, psychologists, coroners, judges, and attorneys, and has consulted for several television series, including *CSI* and *Bones*. She also writes a regular blog for *Psychology Today* and has appeared on numerous crime documentaries. Her most recent books are *Confession of a Serial Killer: The Untold Story of Dennis Rader, the BTK Killer* and *Forensic Investigation: Methods from Experts*.

Introduction: Victimology and Behavioral Evidence

On a mid-September morning in 2014, a dog walker discovered the corpse of 21-year-old Daniel Whitworth propped up against a wall just inside a cemetery. Clutched in his hand was a scrap of paper—a suicide note. He seemed to have been despondent over the death of Gabriel Kovari, 22, whose body had turned up in the same cemetery 3 weeks earlier. Both had died from an overdose of the date-rape sedative, gamma hydroxybutyrate (GHB). In the note, Whitworth admitted that he had injected Kovari during sex to enhance their experience. The death had been an accident, but Whitworth was so overcome that he saw suicide as the only option. The note included an odd addendum: "BTW please do not blame the guy I was with last night, we only had sex and then I left, he knows nothing of what I have done."

The police accepted the note at face value. They decided that Whitworth had killed Kovari. Two cases closed. No further investigation. They did not check on Whitworth's movements prior to death, his susceptibility to depression, who else had crossed his path, the identity of the "guy" mentioned in the postscript, or whether Whitworth even knew Kovari. There was no need; to the investigators, it was open and shut.

Except that these incidents were not as obvious as they seemed. Police are not trained in the signals of false notes used to stage a scene as a suicide. There is little research on this topic, and what research there is suggests that law enforcement gets it wrong nearly 50% of the time, in part because like many people untrained in suicide evaluation, they accept cultural myths. Most death investigators who find a note assume that a death incident is what it looks like: a suicide. This book offers an approach that assists investigators to examine such assumptions, learn a framework for victimology, learn about staging, and recognize the differences between genuine and nongenuine suicide notes.

A key aspect of behavioral evidence is its ambiguity—its potential to be interpreted in more than one way. A piece of writing might be viewed as a suicide note when found near a body or as a piece of evidence in a homicide, if evidence points that way. It might even be unassociated with the death. This is one of the frustrating aspects of interpreting behavioral evidence. It is not as exact as matching DNA, fingerprints, or blood from a scene to a specific source. The interpretation of behavior is based on context, facts about the victim, and probability analysis, that is, what is the *likelihood* that this incident is a suicide? Probability analysis is about making calculations about uncertainty based on representative behavior or on what is known. When making these calculations, especially with ambiguous death investigations, one asks how great is the margin of error? What can be done to improve accuracy? Which factors might shift the interpretation, and how much weight do such factors have compared to others? That is, if a person was depressed over the breakup of a relationship, this could count heavily in a suicidal impulse, but if the breakup was 3 years ago, it would have less weight than if it was the day before. These calculations, which often involve multiple factors, are not necessarily easy to make.

Interpreting some types of behavior relies on clinical or experimental research. This means that investigators who deal with behavioral evidence must know the most recent findings. However, if they feel pressured to close a case quickly, they are more likely to accept assumptions based on shortcuts than to sort through documents or consult mental health experts. This leads to errors.

This book gathers behavioral research for death investigators into a comprehensive, accessible source. It describes the two most prominent forms of death investigation that rely on behavioral evidence—psychological autopsies and criminal profiling—and discusses their development, methods, current status, and contribution to incident reconstruction. Tips are provided for fieldwork and cases are offered for analysis of methods and mistakes, such as the one described in the opening case.

In fact, Whitworth had not killed Kovari, accidentally or otherwise. Whitworth had also not committed suicide. Instead, Stephen Port had met both victims, injected them with GHB, and killed both, posing them similarly in the cemetery and writing the staged suicide note. He nearly got away with it except that he was seen on CCTV footage with another "accidental overdose" victim and arrested. His residence was near the cemetery, so he was investigated for both deaths. Solid links were established between Port and the victims. Port had also killed another man in 2014, whose body he had left in the public entrance to his apartment building. In 2016, Port was convicted of all four murders, along with the sexual assaults of seven other men (*Guardian* staff, 2016).

A more thorough investigation might have raised some red flags. The note was not Whitworth's handwriting. He was not despondent. He was found propped up in nearly the same posture and place as another dead man, with whom he had no connection. In addition, one study shows that notes written to stage a homicide as a suicide often mention the perpetrator in a favorable light! At the very least, the investigation of a death incident should include an analysis of victim behavior and mental state.

All death investigations involve some degree of teamwork, with the likelihood of using experts for more sophisticated areas, such as the analysis of bones, blood spatter patterns, bullet trajectory, and mental state. Best practice requires that investigators learn about items that require specialized knowledge and acquire a list of experts to consult. This list should include a behavioral expert. In turn, behavioral experts who consult for investigations must learn what a forensic investigation involves.

I have been on several death investigation teams and, in order to effectively coordinate my analysis with the other team members, I learned quite a lot about each specialization used. For example, the search for a missing girl, believed to have been killed by her uncle two decades earlier and buried in a cotton field, required that I work with dog handlers, geologists, anthropologists, biologists, criminalists, and law enforcement. First, we evaluated the potential for deception in the uncle's confession that pinpointed the search area (the likelihood was high) and the circumstances of the girl's disappearance (e.g., her state of mind), both of which drew on knowledge from psychological research. Local law enforcement resisted our team's efforts; we used research to support arguments and outline our approach. Psychological finesse was handy for dealing with relatives of the missing girl, and mediation was needed at times for the team to work effectively. The list goes on. There were quite a few areas in which psychological expertise beyond behavioral profiling assisted the process. Knowledge of the other areas of expertise was instrumental in effective behavioral analysis.

DEATH INVESTIGATIONS

A death scene is a location where a death incident has occurred. If not obvious, it should be treated as a potential homicide. Even if seemingly obvious or expected, initial observations should be careful: some scenes are staged and some encompass more than what they seem. For example, expected deaths in hospitals are sometimes hastened by murder (Ramsland, 2007).

The first responding officers should note the victim's position and record a description of visible wounds or injuries (Adcock & Chancellor, 2013). Victims should be photographed or videotaped. These officers should also record any distinct odors, lighting conditions, temperature, and other potentially relevant factors that could dissipate quickly. Besides learning to be good observers, investigators must know how to coordinate resources and look for scientific experts, if needed, with an eye to protecting and documenting chain of custody for later admissibility in court. As cases develop, the totality of the evidence is essential for accurate reconstruction.

Law enforcement will look for evidence left by the perpetrator, as well as potentially transferred to the perpetrator (Locard's exchange principle). Officers must avoid contamination and restrict scene access to only the principal personnel. Crime scene processors must wear specific types of protective gear, such as shoe coverings and gloves (Gilbet, 2010).

If a suspect is present, and probable cause can be established about culpability, officers can make an arrest. Any and all suspects are detained. Under the direction of a detective, officers obtain names of witnesses for questioning. The principle death investigator, a medical examiner, or a coroner as dictated by the jurisdiction, will make decisions about the body.

Outside death scenes involve taphonomic observations, especially if the decedent is under debris, such as dirt or fallen leaves. The discipline of taphonomy clarifies the complex factors involved in the postmortem history of physical remains. It is concerned with the death event, decomposition rate, weather factors, exposure of remains, and collection of potential evidence. Decedents contribute their own individual features to all calculations, for example, weight, type, and amount of clothing worn, quality of nutrition, presence of illness or substance use, and properties of their bones (Bass & Jefferson, 2003; Bass & Meadows, 1990; Ferllini, 2002/2012; Ubelaker, 1997).

Among other specialists might be anthropologists for bone examination, odontologists for teeth, entomologists for insect activity, ballistics experts for gunshot wounds and matching a weapon to a spent casing, geologists for soil sample analysis, and botanists to analyze plant matter. Also, in the lab might be serologists, toxicologists, biologists, and chemists.

Psychological experts tend to participate as consultants in either a psychological autopsy or criminal profiling (Ramsland, 2010). The first method focuses on state of mind to try to support or negate a finding of suicide when this manner of death is suspected but unclear. The second approach attempts to narrow the pool of suspects in a probable homicide or series of homicides and make predictions about future offender activity. (Profiling is also used in other types of serial crimes, such as arson, burglary, and rape, but this book focuses on death investigation.) Both approaches attempt to better understand a victim's state of mind and antemortem activities to resolve open questions relevant to decision-making and developing leads. Both also involve the collection of victim details from a variety of sources, although a psychological autopsy is generally more penetrating and diagnostic. Psychological autopsy and profiling overlap to some extent, especially for victimology, but each approach should be studied as its own investigative tool.

Complete victim backgrounds identify state of mind, risk factors for suicide or homicide, and leads from personal circumstances for more information. Interview protocols assist with collecting behavioral evidence for mapping timelines of a victim's known movements up until the point of death. Strategic and structured interviewing of all relevant parties, along with careful analysis of records, is essential to maximize time and resource allocation.

All death investigators, regardless of what purpose they serve on the team, should follow protocols and resist the tendency to make quick decisions prior to full evidence gathering and analysis. They should move nothing and touch nothing without gloves and should avoid placing their kits on scene-related surfaces. Above all, everything should be documented according to agency protocols. The lead investigators determine whether potential evidentiary items should be collected, the manner of this collection, and the handling of evidence. (E.g., they know to avoid using plastic bags for wet items. Rain-soaked cigarettes from one scene placed into a plastic bag ruined DNA analysis, due to mold.) Crime scene technicians or designated photographers might take hundreds of photos or might use the 360-degree scanners that stitch together a wide scene into a comprehensive overview (Adcock & Chancellor, 2013; Gilbet, 2010). The guiding hypothesis, used to organize evidence and generate leads, must account not only for all of the evidence but also be sufficiently flexible to accommodate new evidence or new angles on prior evidence. As mentioned above, context affects interpretation. Any item can appear to support one interpretation, but with new facts it now supports another one (Gilbet, 2010).

Behavioral evidence interpretation is fundamental for accurate incident reconstruction, but it can be easy to misinterpret. In addition, human motivation, while often predictable, can also be highly mysterious, leaving us with unanswered questions, as in the following case.

Sixteen-year-old Annie McCann went missing from her home in Alexandria, Virginia, on Halloween 2008, while her parents were away visiting her brother. She apparently took their white Volvo, along with $1,000, her favorite clothes, and a box of Cheerios. She left a note suggesting that she'd been depressed and needed to get away from home and start over. She had contemplated suicide, the note said, but had decided instead to run away: "This morning I was going to kill myself. But I realized I can start over instead. I don't want help and I'm no longer scared. If you really love me you'll let me go … Please don't go looking for me" (Hermann, 2012).

McCann's body was found 2 days later behind a dumpster on Lombard Street in Baltimore, Maryland. There were no obvious signs of trauma. The autopsy report determined that she had ingested alcohol and a toxic dose of lidocaine. In the trash near her body was a 5-ounce bottle of Bactine, which she had used at home to treat her recently pierced ears. McCann's DNA was found on the bottle but not her fingerprints. Two other notes that she had written had shown suicidal thoughts, depression, and anorexia.

An investigation turned up information that two young men had placed McCann's body behind the dumpster after they found her dead inside her car. They wanted to take it for a joyride. At first, they were implicated in her death, but eventually it seemed likely that they had found McCann dead in the car, as they claimed. Evidence showed that she had died in the car's back seat. The Baltimore police closed the case as a suicide.

McCann's parents, Daniel and Mary Jane, did not accept this decision. They insisted that the investigation had been superficial. They hired a team of independent investigators, including former New York City pathologist Michael Baden. The team found reason to ask questions about certain items that the police had considered but dismissed. For example, one report stated that just before her death, McCann was seen going into a coffee shop with a dark-haired woman. No one had learned this woman's identity. Perhaps she had spotted an easy mark and lured McCann into a trap. Reportedly, a white man with a goatee was seen abandoning McCann's car before the joyriders discovered it.

Behaviorally speaking, although McCann had thought about suicide and her notes were rambling, the most recent note indicated a change of heart. "Please let me be free," it concluded. "Yes, I'm a 16 year old, almost 17, who knows nothing about the world. But just give me this chance to have my own experience. I love you, and I will be careful." She had taken a lot of money and her favorite clothes. She was a good student, with a good relationship with her parents and brother. No pathologist who was questioned had ever seen suicide by lidocaine before, so its rarity should have been a concern.

One of the joyriders, Daniel Kinlaw, had been convicted of killing his girlfriend 3 years earlier and taking her car. The circumstances seemed too coincidental to believe that he and his friend had just happened upon McCann's car and had callously dumped her body. The McCanns interviewed Kinlaw in prison and decided he had no new information. Yet they remain certain that their daughter was murdered. The homicide detectives are just as certain that they covered every angle and that the girl committed suicide. The stolen car, they said, is just an odd twist.

In this case, little was done to illuminate the victim's inner life. Police officers are generally trained in just the basics of suicide analysis. They generally learn on the job. To examine a few notes in which McCann mentioned suicide is not sufficient support for determining the manner of death as suicide, especially given the odd circumstances. Yet it is also true that families can have a lot at stake in denying and defying a finding of suicide. Since the McCanns are Catholic, religious prohibition could be a strong factor. In addition, a child's suicide often makes parents feel as if they had failed when most needed: They did not see the signs and get her help. Such a realization can be debilitating, throwing psychological weight onto a homicide narrative.

Although there might be no more evidence to find, cases like Annie McCann's demonstrate that a careful psychological investigation can help to make equivocal deaths less ambiguous. At the very least, it can reassure surviving families that all aspects were covered.

****

This book addresses two forms of behavioral interpretations for death investigators. The first part covers psychological autopsy, explaining the history, methods, key developers, and attempts to standardize its practice. This discipline was built on the foundational work that psychologists Edwin Shneidman and Norman Faberow established during the 1960s. From "mode conferences" to suicide notes to suicidology, they left an impressive legacy that provides solid tools for investigators today. The primary goal is to learn as much as possible about a decedent's state of mind via biographical collection and analysis, and to use research to support manner of death conclusions (Shneidman, 1981).

The second approach, criminal profiling, is more renowned and more diverse in its methods and practitioners. Most famous is the FBI's methodology from the Behavioral Science Unit (now Behavioral Analysis Unit), thanks in part to books produced by the first agent profilers and the 1991 film *The Silence of the Lambs* (Ramsland, 2010). Profiling has a longer history, with the involvement of psychologists and psychiatrists from different countries, and even of detectives with no formal training. Although profiling has been admitted more readily into court than psychological autopsies, it has also triggered several appeals and reversals, for reasons similar to why courts resist psychological autopsy.

As mentioned above, both approaches focus on victimology and both rely on behavioral interpretation and probability analysis. Efforts are ongoing to improve the methods and research in order to reduce the margins of error and make procedures more valid and reliable.

This book poses challenges to investigators. It relies on case material to demonstrate methods and issues. The goal is to teach investigators the importance of, and best approach to, behavioral interpretation for death-involved incident analysis.

REFERENCES

Adcock, J. M., & Chancellor, A. S. (2013). *Death investigations.* Burlington, MA: Jones & Bartlett.

Bass, B., & Jefferson, J. (2003). *Death's acre: Inside the legendary forensic lab the Body Farm, where the dead do tell tales.* New York: Putnam.

Bass, B., & Meadows, L. (1990). Time since death and decomposition of the human body: Variables and observations in case and experimental studies. *Journal of Forensic Sciences, 35*, 103–111.

Ferllini, R. (2002/2012). *Silent witness: How forensic anthropology is used to solve the world's toughest crimes.* 2nd edition. Buffalo, NY: Firefly.

Gilbet, J. N. (2010). *Criminal investigation.* 8th edition. Upper Saddle River, NJ: Prentice Hall.

Guardian Staff. (2016, October 6). Stephen Port trial: Police took fake suicide note at face value. *The Guardian.* Retrieved from https://www.theguardian.com/uk-news/2016/oct/06/stephen-port-trial-police-took-fake-suicide-note-daniel-whitworth-face-value-court-told

Hermann, P. (2009, March 2). Too many unanswered questions remain for dead Va. girl's parents. *The Baltimore Sun.* Retrieved from http://www.baltimoresun.com/news/maryland/baltimore-city/bal-mccann0302-story.html

Ramsland, K. (2007). *Inside the minds of healthcare serial killers: Why they kill.* Westport, CT: Praeger.

Ramsland, K. (2010). *The forensic psychology of criminal minds.* New York: Berkley.

Shneidman, E. S. (1981). The psychological autopsy. *Suicide and Life Threatening Behavior, 11*(4), 325–340.

Ubelaker, D. H. (1997). Taphonomic applications in forensic anthropology. In W. D. Haglund & M. H. Sorg (Eds.), *Forensic taphonomy: The postmortem fate of human remains* (pp. 77–90). Boca Raton, FL: CRC Press.

Psychological Autopsies

CHAPTER 1

History and Concepts

The approach to death investigation that includes the most concentrated collection and analysis of psychological material about a decedent is a psychological autopsy. A group of suicide counselors in Los Angeles, California, formalized this practice. Like a physical postmortem autopsy, it involves "opening" the person to examine his or her life and thought processes for evidence that supports a specific manner of death. Most often, but not always, this involves seeking support for a determination of suicide.

Clinical experience adds important dimensions for which most law enforcement investigators have not been trained. Psychological insight can assist with forming the type of questions needed for the decedent's associates and an in-depth analysis of motives. Clinical awareness also reminds investigators to watch for behavioral signals in people who might have staged or altered a death scene. Hence, death investigations can benefit from including a mental health expert. Mistakes regarding state of mind and motive, such as labeling a homicide a suicide or vice versa, can have serious repercussions for decedents' families and for the justice system.

SUICIDAL INTENT

During the development of a hypothesis for death event reconstruction, the focus is on cause and manner of death. The cause is the condition that resulted in the death, such as a disease or injury. *Manner* is a category determined by the coroner or medical examiner. The NASH classification system for death investigators offers four options: natural, accident, suicide, or homicide (Biffl, 1996). A decedent in a crashed car, for example, might have had a heart attack (natural), hit a slick area and crashed (accident), intentionally crashed (suicide), or been placed there by a killer in an attempt to stage the death as one of the other three (homicide). Those deaths that are difficult to categorize are labeled

undetermined or *undetermined—pending*, meaning that further immediate investigation might change its status.

For undetermined death events, more information must be gathered and this usually involves collecting details about the decedent.
Whenever state of mind becomes an issue, the information will be
psychological (Curphey, 1961; Shneidman & Faberow, 1993), especially for possible suicides. Below is an example of a death that was
initially placed in one category but with more information shifted to
a different one.

In 2005, Greg Maurek reported his brother's suicide. Peter, he said,
had come to his house in a foul mood, intoxicated, and had shot himself
in the head. Detectives went to Greg's home. He was sitting outside, seemingly undisturbed. His casual attitude about his brother's death looked
suspicious, as did the fact that Greg had removed his T-shirt, which bore
blood spatter. Inside, around the body, police discovered more items that
alerted them to a scenario that contradicted Greg's narrative.

Peter was dead from a gunshot to his head. On a wall behind him,
investigators saw spots of blood and brain matter. Spatter was present on
the ceiling and on a chair. The shot had been to the back of Peter's head
with a 0.50-caliber semi-automatic handgun, which lay on a desk 6 feet
from the body. The safety catch was engaged. When officers pointed this
out, Greg said he had not touched the gun. He did not like guns. Peter
had brought it. Yet a man who has just killed himself cannot engage the
catch. In addition, the shot was to the back of the head, a location that
few people would choose.

Greg stated that he was not surprised that Peter had decided to kill
himself. He had often talked about doing it. Greg pointed to the chair
where he was sitting, 10 feet from Peter, when Peter shot himself. Blood
had spattered onto him, he said. He showed them his T-shirt. Despite
his protests that he had done nothing and touched nothing, the officers
arrested him.

Approaching trial, experts for each side on blood spatter pattern reconstructed the incident, but their interpretations dramatically
diverged. The prosecution's experts said that the blood on Greg's T-shirt
indicated that during the shot, Greg had been 2 feet away. They also
showed how difficult it would be to shoot oneself from behind, and the
lack of blood spatter on Peter's hand strongly suggested that he had not
held the gun. Their reconstruction seemed definitive.

However, there was a big hole. They had left out Peter's background.
Greg's defense team included a psychologist who had performed a psychological autopsy. He had queried Peter's friends and relatives about
Peter's state of mind. Peter had been a prime candidate for suicide; he
had a number of behaviors referred to as *suicide markers*. He regularly
abused alcohol and had been depressed for a while. In the past, Peter and

Greg's older brother had fatally shot himself in the back of the head, and Peter had admired his courage. He even thought that this method was the best approach. Recently their parents had died, as had Peter's former girlfriend, which had greatly affected him. In addition, Greg lacked a motive to kill Peter.

A blood spatter analyst for the defense demonstrated how the blood patterns in the room could support Greg's version. A "shadow" pattern on the chair showed that someone had sat there when blood flew across the room. Only Greg was in the house, so it had to be him. Peter could have held the gun in a manner different than what the prosecutor's expert showed, making a self-inflicted wound less awkward. The wound analysis precluded the possibility that Greg had shot him from 10 feet away. As for the safety catch, a reconstruction showed that the gun might have hit an item when it bounced on the desk during recoil, knocking it into place. This was not possible to replicate. The psychological evidence persuaded jurors of reasonable doubt. They acquitted Greg ("Maurek found not guilty," 2008).

In this case, investigators had formed a hypothesis quickly and did not consider alternative scenarios. Quite a few factors supported Peter's suicidal state of mind. Psychological autopsies that deliver this type of information can often change the track of an investigation.

IN THE BEGINNING

The formalization of psychological autopsy began in Los Angeles, California, during the late 1950s. The LA County chief medical examiner, Theodore Curphey, had an abundance of drug-related deaths (Curphey, 1961). Often, Curphey and his staff could not distinguish suicides from accidental overdoses. Some might even be homicides. He knew the directors at the Los Angeles Suicide Prevention Center (SPC)—the country's first such clinic. This place had opened in 1958 on the grounds of the Los Angeles County General Hospital, with the mission of learning about suicidal people for the purpose of improved treatment and prevention (Shneidman, Faberow, & Litman, 1961b).

Curphey had once asked Edwin Shneidman, one of the SPC directors and a suicide counselor, to write condolence letters to the relatives of two suicide victims. Shneidman had looked through the records to gain a better sense of the victims. He had discovered a collection of more than 700 suicide notes. Believing that these notes, if matchable to records, would offer fertile data for research about suicidal intent, he had asked to use them. Curphey granted permission. With his SPC colleagues Norman Faberow and Robert Litman, Shneidman acquired grants and set up several studies (Shneidman & Faberow, 1957b).

The SPC had two project directors, a psychiatric director, two clinical psychologists, two psychiatric social workers, a biometrician, and a psychological technician. As experts on suicide, they were likely aware of the 6-year study, published in 1930, that analyzed 93 suicidal deaths among New York City police officers. However, little had been done to set up comparative studies between suicidal and nonsuicidal individuals. In addition, distinctions remained vague among those who were intent on self-annihilation and those who would be labeled *attempters* but not *completers*.

At the time, the predominant social attitude toward suicide was one of condemnation: the act was considered rude and cowardly, showing contempt for society and for God. This attitude filtered into the professional world as well, which had discouraged research on the topic. Shneidman and his colleagues knew that research had to be done if work like theirs was going to move forward. Whenever SPC patients were referred to other agencies or a hospital, the staff followed up to evaluate the effectiveness of various treatment methods. With positive results, they hoped to demonstrate to other professionals how important it was to learn about this subject.

For one project, Shneidman and Faberow (1957a) obtained the names of adult male suicide victims from a 10-year time frame in Los Angeles. Although this limited their findings to a specific geographical area and only to adult males, it was a start for what they hoped would become a much more extensive subject group. They collected case histories of 32 adult male completers ranging in age from 20 to 69 and the same number of men whom they labeled as *attempters, threateners*, and *nonsuicidal*. For analysis, they applied more than 100 factors that ranged from social to familial to psychological. For these subjects, they collected background and diagnostic information along with scores from several standardized tests and personality assessments. In the three categories that contained living subjects, participants were invited to write narratives about themselves, especially as it related to suicide.

Shneidman and Faberow also selected 33 suicide notes and collected as much information as they could on each decedent. To make comparisons between authentic notes and items that might be fabricated, such as in staged scenes, they sought volunteer subjects who had similar characteristics to the selected note-writers. The subjects were to contemplate suicide and write a hypothetical or "simulated" note. The analysts found a number of differences in specific types of thought patterns, which laid an important foundation for future research (discussed in detail in Chapter 3).

In 1957, Shneidman and Faberow edited and published a groundbreaking anthology, *Clues to Suicide*, which included their research on suicide notes. It also included discussions on the logic of suicide, suicide and religion, suicide and law, treatment, suicidal behavior in children, and suicide among the elderly. The final paper in this anthology offered suggestions for prevention.

The primary goal of the SPC clinicians was to save lives (Shneidman & Faberow, 1961). They hoped to affiliate with other public service agencies to form and test hypotheses about suicide for treatment and for research purposes. They had immediate goals for suicide prevention and long-range goals for greater comprehension. They believed that the majority of suicides displayed a "recognizable presuicidal phase" (p. 7), which could be different for attempters versus completers. The clinicians wanted to know the percentage of people in each group who would seek assistance, have long-term depression, threaten suicide, make serious attempts, and indulge in any type of substance abuse. How many were in current relationships, were employed, or had served in the military? What age group had the most successful suicides? What was the most common suicide method? Were methods distinct for different age groups or ethnicities? How did males versus females approach suicide?

Acquiring accurate data was a challenge, but the SPC associates surveyed many local physicians, gathered hospital charts for suicidal patients, and queried the coroner's staff about their suicide cases. They also contacted relatives and associates of the decedents, when possible, and added data to the charts for their four distinct groups: completers, attempters, threateners, and nonsuicidal (Shneidman & Faberow, 1961). With these distinctions and with increasingly more potential participants, they set up more research projects.

The clinicians not only developed a rapid response protocol for emergency cases, but they also discovered how difficult it was to distinguish potentially suicidal people from case details, unless they had certain "red flag" mental illnesses, such as paranoid schizophrenia or chronic reactive depression. The researchers did learn that nearly three out of four men who had committed suicide had attempted or threatened it in the past. Half who had been patients had been recently discharged from a hospital with a positive diagnosis. Within 3 months, they were dead. The staff noted this counterintuitive fact. On psychological assessments, individuals who had threatened but not attempted suicide showed more guilt, were more agitated, and showed a higher level of aggression to test items than attempters (Shneidman et al., 1961a).

With their focused immersion in the subject, the SPC clinicians were ready and willing to assist Curphey. They set up panels for evaluating cases that he sent their way. Shneidman coined the term "psychological autopsy" for the method they devised (Shneidman & Faberow, 1961). As the practice formalized, the death team meetings were called "mode conferences," because manner of death at this time was referred to as "mode." Each conference included the coroner, psychologists, social workers, investigators, a forensic pathologist, possibly a physician, and any other area of expertise that seemed to be required for an accurate evaluation of the death event. Team members not only focused on the case at hand but also considered its potential value for research.

Curphey (1961) appreciated the work of this "Suicide Team." The LA Coroner's Office had recently received a mandate to use more science in death investigations. Curphey realized that, just as toxicologists might sometimes need to consult a specialist for some matters, so also the medicolegal team needed a behavioral specialist for the assessment of motive and intent. "Intention and motivation are neither chemical nor tissue matters; they are psychological in nature. This is where the social scientists can assist the coroner's office" (p. 112). He described the type of information they gathered as primarily psychiatric and psychological, which included communications, self-attitudes, and "detective information" that came up during their analysis. Since they knew best what to look for, they might see more meaning in certain acts than a detective did. Different training informed different perspectives.

In one case, the female decedent's relatives and associates insisted she had not committed suicide, although an autopsy had found a fatal overdose of prescription drugs in her system. The family had hired an attorney to challenge the official ruling. When the Suicide Team investigated, the support for suicide was confirmed: she had been severely depressed, she had a chronic drinking problem, had been under psychiatric care, and had prescriptions for several medications. Two days prior to her death, a psychiatrist had been so concerned that he had recommended hospitalization. The family was aware of all of these markers for suicide yet had resisted their meaning. They believed in religious taboos and were concerned about her soul.

Curphey also explained why the correct mode of death finding is important. Not only does it matter to the surviving friends and family but it can also have religious and financial repercussions. In addition, the correct procedure will make the statistics more accurate and will help to eliminate "fictitious accuracy" that can result from investigators' erroneous impression that they know all the details and that they have interpreted them correctly. Curphey was aware that in many jurisdictions there was no attempt to use a scientific method, so death investigations were often superficial. He noted that an additional benefit to using social scientists for such teams was compassionate therapy for decedents' families.

The primary job of the Suicide Team was to try to establish that a questionable death was a suicide. In the process, the clinicians realized how much misunderstanding surrounded the act of suicide, so they developed ways to inform death investigators and the community about the realities. Some of the most common myths they identified at the time are in Table 1.1 (Curphey, 1961, p. 13–14).

TABLE 1.1   Myths about Suicide
- People who talk about suicide won't do it.
- Suicide happens without warning.
- Mood improvement means the crisis is over.
- Suicide is a single disease.
- Suicidal people are insane.

There is more to suicide than mental illness, Shneidman wrote. "In a sense, self-destruction reflects the relationship of the individual to his community and his civilization" (p. 16). He was keenly interested in broader sociological implications.

The initial procedure adopted a pattern that began with police reports. The SPC would send one of its own investigators to the scene to observe from a different perspective. Only if both reports concurred that an autopsy was needed would the medical examiner perform it. This medical report added more data. Whenever a suicide note was present, the staff engaged a handwriting expert to affirm that the decedent had written it. For equivocal cases, the SPC staff organized a full mode conference. Their discussions involved brainstorming, as well as checking one another's interpretations. They devised structured interviews to use with the decedent's acquaintances or relatives, with special attention on known suicide markers or risk factors. From this information, they reconstructed a narrative. The type of information they used derived from four categories: psychological data, decedent communications, life history, and nonpsychiatric data.

For another research project, Shneidman and Faberow (1961) interviewed a unique group of suicide survivors who had made a serious attempt but had failed. The researchers learned that attempters could range from those looking for attention to those who seriously wished to die. It was rare to find a case that had no shred of evidence for suicidal intent. Within the four categories, the SPC directors identified fifteen distinct items for evaluation, with a flexibly vague sixteenth item for "special features" that might arise that were not covered by one of the other 15 (Leenaars, 2010). These are listed in Table 1.2.

Shneidman et al. (1961) classified suicidal acts as intentional (premeditated), subintentional, and unintentional. That is, some suicidal people know what they want to do (intentional). Some desire to die but suppress it, setting themselves up for fatal danger in a subconscious way (subintentional). Some recklessly engage in known dangerous activities but do not necessarily want to end their lives (unintentional). The researchers also developed a "scale of lethality" to identify four levels of intensity or probability. They examined the decedent's knowledge about the suicidal method used and measured evidence of intent according to the decedent's

TABLE 1.2   The 15 SPC Categories for Psychological Autopsy

1. Identifying factors (name, age, address, occupation, marital status, and religion)
2. Death details (cause and mechanism)
3. Family history
4. Family death history, including illness types and suicides
5. Personality and lifestyle
6. Patterns of reactions to stress and periods of disequilibrium
7. Recent pressures, tensions, or anticipation of trouble
8. Role of substances in life or death
9. Interpersonal relationships, including physicians
10. Fantasies, premonitions, dreams, and fears related to death or suicide
11. Recent changes, such as eating habits, sleep issues, routines, and sexual patterns
12. Information about successes and positive items
13. Assessment of intention
14. Lethality rating
15. Reaction of informants to the death

Note: SPC, Los Angeles Suicide Prevention Center.

degree of planning and participation. A remote location, a suicide note, and the victim's own gun would get a higher score than someone with a history of nonlethal attempts taking pills and phoning a friend for help. From this research, they learned that 62% of suicidal people had communicated their intent to at least one other person. Even when they did not, they often showed it in their behavior.

One case the clinicians examined involved a man who had played Russian roulette dozens of times. According to his widow, he believed he had a failsafe method: he knew what the gun looked like with the bullet near the chamber, so there was no possibility that he would actually kill himself. When he did finally die by this method, it turned out that he had used a gun with which he was unfamiliar. Apparently, he had assumed that it would have the same appearance as the gun he had handled many times before. He was wrong. With no past suicidal ideation, depression, or threats, this death was considered an accident, but it was also an example of an unintentional suicide.

Shneidman proposed that mental health experts who dealt with suicidal people should fully explore the method, motive, and degree of desire to die. They should note if the death occurred on or near a special anniversary, for example, was due to a debilitating illness, or showed complaints that attested to a "psychache," which he defined as a pain too great to bear (Shneidman & Faberow, 1961).

The SPC staff were determined to bring scientific standards to the research on suicide and to persist in using their research as the foundation for a formal and multifaceted discipline. In 1961, they set up the National Advisory Board of the Suicide Prevention Foundation. This gained attention and respect. Soon, they designated personnel for the Center for the Scientific Study of Suicide. They published another edited anthology, *The Cry for Help* (Shneidman & Faberow, 1961). It was twice as long as their first anthology. Using Edvard Munch's *The Scream* as their frontispiece, they included an article on the SPC, statistical comparisons of attempters and completers, emergency evaluation methods, issues with psychiatric populations, a sample investigation, a case history, and a collection of diverse points of view from prominent psychodynamic theorists about suicide. It would serve as a worthy textbook for teaching about suicide in greater detail.

They learned that, no matter how "gentle" their approach was to questioning relatives, postsuicide, information did not necessarily come easily. Some people did not trust them, some did not want to talk about the incident, and some had reason to withhold facts related to a possible suicide. If there was an insurance payout at stake, for example, they were unlikely to be open about an act that would erase the money. This was also true for religious concerns about suicide and the afterlife.

In a few cases, the SPC team found that investigators had made a hasty judgment call and had lost interest too soon. One involved a fully clothed man who had drowned in a hotel bathtub. He had serious financial problems, was suspected of extensive fraud, and had made enemies. This man had informed his wife about an appointment he had in that hotel room. The police wrote it off as a suicide, deciding that he had felt guilty and afraid of recriminations. The Suicide Team believed that most people would not put themselves into a tub fully clothed, so there was reason to investigate this case as a homicide.

From his clinical cases, Litman (1957) focused on the "suicidal crisis," which was a temporary state. He used case histories that had suicidal depression as the presenting complaint, which had complicated psychotherapeutic progress. With help, he found, they can avoid killing themselves and will eventually move on and resume their lives. He thought that quite a few suicidal people experienced this transient phase, although to them at the time it had felt permanent. Litman's success with such patients gave hope to other mental health experts.

As the SPC team showed their worth, Curphey's office established a "case of the week" conference. Several case analyses were later published in order to show other clinicians how to work with police to perform a psychological autopsy. (Unfortunately, few police departments followed Curphey's example.)

The psychological autopsy, they stated, focuses on aspects of personality and circumstances specifically associated with suicide. To identify these factors and reconstruct a life history, they examined recent

TABLE 1.3   Six Types of Suicide Evaluations

- A death recommended for certification as a suicide
- A death that seemed suicidal but was recommended for a finding of accidental
- A probable suicide
- A death that could be a suicide or accident and was thereby undetermined
- A death recommended for homicide investigation
- A death recommended for certification as natural
- An unequivocal suicide in which "therapeutic functions for the bereaved were served"

---

incidents, expressions, illnesses, habits, and changes. As facts were clarified, the cases fell into one of six categories, seen in Table 1.3 (p. 120).

The conferences were progressing well until August 5, 1962, when Curphey presented the team with a case that would place their work into the public eye. World-famous actress Marilyn Monroe had been found dead. It looked like a suicide, but there were suspicious factors. It was a perfect case for the Suicide Team.

TEST CASE

Monroe was just 36, in the midst of an impressive film career. Yet she also sabotaged her success with demands, mood swings, excessive spending, neediness, and unreliability. The first responders to her home had found empty bottles of prescription drugs, which signaled the need for an autopsy with a toxicology report. They also noticed that Monroe's nurse/housekeeper, Mrs. Murray, had called Monroe's psychiatrist, Dr. Ralph Greenson, who had arrived first, followed by her physician. Another half hour had passed before anyone had called the police. In addition, Monroe's nude body appeared to have been posed, rather lying than in a convulsed position typical of a drug overdose. They also thought it was odd that Mrs. Murray was doing laundry. The appearance was that of an altered death scene, if not outright staged, and a potential cover-up. It would not take long before plots were hatched over Monroe being the victim of a homicide, specifically a politically entangled homicide with significant international ramifications.

Curphey assigned the autopsy to Deputy Medical Examiner Thomas Noguchi, who had studied the latest scientific methods. Noguchi was acutely aware that the world was watching (Noguchi & DiMona, 1983). He wanted no errors, although he could not control all areas of the lab. As he inventoried the pill bottles gathered from the scene and evaluated the medications found inside the dead actress, he speculated that Monroe had suffered acute barbiturate poisoning—an overdose of Nembutal and chloral hydrate. He sent samples of her stomach and intestines to the toxicology lab, but reportedly the technicians thought the case had been closed as a suicide—that's what the headlines said—so they had performed just a rudimentary blood and liver test before destroying the rest of the samples.

Due in part to this set of miscommunications, as well as to resistance to a finding of suicide from those who knew the ill-fated Monroe, rumors spread that President John F. Kennedy and his brother were implicated—especially when no one could locate Monroe's diary. People suspected that it held secrets about her liaisons with these men, and possibly some classified material.

As the medical examiner who covered Hollywood, Curphey was used to celebrity deaths and media reports, but this one was in a category all its own. Monroe was young and beautiful, internationally renowned, and she appeared to have plenty of secrets. Feeling intense pressure to get this case right, Curphey gathered his SPC team. They tried to work in secret, but this proved challenging, as some of Monroe's associates did not trust them and would not talk. There were also leaks to the media. The team assured those whom they interviewed that the process would remain confidential. They spoke with Monroe's agent, her business associates, friends, psychiatrist, former husbands, and housekeeper. They studied the police reports and interviewed the first responders and detectives. They tried to avoid confirmation bias as they gathered details about Monroe's financial difficulties, recent successes and failures, exchanges with people during the day before she died, and achievements that she had anticipated.

Despite setbacks that supported a finding of suicide, Monroe had reasons to live. Several associates who saw or spoke to her during the hours before she died said she had seemed optimistic. Close friends described how she often forgot which drugs she had taken. She had a history of overdosing, sometimes just to get attention. They believed the overdose was accidental. Even Dr. Greenson, who had been at Monroe's home that day for several hours, was convinced it was an accident (Welkos, 2005).

Still, Monroe suffered from depression. Her recent career setbacks and her cash-flow problem could have made her feel trapped. Her marriages had ended in failure and she had suffered miscarriages that had deeply distressed her. The Suicide Team concluded that she fit the profile for suicidal depression, a psychache.

Noguchi agreed, although he later admitted in his own book that the lack of yellow capsules in Monroe's stomach had puzzled him. Since her intestines had been destroyed, he did not know if the pills had moved into them. He also could not explain why she was discovered neatly laid out, yet it had seemed to him more like a publicity concern than a homicide staged as a suicide.

Over the years, other facts have surfaced that the Suicide Panel did not know. In 2005, a former prosecutor, John Miner, revealed that Greenson had let him listen to tapes of Monroe's therapy sessions. He said he had heard no hint of suicidal depression. He called for a re-autopsy, but the district attorney said there was insufficient cause. Nevertheless, the LA office now admits that the overdose could have been accidental (Welkos, 2005). This shift in attitude could come only from adding more psychological factors to the review.

QUALITATIVE ANALYSIS

Shneidman and Faberow (1957a) had collected the aforementioned suicide notes from the coroner's office. For Shneidman, seeing this valuable resource had been a revelatory moment (Leenaars, 2010). The note-writers ranged in age from 13 to 96. With qualitative content analysis, Shneidman and Faberow used a tool called the Discomfort-Relief Quotient to compare the frequency of "discomfort thought units" in suicide notes to "relief thought units." In other words, they went through each phrase in a selected number of usable notes to isolate distinct thoughts that were in complete or near-complete form. They could then rephrase individual expressions as general themes and make comparisons across notes. "It hurts too much to keep going," could be rephrased as "The subject complains of psychache." This method was not a scientific measurement, *per se*, but they used inter-rater agreement with other professionals for reliability. Qualitative analysis allowed them to see similarities and differences more easily. "The subject communicates that he is preoccupied with someone he lost," for example, can cover many different personal forms that express this theme. Many of the notes were emotionally neutral: the person gave instructions, discussed friends or relatives, indicated where to find important papers, designated recipients of personal items, or provided a list of chores to accomplish.

They found that authentic notes contained more "thought units," as if the suicidal people wanted to make the most of this final communication. They expressed more psychological discomfort, as well, and more anger and self-blame. Shneidman and Faberow thought that those who took the time to write a note were trying to exercise power or exact one last infliction of punishment. The writers of simulated notes seemed to form more abstract ideas. They did not refer much to personal circumstances. Although this study involved a small number of artificially selected subjects, all of them male, it would inspire a much more comprehensive and diverse study of suicide notes in the future.

Over the years, Shneidman (1993) studied many more modes of suicidal expression. He found that a strong factor in authentic notes was indication of a psychache. Eventually, he formed themes from these expressions into five clusters of personal need: (1) thwarted love or acceptance, (2) a fractured sense of control, (3) a damaged self-image, (4) ruptured relationships, and (5) excessive anger. These categories formed the basis of the Psychological Pain Assessment Scale as a predictive device (1999).

The SPC's efforts laid a foundation for the emerging discipline of suicidology, another term that Shneidman also coined. Not all suicidologists would get involved in psychological autopsies, but the research in which other professionals engaged would provide databases for many more dimensions of suicide. Along with this would come pressure to bring rigor into the methods. What the SPC had envisioned when they defied social attitudes was taking shape.

COGNITIVE ISSUES FOR INVESTIGATORS

At times, it can be difficult to know how to proceed with a death investigation, and a case can trigger disagreement among personnel. TM, age 54, was found in the basement of his home, dead from a gunshot wound. He was lying to the right of the stairs in an unfinished space, used for storage. A woman living in his home called 911 to report it. Police decided it was a suicide, despite the odd circumstances. The decedent had used a 12-gauge Remington shotgun to shoot himself in the groin. It lay six feet from the body, with the barrel pointed away. A gun case upstairs contained four shotguns, with ammunition.

The investigators believed that the decedent had understood from his experience as a hunter that a shot to an artery would be fatal. However, there was reason for a deeper investigation.

The woman who called 911 resided in the home, but TM had told people he wanted her to leave. TM's son said that TM suffered from hypertension but had not been despondent and had not been a substance abuser. He had no history of suicidal thoughts or attempts. He had been fine the day before and had made plans with his son. The son said that the housemate had no source of income, was mentally unstable, and was not welcome at their family events. TM had seemed happy that she was going to move out.

The woman contradicted this narrative. She said she had decided herself to move out and had made arrangements. She had gone to take a nap that morning but got a call on her cellphone from TM, who said he had a gun to his head and was going to shoot himself. She tried to dissuade him. She called 911 and heard a pop downstairs. She did not go look in the basement. When police arrived and offered to transport her to the shelter where she said she was going, she decided to remain in the house. She claimed that TM had sexually and verbally abused her. Under questioning, she gave conflicting stories about when she had heard the sound of the gun, and her 911 call had sounded rehearsed.

Neighbors confirmed that there was tension in the home and that TM wanted his housemate to move out. Nothing about his demeanor on the morning of his death had alerted anyone who spoke with him to a despairing state of mind.

The shotgun did not show any blood or tissue on the muzzle and dust covered the barrel. There was dried blood on TM's thumb and index finger, but no spatter. The shotgun blast was directed straight backward through the lower abdominal wall. The police decided that he had leaned the gun butt against the wall to shoot. TM's life insurance policy and paperwork related to his two cars was found on the front seat of one car, suggesting that he had gotten his affairs in order.

Several investigators wanted to close the case; others resisted. Those who wished to close it dismissed the new information, because they had already made up their minds. This is a common problem in death investigations. A threshold diagnosis, made before all the relevant facts are gathered, can lead to the cognitive errors known as *tunnel vision* and *confirmation bias* (Rossmo, 2008). This means that investigators can fail to see or might minimize factors that fail to fit their idea of what happened. Erroneous determinations can result in heartaches for families, innocent people being falsely arrested or convicted, and killers going free. Cognitive errors happen when investigators act in haste or think a scene is obvious. It takes work to resist the impulse to take shortcuts.

This case remained undetermined, because the primary investigators reached an impasse. The longer it goes without investigation, the less likely it is that this case will be resolved. We will see similar cases as we move along, because human behavior can yield several different interpretations. If minimal information is collected, superficial conclusions will be reached. However, the cases explored thus far show that patience and probing beyond the surface can reveal important facts about a decedent's state of mind.

Techniques for performing a psychological autopsy are fully described in the next chapter, with updated research since the days of the SPC. Shneidman changed his mind several times about suicidal behavior. More research added more data. Once a relatively unknown method, increasingly more investigators see the value of a psychological autopsy for making accurate decisions about the manner of death.

REFERENCES

Biffl, E. (1996, Fall). Psychological autopsies: Do they belong in the courtroom? *American Journal of Criminal Law, 24,* 123–146.

Curphey, T. J. (1961). The role of the social scientist in medicolegal certification of death from suicide. In N. L. Faberow & E. S. Shneidman (Eds.), *The cry for help* (pp. 110–117). New York: McGraw Hill.

Leenaars, A. A. (2010). Edwin S. Shneidman on suicide. *Suicidology Online, 1,* 5–18.

Litman, R. E. (1957). Some aspects of the treatment of the potentially suicidal patient. In E. S. Shneidman & N. L. Faberow (Eds.), *Clues to suicide* (pp. 111–118). New York: McGraw Hill.

Maurek found not guilty. (January 22, 2008). *ABC News.* Retrieved from http://www.kswo.com/story/7758647/maurek-found-not-guilty-in-murder-trial

Noguchi, T. T., & DiMona, J. (1983). *Coroner.* New York: Pocket.

Rossmo, D. K. (2008). Cognitive biases: Perception, intuition, and tunnel vision. In K.D. Rossmo (ed.), *Criminal investigative failures* (pp. 9–21). Boca Raton, FL: CRC Press.

Shneidman, E. S. (1993). *Suicide as psychache: A clinical approach to self-destructive behavior.* Lanham, MD: Jason Aronson.

Shneidman, E. S. (1999). The Psychological Pain Assessment Scale. *Suicide and Life-Threatening Behavior, 29,* 287–294.

Shneidman, E. S., & Faberow, N. L. (1957a). Some comparisons between genuine and simulated suicide notes in terms of Mowrer's concepts of discomfort and relief. *Journal of General Psychology, 56,* 251–256.

Shneidman, E. S. & Faberow, N. L., eds, (1957b). *Clues to suicide.* New York: McGraw-Hill.

Shneidman, E. S., & Faberow, N. L. (1961). Sample investigations of equivocal suicidal deaths. In N. L. Faberow & E. S. Shneidman (Eds.), *The cry for help* (pp. 118–128). New York: McGraw Hill.

Shneidman, E. S., Faberow, N. L., & Litman, R. E. (1961a). A taxonomy of death – a psychological point of view. In N. L. Faberow & E. S. Shneidman (Eds.), *The cry for help* (pp. 129–135). New York: McGraw Hill.

Shneidman, E. S., Faberow, N. L., & Litman, R. E. (1961b). The suicide prevention center. In N. L. Faberow & E. S. Shneidman (Eds.), *The cry for help* (pp. 6–18). New York: McGraw Hill.

Welkos, R. (2005, August 5). New chapter in the mystery of Marilyn Monroe: In her own words? *Los Angeles Times.* Retrieved from http://articles.latimes.com/2005/aug/05/entertainment/et-marilyn5

CHAPTER 2

The Consulting Suicidologist

A 911 call on May 15, 2006, reported the discovery of 56-year-old Bob McClancy, found dead in the recliner in his home. A gun was in one hand and a bottle of prescription pills was in the other, with a few pills scattered on top of him. The 911 caller, Chuck Kaczmarczyk, was a friend of Bob and his wife, Martha Ann. Kaczmarczyk had met Bob in a veteran's treatment program for PTSD, and since he lived not far from their home in Coker Creek, Tennessee, he had been helping with Bob's psychological issues. A former police officer with military background, Bob had been taking medications for depression and insomnia. He had found solace in animal rescue and his family but still had trouble with flashbacks.

The 911 dispatcher wanted Kaczmarczyk to attempt CPR. He said he knew how, but that he had found a "do not resuscitate" order on the kitchen table. He was unwilling to defy his friend's wishes. The police arrived and found that the pistol had not been fired, but McClancy was dead. There was white foam around his mouth, but his position looked posed. Martha Ann came home from work and nearly collapsed from grief. There was no suicide note, but a history of complaints attested to probable depression.

One detective thought that Kaczmarczyk seemed oddly calm over the loss of his best friend, so he took him in for questioning. The former military man gave straightforward, unemotional answers, so it seemed that this demeanor was his personal style. Oddly, he admitted taking photos of the body, but there was nothing illegal about it. The drug overdose was from McClancy's own prescriptions, so the coroner closed the case as a suicide. The detective thought the case should be further investigated but had no leads.

McClancy was buried and his family mourned. But this death was not a suicide. Kaczmarczyk had been having an affair with McClancy's wife and together they had plotted and staged it. Surprisingly, they kept the photos that Kaczmarczyk had taken. Six years later, Martha Ann's adopted son discovered them.

At this point, his mother had already been indicted for another crime. She and Kaczmarczyk had pretended to grow close in their shared grief over Bob and they eventually married. They had then proceeded to commit extensive fraud, collecting up to half a million dollars from Bob's military benefits and from the Veterans Administration's disability fund.

When police investigated them for McClancy's murder, each suspect pointed a finger at the other. Kaczmarczyk had made the call to 911 and was alone with the body, so it was easy for Martha Ann to deny knowing about the murder. Now divorced, he took a deal and said she not only knew but also had dispensed the pills. In 2016, a jury convicted her of conspiracy and attempt to commit murder, and the judge sentenced her to 50 years in prison (Harper, 2016).

THE SCIENCE OF SUICIDE STUDIES

Suicide is the act of self-inflicted, self-intentioned cessation of life (Shneidman, 1981b). It is a "human malaise with considerable psychological variability" (Leenaars 1992, p. 347). As noted in Chapter 1, Shneidman and Faberow founded the discipline of suicidology, the scientific study of suicide risk and prevention (Reiter & Parker, 2002; Shneidman, 1967). This chapter and the following one collect the findings of this field as they apply to the procedure of psychological autopsy. Some facts about suicide are counterintuitive, as are the methods that some people have chosen to end their lives. These chapters cover myths, current research, methodologies, cluster suicides, suicide shrines, analyses of first responders to death scenes, and the evaluation of suicide notes. Unusual suicide methods are included, to assist investigators in broadening their awareness of mental states and mental illness.

First, a brief history. During the late eighteenth century, suicide was listed as a mental disorder. In 1897, Emile Durkheim published a sociological study, *Le Suicide*. Sigmund Freud said little about the act, except as an expression of Thanatos, the death instinct. He viewed suicide as murder. (Some theorists have speculated that Freud's death was a physician-assisted suicide). Around the same time as the SPC opened, Robins, Gassner, Kayes, Wilkinson, & Murphey (1959) published their study of 134 cases. They had performed systematic interviews with family and associates of the decedents to identify whether the decedents had communicated their intent. More than two-thirds (69%) had expressed suicidal ideas and 41% had made specific statements. Most expressions had been repeated to a number of people. (Yet the myth persists that people intent on suicide keep it to themselves.)

Scholars in this field met in 1968 to found the American Association of Suicidology (AAS). Its members established a journal, *Suicide and Life-Threatening Behavior*, for professional networking and communication. This inspired more clinicians to conduct research and consult with other agencies on suicide cases. In 1987, the American Suicide Foundation funded suicide research that investigated the effect of medication on severe depression. Although the emphasis of the AAS is on treatment and prevention, every journal issue also addresses items that would benefit investigators. For example, a common belief is that people often commit suicide on a whim, but Joiner (2010) dismissed this as a notion found only in fiction. (It does seem to be implicated in some suicides, however, such as adolescent cluster suicides and anger-based suicides meant to punish someone.)

Investigators might learn the difference between suicidal self-injury and nonsuicidal cutting or discover that seemingly impossible suicides do happen, such as the man who stabbed himself 83 times. They can read survivor accounts and gain practical methods of brief assessment. The types of research covered include adolescent risk factors, suicide in the military and among veterans, improvements on psychological autopsy, social support systems, treatment outcomes, suicide counseling in the LGBT community, traits of attempters versus completers, temperament and risk, suicide hotspots, suicide contagion, social media suicides, and gender, age, and racial differences. The statistics shift with each annual survey, and new angles are discovered and explored. Investigators should know about these resources.

Suicide holds steady as the tenth leading cause of death in the United States, with about 80–90 occurring per day and a steep rise over the past few years for women (Tavernise, 2016). In 2014, there were 42,773 identified suicides in the United States. Suicide rates spike during the spring, especially on Mondays (Joiner, 2010). Males take their lives at a rate of 3.6 times that of females, but three to four times more females make a suicide attempt. More women are committing suicide now than in the past (Tavernise, 2016).

Although few suicide completers leave an explanation, three out of four had given signals about their intent (Joiner, 2005), echoing the findings from the earliest study. Over 60% who threaten to kill themselves do make an attempt or complete the act. Some people are clumsy or naive about their methods, but the fact of an attempt made is more significant for risk evaluation of a suicidal individual than the selected method. However, one study found that only 4% of attempters who survived viewed their intent as "very serious" (Joiner et al., 2002). Past attempts best predict future attempts, with 75% of completers having made at least one prior attempt, but usually more. The most successful group of completers is the elderly, who might be better researched and less ambivalent. Around 90% of people who commit suicide have a mental illness, mostly clinical depression or bipolar disorder. Other mood disorders, as well as substance abuse, are also factors (Tavernise, 2016).

Joiner (2010) found that people erroneously believe that suicide is an "easy" escape, is done for revenge, is unstoppable once set in motion, and is reserved for adults. They also believe that suicidal people do not make plans, most people who take their lives leave a note, these notes explain motives, and most people who decide to end their lives look depressed. Police officers share these ideas as well, which can affect their decisions at scenes.

Although only one out of four completers have written a suicide note (few of which explain anything), *three* out of four have given definite prior clues. Most often, the method involves a firearm. Although 60% of threateners do make an attempt, most report ambivalence about dying. Some hope for rescue. Still, the risk for suicide remains even after a person is thought to have improved, post-treatment. Some have merely achieved clarity about their decision and are now relaxed.

The extensive research offers a summary of key elements for the risk of completion. Shneidman (1981a) identified four, as seen in Table 2.1.

Shneidman had looked for evidence of psychache (Shneidman & Faberow, 1961), whereas Joiner et al. (2002) identified two primary psychological states that could erode the instinct for self-preservation: perceived burdensomeness toward kin (PB) and a sense of low belongingness (LB). They examined a study of 40 suicide notes that separated completers (13 males and 7 females) from attempters (8 males and 12 females), finding more PB and LB for completers than other motives, such as psychache, hopelessness, a desire to control others, and a desire to control one's own feelings. Completers who expressed PB and/or LB had also selected more lethal means than attempters, such as guns, electrocution, and hanging. The researchers surmised that interpersonal factors such as deteriorating relationships might weigh more in the decision to die than intrapsychic factors such as depression. Those people who talk about suicide using the most immediate and lethal means can be identified for treatment.

There have been several detailed qualitative studies of suicidal people in an attempt to identify key factors. These date back to the SPC Mode Conferences. Ten members from the staff participated in one

TABLE 2.1   Shneidman's Four Elements of Suicide Risk

- Heightened inimicality (self-animosity)
- Exacerbated perturbation (uneasiness, anxiety, and psychache)
- Increased constriction of intellectual focus
- Cessation as a perceived solution

for publication (Los Angeles Suicide Prevention Center, 1970). They looked at the case of a Caucasian male, 65, found dead in bed with a self-inflicted gunshot wound to the forehead. He had used his favorite revolver. The group interviewed the decedent's wife, employer, physician, and five of his close friends. They found repeated confirmation of his life circumstances, but few respondents knew much about his childhood. He was generally cheerful, active, and admired. He liked to golf and garden and did not drink. He had no financial troubles, but his wife of 35 years had been ill. No one interviewed accepted the finding of suicide. On the day he died, he had played golf and participated in planning a Masonic event.

The SPC staff went over items they considered important, such as the decedent's health status and knowledge of handling guns. He had lost sight in one eye and was losing it in the other. The analysts thought it was interesting that no one had mentioned this except the physician, and he had added a 2-week bout of depression. They thought that the missing information from the decedent's childhood might hold a clue, especially as this self-sufficient man faced retirement and the loss of a routine and sense of meaning.

There are problems with this approach. The more they talk, the more they lean on speculation, making assumptions consistent with what they know of other cases. There are no controls in place to keep them from projecting their own meanings onto the decedent's mental state. They examine the facts but fail to use research to assist. They ultimately decided against accident or homicide, which left them with suicide. They decided that the decedent did not have adequate internal coping mechanisms for the dramatic changes he faced in the future.

The SPC staff (1970) also undertook a psychological autopsy of the death by gunshot of author Herman Melville's 18-year-old son, Malcolm. This was a new idea: perform a postmortem psychological analysis of a person long dead, whose death has unresolved issues. They could question no one. They could consult only extant records. They would be unable to corroborate their ultimate decision. Yet, having several experts all trained in the same methodology examine a case together helped to establish protocols for "distance diagnosis" of this kind. They also just found it fascinating (Shneidman, 1970).

At the time of the incident, some people thought that Malcolm had killed himself, but others called it an accident. There was even talk of homicide, since Melville was known to be abusive to his children. They found that Herman was prone to extreme bouts of depression that probably had infected his firstborn son's sense of himself. Suicide was a repeated motif in Melville's novels, which Malcolm might have realized. In any event, he would have absorbed the emotional tone of the family home as Herman wrote such dark and intense literature. Most of the

SPC clinicians believed that Malcolm had killed himself. An accident seemed unlikely, since he had known how to handle a gun. They thought the records were sufficiently extensive to make an educated clinical evaluation (Shneidman, 1970).

They expected that psychological autopsy would be useful in other historical cases. Knoll (2008) would later see it as a fruitful approach for understanding the factors that led up to Ernest Hemingway's suicide. It has been applied to Julius Caesar, King Tut, Adolf Hitler, and other historical figures whose deaths were not necessarily equivocal. Postsuicide study of some individuals seemed to be a valuable venture to add to databases. (Purists believe that this approach should not be called a psychological autopsy.)

Cross, Gust-Brey, & Ball (2002) used the method of life-and-death dissection to examine the thought processes of a gifted college student (99th percentile) who had killed himself, comparing their results with three other cases. They conducted interviews over 4 years and found that a collection of unique traits and beliefs specific to the gifted population were also potential indicators of suicidal behavior. The subject had trouble in two primary areas, self-esteem and romance, and he had developed irrational beliefs, isolating himself from a community that might have helped him to think more positively. The four cases provided a list of predictive signals, seen in Table 2.2.

The Threat Assessment Group also performed a "psychiatric autopsy" on Dylan Klebold and Eric Harris, the high school shooters who killed a dozen students and a teacher in April 1999 before ending their own lives. Several psychiatrists and a former FBI profiler went to Littleton, Colorado, to ask the shooters' friends and family about the boys and to examine their writings and films. The purpose was to learn what had motivated the suicidal mass murder plan and to pinpoint risk factors for such violence that might be found in other angry adolescents. Although the researchers

TABLE 2.2   Predictive Suicide Markers in Gifted Children

- Minimal prosocial associations
- High excitability but disdain of emotions
- Difficulty separating fact from fiction
- Overidentification with negative characters or themes
- Conflicted
- Self-directed guilt
- Confused about the future
- Egocentric value systems
- Viewed suicide as honorable; ideation present for years
- Past attempts at self-harm
- Experienced disintegration
- Constricted thinking

lacked the involvement of both sets of parents, which left a significant hole, they managed to learn important things about the state of mind of both killers, including the impact they had on each other. Warning signs include threats, inappropriate communications to peers, secretive behavior, anger, depression, and suicidal thoughts ("Documentary says," 2002).

METHODS AND MEASURES FOR PSYCHOLOGICAL AUTOPSY

Up to 20% of deaths around the United States are considered equivocal or controversially determined, although some experts say this figure is closer to 10%. Mental health professionals or death investigators with specialized training generally conduct psychological autopsies. A team on which mental health professionals with relevant experience are represented can also undertake them (Cavanagh, Carson, Sharpe, & Lawrie, 2003).

Evaluators consider cause, manner, motive, intent, lethality, and mental state (Scott, Swartz, & Warburton, 2006). Whether for lack of time, concern, or resources, some deaths are erroneously coded. It helps to know the research data. For example, Fischer (2016) stated that suicide is statistically the third leading cause of death for adolescents, but the number is underreported in many places to spare families.

For deaths that seem obvious, such as Bob McClancy's above, little more is done to investigate. Without clear evidence to the contrary, death investigators rarely believe that a suicide note is staged or fake. Yet an accurate manner of death is important for families and for communities. Psychological autopsies use known facts about suicide to look beyond the surface of a person's life. Most people are more complex than their typical persona suggests. They have a public face but often have secrets.

When David Duyst called in his wife's suicide in Grand Rapids, Michigan, in March 2000, there were several strong indicators that Sandra had been depressed. The year before, she had been kicked in the head by her horse and had seemed to friends and family to have grown irritable and dispirited. Voice mails from Sandra to Duyst 3 months before her death suggested her life was over. She could not go on and she urged him to carry on alone. The gun used was found near her hand. Nothing looked unusual until the autopsy. The pathologist found two entry wounds, and the first shot had destroyed her motor control, so she could not have fired twice. The gun did not have a defect.

Later, a note written by Sandra was found in a cabinet. It warned the reader that her husband wanted her dead. The "horse kick" had actually been the result of his hitting her with an axe after they had argued over his affair with his secretary. No wonder she had been depressed! With this knowledge, investigators listened to the voice mails from Sandra once more.

This time, they heard a different tone. Her voice was angry. She wanted to end her *marriage* not her life. In addition, there was a new insurance policy on Sandra for half a million dollars, financial problems for Duyst, and blood found on the clothing he had worn when he said he had discovered his wife dead. Duyst was brought to trial and convicted (Reens, 2011).

The first generation of psychological autopsies produced detail-rich reports on suicidal states of mind that were like mini-biographies, but they suffered from subjectivity, questionable methodology, incompleteness, and inconsistency among researchers. Initially, since there was so little data, counselors who specialized in suicide just hoped to assist. No one viewed the first efforts as scientific. This made it difficult to use suicidal analysis in court. Researchers who followed later tried to impose more rigorous controls and standardized procedures.

UPDATED ANALYSES

Building on Shneidman's tool, Bruce Ebert (1987), a clinical psychologist and a captain and chief of psychological services in the Air Force, developed an extensive guide for psychological autopsies. He also considered legal ramifications. He reviewed how the technique had been used to analyze aircraft crashes, homicide investigations, and hospital deaths. He added more categories, for a total of 26. Within each category, Ebert listed more specific aspects, for 100 separate factors. Again, his list was intended as a guide. The analyst was not required to review or acquire answers to all 26 but simply to collect as much information as possible.

Among Ebert's factors are mood, stressors, expressions of suicide, relationship issues, family death history, feelings about suicide, reconstructing the death event, a change in eating or sleeping habits, suicidal threats, preoccupations, history with drugs or alcohol, shifts in mental state, and behavior suggestive of bringing significant things to a close. In addition, professionals conducting a psychological autopsy should review the police and coroner's report and examine the decedent's educational and military history and familiarity with methods of death. For organizing all of this data, he suggested making a chart that lists items under each of the NASH categories. An example is seen in Table 2.3.

Ebert believed that a detailed psychological autopsy that gathers information from a variety of sources can enlighten investigators about psychological states better than do standard diagnostic assessments, such as personality inventories. Adding a full death reconstruction shows quite a lot about a decedent's mental state.

The CDC hoped to create a rigorous scientific approach (Rosenberg et al., 1988). The agency convened a working group that included

TABLE 2.3   A NASH Chart for Sandra Dyst

Manner	Natural	Accident	Suicide	Homicide
Physical	NA	NA	Prior head injury; gun found nearby; voice mails	Two gunshots; impossible; blood on suspect clothing; 911 caller
Psychological	NA	NA	Depression; irritable moods; statements of closure and hopelessness	
Life circumstances	NA	NA	Difficult marriage; note about husband's assault; husband's affair with secretary	Difficult marriage; husband's affair with secretary; new insurance policy; husband's financial difficulty

Note: NASH, natural, accident, suicide, or homicide.

different types of death investigators, along with statisticians, to develop accurate suicide rate statistics. These findings would assist with updating policies that had an impact on public programs. Focusing on intention and method, they established 22 criteria, which became the Operational Criteria for the Determination of Suicide. Eventually, these criteria were combined with 33 more to create the Death Investigation Checklist. This, in turn, evolved into the 16-item Empirical Criteria for the Determination of Suicide Checklist (ECDS). Among its items are results from autopsy reports, investigative reports, and witness reports, as well as items about the decedent's personality, intent, and evidence of depression or bipolar disorder. The ECDS scoring system can be tested among professionals. In one study, 70 medical examiners applied the ECDS to 126 recent deaths. They were correct 100% of the time for suicides and 83% for accidents (Jobes et al., 1991). However, the score does depend on the quality of the raw data.

Knoll (2008) drew together a variety of studies from the past 50 years to provide a formal definition of *psychological autopsy*: "a postmortem investigative procedure requiring the identification and assessment of suicide risk factors present at the time of death, with the goal of enabling a determination of the manner of death to as high a degree of certainty as possible" (p. 393). He associated the quality of the method with the training and clinical experience of the practitioner.

Categorizing suicidal people depends on goals. For a statistical overview, categories tend to align according to age groups, gender, race, and ethnicity. There are also studies for types of weapons used, differences between attempters and completers, and types of mental illness evident. The Self-Directed Violence Classification System (SDVCS) offers a standard nomenclature, used by military organizations, for thought patterns related to suicide. Its 22 items are reportedly culture neutral. The SDVCS comes with a decision-tree–based clinical tool that focuses on manifestations of suicidal thoughts, preparation, and type of self-directed violence.

The Food and Drug Administration has recommended the Columbia Classification Algorithm for Suicide Assessment (C-CASA) for coding behavior during drug trials. It consists of eight classifications, including completed, attempted, self-harm, ideation, and preparatory acts. Matarazzo, Clemans, Silverman, and Brenner (2013) combined the SDVCS and the C-CASA to increase clarity and efficiency, enable better comparison studies, and improve communication among suicide researchers and therapists.

At times, people who knew the decedent have motives for concealing what may have happened, so the investigator must recognize the potential for deception. The McClancy case that opens this chapter involved a pair of liars committing murder, forgery, and insurance fraud. Formal studies on the role of deception detection techniques during structured interviews would be a valuable contribution to training.

Some mental health professionals estimate that a comprehensive psychological autopsy could take around 30 hours. Knoll (2008) suggests 20–50 hours. The amount of time involved depends on the ultimate goal and sometimes on available funds.

Over the past few decades, precursor conditions have been isolated and better identified, especially the presence of specific forms of mental illness such as bipolar disorder and reactive depression (Conner et al., 2012). The AAS offers certification in psychological autopsy following an educational seminar that covers the history and methods of psychological autopsy, medicolegal and ethical issues, and current research on subject areas such as suicide clusters, suicide risk factors, investigative errors, military suicide protocols, and clinical angles on suicide. Participants also learn about methodological limitations. The AAS conducts practicum exercises and supervises method application. They are particularly concerned that trainees follow the structured interview protocol, to help standardize the practice. The organization models the method and demonstrates questions to ask that will elicit productive data (Berman, 2006; Juhnke, Granello, & Lebron-Striker, 2007). The AAS method follows the pattern in Table 2.4.

For quick evaluations in the field, the AAS has developed a mnemonic device (Juhnke et al., 2007). Each letter in the phrase corresponds

TABLE 2.4   Basic Method of a Psychological Autopsy

1. Identify people to interview, including professionals.
2. Identify goals.
3. Acquire official records.
4. Form questions to meet goals, specific to interviewees.
5. Send letters requesting appointment.
6. Start with people who knew decedent best.
7. Follow up with a phone call (be sensitive).
8. Make arrangements; set date and place.
9. Conduct taped interviews, with signed consent form and prepared questions.
10. Transcribe interviews and store data safely.
11. Request other needed records.
12. Follow up on failed contacts.
13. Review and reconcile data.
14. Analyze data with known research (e.g., clusters, hotspots, and special features).
15. Write report.

to a significant risk factor. The phrase to remember is this: "IS PATH WARM." The factors are as follows:

I   Ideation (thoughts, writings, artwork, and verbal expressions)
S   Substance abuse

P   Purposelessness (no reason to keep going)
A   Anger
T   Trapped
H   Hopelessness (negative sense of future)

W   Withdrawal
A   Anxiety (agitation and fitful sleep habits)
R   Recklessness (impulsive and engaging in risky behavior)
M   Mood changes

Those at high risk will often show several indicators, which can be ascertained from answers to specific questions put to friends, coworkers, and acquaintances. They might have prior attempts or threats or talk a lot about suicide. They might have a "game over" mentality or fail to take care of themselves in a healthy way. They might have rigid personalities that cannot deal with recent events that robbed them of control. They might have stopped socializing.

The formula, meant to augment clinical judgment, still provides a deeper evaluation than is currently used by police for the potential to harm oneself and others. Friends, family, and coworkers will have noticed some of these behaviors. Officers can be trained to use this mnemonic so they can alert an at-risk individual's family or make a referral for intervention. Counselors might also find it useful.

Death investigators must consider the totality of the circumstances rather than become too focused on a single aspect. In addition, they must consider the potential for bias to infect an evaluation (Rossmo, 2008). An ambiguous piece of writing at a death scene can be interpreted as a suicide note, which will skew the entire investigation. It is important to not only analyze the death scene with respect to victim behavior but also to integrate this analysis with witness interviews and evidence from the investigation. Investigators must consider not just what is *present* but also what is *absent* that should be present. (If a man states that he heard the shower running before he found his wife hanging in the shower stall, then water should be present on her, on the walls, and on the stall floor.) The consultant's primary role is to crystallize the psychological factors that decrease interpretive ambiguity. Probability analysis uses research databases to support findings that offer accuracy and closure (Knoll, 2008; Reiter & Parker, 2002).

To develop a sense of the person's final days and hours, a psychologist might use any number (or all) of the sources listed in Table 2.5, with the awareness that anyone interviewed might be hiding something or might intentionally or unintentionally contaminate the process. Collateral records and interviews with those who knew the decedent are primary sources. The following list is not exhaustive.

Suicidologists offer other tips, based on experience, to assist with data gathering. They suggest avoiding interviews on important anniversaries. Also, with relatives and close friends, it is best to avoid using the term "decedent," and the suicide should be referred to as a "sudden death" (Scott et al., 2006). The resulting report should provide an

TABLE 2.5   Sources for Psychological Autopsy

- First-responder interviews, other law enforcement personnel
- Autopsy and police reports
- Death scene photographs and videos
- Forensic experts for certain areas, when needed
- Suicide note (or other type of suicidal expression)
- Social medial posts
- Journals, diaries, blogs, and webcasts
- Correspondence
- Decedent's artwork or poetry
- Family members
- Close friends, acquaintances
- Coworkers
- Former spouses
- Records (school, military, work, medical, and prescriptions)
- Archival data (suicide research; risk prediction)
- Changes in behavior, wills, or life insurance policies
- Family history of mental illness or suicide

accurate sense of the victim's personality, habits, and behavior patterns, specifically including recent or dramatic changes.

In one case, a man was found in his own bed, shot with his favorite gun, but he was shot with his right hand and everyone who knew him swore that he was left-handed. His sister was suing the county over their determination of suicide, but at the coroner's inquest it turned out that she had not spoken to her brother in nearly a year. She did not know his recent state of mind. His closest friends, who were also certain his death was not a suicide, admitted that they brushed him off whenever he wanted to talk about things that bothered him. One friend said that the decedent was afraid of his stepson, who lived in his house, yet there was no lock on the decedent's door and he died at home in his own bed. His behavior contradicted the information. It was important to note that everyone who challenged the coroner's decision had not known the decedent as well as they had claimed. Evaluation of archival data, confirmed by a medical examiner with more than four decades of experience, indicated that left-handed people shoot themselves with the right hand about 10% of the time. With no evidence to the contrary, the decision was affirmed (Attendance at coroner's inquest, 2015).

RISKS AND RED FLAGS

Ten minutes after Ashley Fallis said goodbye to her family after a New Year's Eve party in Evans, Colorado, she was dead. Her husband, Tom, called 911 at 12:50 AM to report that Ashley had shot herself in the head. He sounded distraught, desperate to save her. An emergency team rushed this mother of three to a hospital, but she soon expired.

Fallis explained that he was in the walk-in closet when Ashley came into the bedroom, retrieved her own gun from under the mattress, and shot herself. He could not explain why the room was disturbed in ways that looked as if a violent physical fight had occurred. Pictures were torn off the wall and a neighbor claimed to have heard Ashley yell, "Get off me!" A large flashlight lay next to her body, and her body bore fresh bruises. Fallis' chest also had a number of red marks and scratches.

Fallis was taken in for questioning. He said that his scratches were from shaving his chest and denied that his wife had yelled anything. He insisted that he had not killed her. The police accepted this and closed the case in March as a suicide.

However, Ashley's relatives were suspicious. They thought Fallis, a corrections officer for the Weld County Sheriff's Office, was controlling and intimidating. A reporter re-interviewed witnesses and found inconsistencies between what they said and the official statements. One young man said he had overheard Fallis confess to his parents, but the police had done nothing with this seemingly important piece of information.

The case was reopened, with other agencies handling it, but since the death had not initially been treated as a potential homicide, valuable evidence had been lost, neglected, or mishandled. Fallis was charged with second-degree murder.

A forensic animator gathered facts from death scene photos and measurements of the room but could not make a definitive case for guilt or innocence. During a 2-week trial, evidence was presented that an intoxicated Ashley had been depressed, had stopped her antianxiety medication, had recently suffered a miscarriage, and had a suicidal past. A few months earlier, she had written a suicide note. Ashley had a number of risk factors for suicide. Yet blood spatter patterns and blood on Fallis' shirt contradicted his account. No one closely examined the scratches on him to determine if his account was accurate. The amount of blood on the wall indicated that Fallis was near his wife when the shot was fired. Experts vigorously debated, and Fallis was cleared in virtue of reasonable doubt. The manner of death was reinstated as a suicide ("Tom Fallis trial," 2016). Investigating more carefully from the start by preserving evidence might have made a difference.

People who are vulnerable to suicidal thoughts vary with age, gender, social demographic, and ethnic group. Table 2.6 helps to classify a person as being at risk.

TABLE 2.6   Factors in Potential for Suicide

- Discussing, asking about, or researching suicide
- Looking up suicide online
- Unresponsive depression, resistance to treatment, and other serious mood disorders
- Loss of purpose
- Serious eating disorder or body dysmorphic disorder
- Significant shift in sleeping habits
- Agitation and unrelenting anger, leading to threats
- Repeated high-risk or impulsive behavior
- History of frequent mobility
- Losing interest in subjects or people once cherished
- Feeling trapped, afraid
- Putting affairs in order, changing a will
- Sudden mood switches, specifically from fear or agitation to calmness
- Visiting or calling people to say goodbye
- Obsessing over a divorce, a loss, a humiliation, or a personal affront
- Self-abuse, especially a recent habit
- History of parental abuse
- Recent exposure to suicide of someone cherished
- Suicide in the immediate family
- Giving important things away, closing accounts
- Financial difficulties that seem insurmountable

For adolescents, risk factors also include substance abuse, the death or suicide of a friend, family loss, homosexuality, bullying, rapid cultural change, media reports on suicide (especially cultural icons), and impulsiveness (Cross et al., 2002).

However, precursor behaviors can also alert investigators to how vulnerable a decedent had been to a staged suicide, as the opening case demonstrated. The following case has similar features.

Darryl Sutorius, a successful heart surgeon in Cincinnati, Ohio, suffered from serious depression and had threatened to commit suicide several times after his first marriage ended. Eventually, through a dating service, he found a new wife, Della "Dante" Britteon, 10 years younger (Vaccariello, 2013).

On February 19, 1996, Sutorius failed to come to work or answer his pager. Police went to his home to search. Della let them in. When they were in the garage, she called to them that she had found her husband. He was on a couch in the basement, dead. There was a wound to his right temple and a gunshot hole in the couch. At first, his death seemed consistent with suicide, and a superficial evaluation would have shown the requisite state of mind. He was in the middle of filing for a divorce and had been upset over his lack of success a second time. He had been seeing a psychiatrist.

However, odd things at the scene suggested that a full investigation was in order. The gun was registered to Della, and she had purchased it just a day earlier. She would inherit over $1 million with her husband's death. Her actual name was Della Hall, this was her fifth marriage, and she had a history of violent threats and assaults involving other men. She had told Sutorius numerous lies about herself. She was a high school dropout who had never held a job. Even her mother told the police that Della was mentally abusive and had mostly likely killed Sutorius. It was Della who had suggested that he see a psychiatrist, as if hoping to use this to confirm depression. In addition, she had been telling people that Sutorius was abusive. It was a setup.

Blood spatter patterns on the couch where Sutorius had died indicated that someone had shot him from an odd angle. It looked as if someone had flung blood against the couch below him, where no blood could have landed had he shot himself. Most telling, his right hand was spattered with blood on both sides, so he could not have held the gun. In addition, although it is not unusual for someone to take a practice shot before killing themselves, in this case, the gunpowder residue was on top of blood spatter. Someone had shot the couch after Sutorius was shot.

Della Sutorius was arrested on February 27. A long history of her abuse of men and suspicion in other disappearances went against her, as did a psychiatrist who stated that Sutorius was not suicidally depressed but had been afraid of his wife. She went to trial and was convicted.

MISTAKEN SUICIDES: AUTOEROTIC ACCIDENTS

Some people who have been found hanged, bound, drowned, gagged, electrocuted, suffocated, or shot did not commit suicide. They were seeking sexual gratification with a dangerous device and their safety mechanism failed. Autoerotic asphyxia, also called *asphyxiophilia*, involves reducing oxygen intake to produce euphoria during arousal. Estimates place autoerotic fatalities (AEFs) between 500 and 1,000 annually, which leaves a lot of room for error (Sauvageau & Geberth, 2013; Scott et al., 2006).

Investigators unfamiliar with AEFs, or having never seen one, might confuse them with suicides, but they are typically accidents. (Some have been done as part of a suicide ritual, but this is rare.) Some have obvious features, such as pornographic photos or books opened to a specific page, sexual clothing or paraphernalia like handcuffs and whips, ropes, masks, autoerotic instructions, a collection of pornographic videos, neck padding (to avoid visible bruises), and nonlethal bindings, but some victims—especially females—have no such indicators. AEFs are *not* part of a death in the midst of dangerous consensual sex. Rescue mechanisms can be a chair or stool close to a hanging victim, a knife or pair of scissors to cut a line, a switch, or an air tube that got clogged because the mechanism failed. However, the absence of a distinct means of escape should not be confused with a desire to die. Sometimes, the practitioner relies on personal judgment (Sauvageau & Geberth, 2013).

The most common asphyxiating device is a noose, but sometimes practitioners tie a rope around the abdomen, place a bag over the head, inhale chemicals, use anesthetics, or immerse themselves in water. One young man enjoyed mud eroticism and he was found dead in a tub of hardened plaster. He had slipped and breathed it into his lungs (Goodman, 2009). Another man who was found in his basement, burnt in several places and bound in chains, resembled the victim of an assault. However, a full-length mirror attached in a strategic place showed that he had been viewing himself. Drug paraphernalia and forceps lay nearby and the victim had once been caught in autoerotic activities by a relative (Sauvageau & Geberth, 2013).

AEF victims might have encased themselves in something like duct tape or plastic, or investigators might find aerosol inhalant containers for CO_2 or nitrogen, as well as evidence of drug use. One man had rigged up a Russian roulette device that proved to be defective and another used an elaborate electrical system that had short-circuited. Power tools are also common, and some people use automobiles. One man liked to balance the leg of a heavy piece of furniture on his throat; a couch had proved to be too heavy. A 19-year-old male died from a massive compression of the thorax when he dressed in a pressure suit for military pilots and overinflated it with an air compressor, impeding his ability to breathe (Sauvageau & Geberth, 2013).

To educate investigators in paraphilias, this section summarizes studies of autoerotic incidents and shows the range of ways people have died. It also explains why some first responders fail to recognize the evidence of accident versus suicide.

A strange and seemingly impossible suicide involved a young man found dead in his apartment. He was fully bound in duct tape from his mouth to his ankles. The windows and doors were locked. Because the ends of the duct tape seemed to be beyond the decedent's reach, this was assumed to be a homicide. Yet once the tape was removed, the decedent was found in a black nylon body suit and diaper. A ball gag was found in his mouth, taped over with duct tape. A full investigation revealed a surprise: the decedent had visited Internet sites on mummification, which demonstrated how to bind oneself in this particular manner. Warnings were posted about the dangers of this method of oxygen restriction, but some people had described the euphoria of their near-death experiences in glowing terms. More diapers in the decedent's apartment suggested that this was a regular practice. Extensive wrapping like this is referred to as *cocooning*.

The victims are predominantly adolescent males, but women and even children have engaged in this practice as well. Hazelwood, Dietz, & Burgess (1983) researched 157 cases, finding 5% female. (With the availability of many types of websites on this subject, this percentage has probably risen.) Almost three-fourths of the victims were younger than 30. Most were found in isolated locations, closets, or locked rooms, with signs of masochistic behavior. Some had used mirrors.

In some cases, the AEF occurs underwater. A young man went into the water in a homemade plastic bodysuit. Over this, he had donned a snowmobile suit. He had also created an elaborate system of chains and anchors. His body was found submerged. His mistake was using an air tube, attached to a floating device, which was too constricted to allow oxygen intake with the expulsion of carbon dioxide. Signs that this death was an accident were the way he had wrapped his genitals and his membership in a club for autoerotic practitioners.

A woman's device failed when her hair got caught in the mechanism. A young man wrapped his mouth and eyes with duct tape, removed his clothes, and hanged himself from a metal ladder inside a vertical sewer pipe. During the autopsy, a pocket watch was found in his mouth. It turned out to have belonged to his deceased grandfather. There were signs that this had been an autoerotic hanging but for the ultimate purpose of suicide.

A correct death determination matters to surviving friends and relatives. Suicide clauses on insurance contracts block payouts for suicide and some religions view suicide as a sin. Although AEFs can be embarrassing, they rarely have the shattering emotional impact that a suicide has.

Many autoerotic accidents are clearly associated with paraphilias, some of which are unique and unexpected. There are thousands of fetishes and paraphilias, limited only by the human imagination. Among them are drinking blood or urine, infantilism, masochism, nymphomania, transvestitism, enemas, skin arousal, ropes, and thunder (Shaffer & Penn, 2006).

Sheleg and Ehrlich (2006) provide a history of asphyxiophilia, dating back to 1856. A summary of psychiatric knowledge from 1968, which still holds true, offered clues for death investigators:

1. The deaths were a complete surprise to relatives.
2. There was no known psychiatric history or obvious motivation for suicide.
3. Signs of preparation and bondage activity suggested habitual practice.
4. The victim was typically an intelligent Caucasian male.

Typically, the practice begins with tentative experimentation. Males generally start during adolescence. As the person grows older, his technique often becomes more elaborate, often involving bondage. It might also become more extreme, as the initial edginess wears off. In sum, the devices used to constrict oxygen can kill a person in a way that resembles suicide. Knowledge about AEFs should be part of training for investigators.

ADDITIONAL CONTEXTS FOR PSYCHOLOGICAL AUTOPSY

Aside from determining the manner of death in official investigations, psychological autopsies may serve other purposes. We mentioned distance diagnosis in historical cases, but they also can address questions about testamentary capacity prior to death, gain actuarial data, help with contested insurance or malpractice claims, show evidence of staging, assist with expert testimony, address product liability, and provide comfort (postvention) for survivors.

One study focused on qualitative postsuicide interviews with relatives. The sample consisted of key people in the lives of 17 suicide victims from 2005, totaling 97 individuals between 10 and 82.

No more than 18 months had passed between the death and the interviews. Using interpretive phenomenological analysis and a data program for organization, they found that most of the survivors benefited from the opportunity to express themselves and offer insight. They also wanted to help others. As they learned more about the decedent, they better understood and felt less guilty. This result will assist with policy decisions for researchers and review boards that have decided, without research, that it is unethical to handle vulnerable populations such as the postsuicide bereaved. Only a few participants had mixed feelings and none found the experience to be negative. The youngest participants had been frightened, and they appreciated being able to learn more. This study opens the door for further research, which the study authors believe will enable friends and family of suicide completers to take comfort in finding meaning (Dyregrov & Dieserud, 2011).

Following the death in 1976 of eccentric billionaire Howard Hughes, Dr. Raymond Fowler, then President of the American Psychological Association, accepted an assignment to perform a psychological autopsy. No one questioned Hughes' manner of death from heart failure, but there was reason to question his mental state while alive, as he made important decisions regarding his will (Fowler, 1986, 2006).

Fowler relied on biographical material, interviews, Hughes' personal writings, business memos, and personal letters to reconstruct the mentally unstable recluse's life. Hughes, he found, had difficulty with other people and had experienced several nervous breakdowns, not to mention sustaining serious head injuries during accidents. He had become highly paranoid and obsessive–compulsive. Occasionally he could pull himself together to make a public appearance, but mostly he kept to himself. Fowler concluded that Hughes was mentally disturbed but had never been psychotic. His business decisions, including his will, had been made appropriately.

SUMMARY

Suicidology is a specialized field that not only supports the method of psychological autopsy but can also be used for other tasks. Because myths and misunderstandings about suicide can influence investigators, it is important to keep up with the research. Psychological autopsy can assist in eroding lingering mysteries about a decedent's death event. The procedure has become increasingly more rigorous as an investigative method, with applications in many areas, including public policy. In the next chapter, we look at unusual suicides and the evolution of research on suicide notes.

REFERENCES

Berman, A. (2006, July/Aug). Risk assessment, treatment, planning and management of the at-risk suicide client: The "how to" aspects of assessing suicide and formulating treatment plans. *Family Therapy Magazine, 5*(4), 7–10.

Cavanagh, J. T. O., Carson, A. J., Sharpe, M., & Lawrie, S. M. (2003). Psychological autopsy studies of suicide: A systematic review. *Psychological Medicine, 33*, 395–405.

Conner, K. R., Beautrais, A. L., Brent, D. A., et al. (2012). The next generation of psychological autopsy studies. *Suicide and Life-Threatening Behavior, 42*(1), 86–103.

Cross, T., Gust-Brey, K., & Ball, P. (2002). A psychological autopsy of the suicide of an academically gifted student: Researchers' and parents' perspectives. *Gifted Child Quarterly, 46*(4), 1–18.

Documentary says Columbine warning signs were overlooked. (2002, March 29). *Lubbock Avalanche Journal.* Retrieved from http://lubbockonline.com/stories/032902/upd_075-8505.shtml#.WRunZsm1s_V

Dyregrov, K. M., & Dieserud, G. (2011). Meaning-making through psychological autopsy interviews. *Death Studies, 35*, 685–710.

Ebert, B. (1987). Guide to conducting a psychological autopsy. *Professional Psychology Research and Practice, 18*, 52–56.

Fischer, D. (2009, Sept/Oct). Equivocal cases of teenage suicide. *The Forensic Examiner, 18*(3), 9–12.

Fowler, R. D. (1986, May). Howard Hughes: A psychological autopsy. *Psychology Today*, 22–23.

Fowler, R. D. (2006). Computers, criminals, an eccentric billionaire, and APA: A brief autobiography. *Journal of Personality Assessment, 87*(3), 234–238.

Goodman, G. (2009, Summer). An atypical autoerotic death by mechanical asphyxiation. *The Forensic Examiner, 18*(2), 71–73.

Harper, M. (2016, June 24). McClancy sentenced to 50 years for killing husband. *Advocate and Democrat*, p. 1.

Hazelwood, R. R., Dietz, P. E., & Burgess, A. W. (1983). *Autoerotic fatalities.* Lexington, MA: Lexington Books.

Jobes, D. A., Casey, J. O., Berman, A. L., et al. (1991). Empirical criteria for the determination of suicide manner of death. *Journal of Forensic Science, 36*(1), 244–256.

Joiner, T. (2005). *Why people die by suicide.* Cambridge, MA: Harvard University Press.

Joiner, T. (2010). *Myths about suicide.* Cambridge, MA: Harvard University Press.

Joiner, T. E., Pettit, J. W., Walker, R. L., Voelz, Z. R., Cruz, J., Rudd, D., & Lester, D. (2002). Perceived burdensomeness and suicidality: Two studies on the suicide notes of those attempting and those completing suicide. *Journal of Social and Clinical Psychology, 21*(5), 531–545.

Juhnke, G. A., Granello, P., & Lebron-Striker, M. (2007). *IS PATH WARM? A suicide assessment mnemonic for counselor.* Alexandria, VA: Professional Counseling Digest. (ACAPD-03).

Knoll, J. L. (2008). The psychological autopsy, Part I: Applications and methods. *Journal of Psychiatric Practice, 14*(6), 393–397.

Leenaars, A. A. (2010). Edwin S. Shneidman on suicide. *Suicidology Online, 1,* 5–18.

Leenaars, A. A. (1992). Suicide notes, communication and ideation. In R. W. Maris, A. Berman, J. T. Maltsberger, & R. I. Yufit (Eds.), *Assessment and Prediction of Suicide,* pp. 337–361, New York, NY: Guilford.

Los Angeles Suicide Prevention Center (1970). Psychological autopsy: No. 1. *Bulletin of Suicidology, 7,* 27–33.

Matarazzo, B. B., Clemans, T. A., Silverman, M. M., & Brenner, L. A. (2013). The self-directed violence classification system and the Columbia classification algorithm for suicide assessment: A crosswalk. *Suicide and Life-Threatening Behavior, 43*(3), 235–248.

Reens, N. (2011, March 16). *David Duyst continues to appeal conviction for wife's murder.* Retrieved from http://www.mlive.com/news/grand-rapids/index.ssf/2011/03/david_duyst_continues_to_appea.html

Reiter, H., & Parker, L. B. (2002). Psychological autopsy. *The Forensic Examiner, 11*(3), 22–26.

Robins, E., Gassner, S., Kayes, J., Wilkinson, R. H., & Murphey, G. E. (1959). The communication of suicidal intent: A study of 134 consecutive cases of successful (completed) suicide. *American Journal of Psychiatry, 115*(8), 724–733.

Rosenberg, M., Davidson, L., Smith, J. C., et al. (1988). Operational criteria for the determination of suicide. *Journal of Forensic Science, 33*(6), 1445–1456.

Rossmo, D. K. (2008). Cognitive biases: Perception, intuition, and tunnel vision. In K. D. Rossmo (Ed.), *Criminal investigative failures* (pp. 9–21). Boca Raton, FL: CRC Press.

Sauvageau, A., & Geberth, V. (2013). *Autoerotic deaths: Practical forensic and investigative perspectives.* Boca Raton, FL: CRC Press.

Scott, C. L., Swartz, E., & Warburton, K. (2006). The Psychological autopsy: Solving the mysteries of death. *Psychiatric Clinics of North America, 29,* 805–822.

Shaffer, L., & Penn, J. (2006). A comprehensive paraphilia classification system. In E. Hickey (Ed.), *Sex crimes and paraphilias* (pp. 69–94). Upper Saddle River, NJ: Pearson.

Sheleg, S., & Ehrlich, E. (2006). *Autoerotic asphyxiation: Forensic, medical and social aspects.* Tucson, AZ: Wheatmark.

Shneidman, E. (1967). *Essays in self-destruction.* New York: Science House.

Shneidman, E. (1970). The death of Herman Melville. In E. S. Shneidmen, (Ed.), *The psychology of suicide* (pp. 587–613). New York: Science House.

Shneidman, E. (1981a). Suicidal thoughts and reflections. *Suicide and Life-Threatening Behavior, 11,* 98–231.

Shneidman, E. (1981b). The psychological autopsy. *Suicide and Life-Threatening Behavior, 22*(1), 107–174.

Shneidman, E. S., & Faberow, N. L. (1961). Sample investigations of equivocal suicidal deaths. In N. L. Faberow & E. S. Shneidman (Eds.), *The cry for help* (pp. 118–128). New York: McGraw Hill.

Tavernise, S. (2016, April 22). U. S. suicide rate surges to a 30-year high. *The New York Times*, pp. A1, A15.

Tom Fallis trial: Doctor says Ashley Fallis had many risk factors. (2016, March 28). *The Denver Post.* Retrieved from http://www.denverpost.com/2016/03/28/tom-fallis-trial-doctor-says-ashley-fallis-had-many-risk-factors/

Vaccariello, L. (2013, May 15). Hearts of darkness: The short, unhappy marriage of Darryl and Dante Sutorius. *Cincinnati Magazine.* Retrieved from http://www.cincinnatimagazine.com/features/hearts-of-darkness-the-brief-unhappy-marriage-of-darryl-and-dante-sutorius/

CHAPTER **3**

Suicide Categories, Oddities, and Notes

Lt. Charles "GI Joe" Gliniewicz was popular in his town. For three decades as a police officer, he had volunteered his spare time to boys who participated in the Explorer Club in Fox Lake, Illinois. Yet, he was nearing retirement and he hoped to turn his energy to other things. No one expected what happened.

On the morning of September 1, 2015, Gliniewicz called his dispatcher. He needed backup. He was in pursuit of three suspicious men. He gave the location. Yet, the arriving officers found Gliniewicz dead, apparently killed with his own weapon. He wore a bulletproof vest, but this time it had not worked. His gun lay in weeds nearby.

This homicide shocked everyone. Tremendous resources were expended to locate and arrest the shooter, at considerable expense. This man was a hero. They were going to do everything possible to get justice for him and his family. It seemed such a tragedy that this much-honored officer had been killed just before he retired.

Yet, the first responders had doubts. They thought it could have been suicide. In addition, Coroner Thomas Rudd could not rule out an accident. So, homicide, suicide, or accident, which one was it? If a NASH chart were made, factors would line up in each category. It took a deeper investigation to see that Gliniewicz had secrets. He was not the man that everyone believed him to be. Despite his clean-cut, generous image, Gliniewicz had a history of complaints for harassment. He had also committed several ethical violations. A new auditor had been about to check his accounts for the Explorer's fund. Once these books were opened, it was clear that he had embezzled thousands of dollars. A check on the text messages that Gliniewicz had recently deleted showed that he had considered having the auditor killed. It now seemed that his death was a suicide staged as a homicide, possibly to protect his reputation.

There were behavioral clues, starting with his call for backup. It had not been urgent. In fact, he had been in the area for 20 minutes.

Apparently, he had used the time to set up the scene and delete his texts. He had positioned his baton to appear to have been dropped while in pursuit or during a struggle. He had then shot himself twice, because he had known that this is rare for suicides and would help to deflect the investigation toward homicide (Constable & Filas, 2015). Ultimately, Gliniewicz had failed. In November, the official manner of death was changed to suicide.

SUICIDAL BEHAVIORS AND INVESTIGATIONS

It can be difficult to know when someone has committed suicide, staged it, died in an autoerotic fatality or bizarre accident, or been the victim of a suicide staged by a killer. This is why investigators must become familiar with cultural myths and be aware of the human tendency to dismiss a suicide based on personal ideas about what they would or would not do. If they think that a specific method is too painful or unlikely, they typically decide that it could not have been suicide, but people are full of surprises. Suicides can have rather bizarre aspects, so this chapter offers examples of some behaviors that investigators might encounter. In addition, we examine the phenomenon of suicidal people who infect or affect others, sometimes by alluring doctrines and sometimes by force. The final part of this chapter includes studies of suicide notes with the aim of developing a practical field tool for investigators who find items that look like a suicidal expression at a scene.

STRANGE SUICIDES

A look through a suicide database will turn up unique and startling suicides. For example, Joiner (2010) described a case where two men who lived together and were in despair over a failed business decided to end their lives. They planned to remove their hands with a circular saw. To ensure that someone found their bodies, they sent a note to their landlord. One of these men had lost both hands and the other just one before the landlord found the note before they had expected, burst in, and saved them. (Joiner does not say whether they survived.) In unrelated cases, four women used table-mounted circular saws to slice into their necks, and one man cut off his arm with an axe (and a dog ran off with his hand). In Philadelphia, in 2015, a man cut into his wife's stomach with a chainsaw before turning the running blade on himself in the same manner.

A female engineer, just 32, built a guillotine with a running chainsaw as the descending blade. Tournel et al. (2008) described how she had designed it, purchased the items she needed, and set to work. She made weights from water bottles, designed to pull the saw downward. It rested on rubber bands, so as not to vibrate off-track. She started the engine with a remote control. Then she lay face down with her neck on the block she had designed and waited for the saw to decapitate her. It worked. It was a startling case, presented to groups of death investigators to show what people might do. The woman had been mentally ill, but she was nevertheless exacting and methodical. She knew what she was doing and she did it patiently. It is not a scenario that anyone would envision, but it did happen. Officers must be trained to accept such behavior.

Geberth (2015) describes a case of a man who was found in his home, stabbed nearly 100 times. The investigating officers insisted it had to be a homicide, but there was no evidence of another person in the room where it happened. No one could have walked away from that blood soaked scene without leaving a trail of blood drops or footprints. A victimology showed plenty of evidence for suicide: chronic depression, acts of closure, and serious financial difficulties. Most of the stabs had been shallow, similar to hesitation marks made by suicidal people.

In Austria, a teenager who played a computer game in which monsters were beheaded with chainsaws turned a real chainsaw on himself. Campman et al. (2000) reported chainsaw suicide cases in the same county, 3 years apart. First, a 69-year-old man was found lying next to a running chainsaw, held in the "on" position with a clamp. Apparently, he had lain down onto the running blade. The second man, 40 years younger, was homeless, depressed, and without support from family. He parked his truck, sat on the ground next to the open door, and started the saw. He leaned back against it.

Other unusual suicide methods have involved a nail gun, a hammer, a power drill, and a meat thermometer; one person even used instant hardening construction foam shot down his throat and over his nose. Another tied a rope around a fire hydrant and used his jeep to decapitate himself. Then there was a man who had rigged up a way to shoot himself simultaneously with a shotgun and a handgun, while yet another positioned a steamroller that he owned to crush his head. A 61-year-old man plunged to his death from a helicopter after he hired it to take a scenic tour. He had booked the trip for two, but only he arrived to board. The pilot reported that this man had asked him to fly higher and higher, which had seemed suspicious, but he complied. The man had paid for the trip. Then it happened. They were quite high when the passenger removed his seatbelt and opened the door. The pilot tried to grab for him but got only his ripped shirt as he jumped.

Use of a trash compactor is highly unusual. This machine is meant to pack trash into a small parcel. A 52-year-old male with a history of depression tried to reconcile with his estranged wife. While in her apartment building, he squeezed himself into the tight chute for trash, ending up eight floors below in a compacter. He had multiple blunt impact injuries, including fractures of every rib. Numerous superficial cuts and a larger wound on his wrist, along with blood inside the apartment, suggested that he had first tried cutting his wrist.

The array of things that people can think of to use to end their lives is limited only by their imaginations and the methods available. To know the literature on such cases often means membership in an organization that keeps track of, and publishes details about, unusual cases. Two such organizations are the American Association of Suicidology and the American Academy of Forensic Sciences.

SUICIDE CONTAGIONS, INSPIRATIONS, AND CLUSTERS

Suicide contagion is the negative impact of a suicide on vulnerable or impulsive people, triggering attempts and completions. These can happen as a widespread cultural response, a local suicide cluster, or an echo cluster. In the United States, about 5% of suicides annually occur as part of a cluster, mostly among teenagers and college students (Smith, 2012). Strangely enough, they tend to occur in affluent Caucasian communities (Chung, 2015; Smith, 2012). However, recorded contagions date back further.

In 1774, Goethe published a novel, *The Sorrows of Young Werther*. The main character killed himself with a pistol. The novel triggered a wave of "emulation suicides," especially among fans of the novel who identified with the character so strongly that they even dressed like him. Some suicidologists call copycat suicides like these a result of the Werther effect. The instigating suicide serves as a model. If publicized in detail, it presents a method and seems to give permission to those who have contemplated suicide to go ahead and do it. A spike in female suicides followed the 1962 overdose suicide of Marilyn Monroe, mostly with pills. Rock star Kurt Cobain's suicide by shotgun in 1994 had a similar effect (not as dramatic), as did actor–comedian Robin Williams's depression-based self-asphyxiation in 2014. The more similar the suicidal celebrity is in age and race to vulnerable people, the more likely it is that reactive suicides linked to the initiating one will use the same method. News accounts have a stronger impact than suicides in fiction, and televised stories will inspire more copycats than will newspaper accounts (Joiner, 2010).

Mesoudi (2009) reported on the celebrity contagion effect, based on a simulation study that used 1,000 digital personalities. They were "residents" of a community that had a specific set of social rules and values. Ten groups of 100 represented different layers of social strata.

Simulations of celebrity suicides were introduced, along with accompanying media coverage. The "citizens" showed a rate of suicide similar to that of actual societies. Ma-Kellams, Baek, and Or (2016) found that depressive affect predicted the likelihood of a response to a publicized celebrity suicide, along with access to death thoughts and attitudes about suicide as an acceptable act. However, media coverage that corresponds to World Health Organization guidelines appears to help reduce copycat suicides (Lee, Lee, Hwang, & Stack, 2014).

One type of copycatting, suicide clusters, occurs in two basic forms: point clusters and mass clusters (Chung, 2015). Point clusters involve a number of suicides related closely in time and location. Mass clusters typically occur in response to a highly publicized suicide and are not necessarily near one another (especially thanks to global Internet coverage). The numerous hanging suicides of teenagers in Bridgend, Wales, between 2007 and 2012 might be an example. Echo clusters sometimes occur on an anniversary or in response to sudden interest in an earlier cluster (Chung, 2015; Smith, 2012).

Smith (2012) reported on clusters in Lake Forest, Illinois; Palo Alto, California; and Monmouth County, New Jersey. There have also been clusters on college campuses, like the one in 2003–2004 at New York University (5), at Cornell in 2010–2011 (6), and at the University of Pennsylvania in 2013–2014 (6). Most seemed to be sparked by an initiating suicide that received a lot of media attention. The succeeding deaths generally used the same method. In instances in which a suicide is heavily publicized or teenagers are creating online shrines to deceased friends, investigators should be on the alert.

Investigators must also be aware of "suicide shrines" or "suicide magnets," which can inspire "suicide tourism." This means that (1) people travel to where they will get an assisted suicide, (2) people travel specifically to kill themselves at what they perceive is a special place, and (3) shrines where suicides routinely occur can also attract gawkers. The Eiffel Tower, the London Underground, the Golden Gate Bridge in San Francisco, Gap Park in Australia, Britain's Beachy Head cliffs, Japan's Aokigahara Woods, Niagara Falls, and tall structures such as the Empire State Building have long been suicide shrines, as have several natural wonders around the world. In 1933, a woman jumped into a volcano to achieve spiritual transformation. This started a narrative that soon attracted more than 100 others to perform similar fatal feats. Another "spiritual suicide" involved a man taking mind-altering drugs who slammed his head against 15 trees until he finally expired.

Some theorists believe that contagion can be attributed to imitation, although this has not been studied. Joiner (2005) tried to explain the phenomenon of suicide clusters as "assortative relating." That is, like-minded people, for example, people vulnerable to suicide, tend to hang out together, so it would make sense that several of them were adversely affected by the suicide of one of them. This could "prearrange" suicide clusters.

An array of negative events could activate the cluster, or the group could have habituated to the idea of suicide by having discussions about it. This might give them courage and justification, as well as ideas about how to accomplish it. Joiner cites his study of college roommates. Those who chose to room together were more similar on a suicide index than those who were randomly assigned to be roommates. He interprets "belongingness threats" as a high-stress event. If suicides by peers, an event that dissolves the belongingness of the group, are not well buffered by other social support systems, this can cause a great deal of stress. However, several suicide researchers found that there were numerous factors in each incident. Some have surmised that the immature teenage brain fails to have a "braking system" and thereby is more prone to an impulsive suicide when life is not going well. Teenagers tend to have less ability to view life as a series of stages.

Public suicides, too, can trigger contagions. Public suicide has many facets. Such an act is often a political or social statement, or it can be a way to resist one's sense of anonymity.

In 1974, the host of a talk show, Christine Chubbuck, did a news story on suicide. On the show, a police officer demonstrated how to commit suicide with wadcutter target bullets. Chubbuck paid close attention. She had been depressed. She apparently had decided to end it. One day, Chubbuck read several news stories on the air before she said, "In keeping with Channel 40's policy of bringing you the latest in blood and guts, and in living color," she said, "you are going to see another first—attempted suicide." She then pulled out a gun and shot herself.

Several people have killed themselves while streaming a live webcam. Alexander Biggs, a mentally ill man in Florida, posted his suicidal intentions online. He inserted a viewing link into a blog, along with his suicide note. Those who hit the link saw him lying on a bed, heavily drugged. Over a period of 12 hours, viewers debated over whether to notify the authorities before someone finally did. By this time, Biggs was dead (Joiner, 2005).

A 20-year-old in Canada known as "Stephen" attempted suicide in his dorm room while live streaming. According to reports, Stephen had posted that he was "an oldfag [sic] who ... would finally give back to the community. I am willing to be an hero on cam for you all." Another user set up a chat room, which soon reached 200 participants. As they watched, Stephen took pills, drank vodka, lit a fire, and crawled under his bed. The room began to fill with smoke as he typed a message to the effect that he was dead. Firefighters broke in and saved him (Visser, 2013).

On March 21, 2007, Kevin Whitrick, a 42-year-old electrical engineer, was in an "insult" chat with about 60 people. As the others watched, Whitrick slung a rope over a joist in his home, stood on a chair, and hanged himself. Some viewers, thinking it was just a show, made fun of him, but one alarmed person contacted police. They arrived too late.

In 2017, several people used Facebook Live to commit suicide online. In April, Arjun Bharadwaj showed himself drinking and eating a meal in a hotel room on the 19th floor, after which he broke the window and jumped out. He was 24, addicted to drugs, and depressed over his life. In Alabama in April, James Jeffrey shot himself in the head following the end of a relationship. Wuttisan Wongtalay hanged his infant daughter in Thailand before he killed himself.

Although many called for Facebook to remove the live streaming feature, this would not address the impulse to make one's death into a live production. Social media has made many aspects of private life public, so those with the need for attention or to make a statement can always find a way. (Note: Facebook did develop policies for responding to these situations more effectively.)

MASS SUICIDES

There is little an investigator can do about a mass suicide or a suicidal mass murder. However, these suicidal acts do have precursors as well. Sometimes it is possible to see it coming. When self-named prophets like Jim Jones and David Koresh teach "end times" philosophies, the probability for mass suicide of their cult rises.

On Saturday November 18, 1978, members of the Peoples Temple in Jonestown in Guyana, South America, were faced with a dreadful decision. A small party of their officials had followed Congressman Leo Ryan to the airstrip, killing him along with a Temple defector and some journalists. Those officials had returned to Jonestown to start the "White Night."

The cult members had been repeatedly prepared for the end, drilling over and over. Jones had warned them about the approaching persecution, trained them in how to commit suicide, and made its inevitability part of their beliefs. In the end, there were more than 900 deaths and no one could say how many had willingly poisoned themselves. Some ran away (Moran, 1999). What was once a religious refuge had become a massive pile of decaying corpses.

Jones was among those leaders who believed that he "owned" his flock. If he decided it was time to die, he would take them all with him. He had prepared them. He spoke for them and decided for them. This is a red flag. What he did, with his rituals of preparing to die and brainwashing his followers with paranoid delusions, could be viewed as a gradual form of mass murder.

The Solar Temple suicides in 1994 were similar. When the two leaders, Jo Di Mambro, 69, and Luc Jouret, 47, decided it was time to go (as fraud investigators looked into their financial mismanagement), they made that decision for all members in the Order of the Solar Temple. Dozens of these deaths were willing suicides, but several members were murdered (Palmer, 1996). Over a year after the first series of mass suicides, 16 more people were found dead in France. They were arranged in a wheel-like pattern. Over a year after that, another mass suicide in Quebec brought the total deaths to 74. As police learned about it, they were able to prevent another outbreak in 1998. A psychologist had gathered over two dozen followers to join her in ending their lives. This time, the mass suicide was thwarted.

Hoffer (1951) delineates key factors that promote self-sacrifice for ideologies. They include identification with a collective ideological mentality, devaluing the present situation, having unified emotions (usually fear and hatred, with a target), a loss of individuality, adherence to a charismatic leader, and acceptance of death as part of a spiritual transformation. The red flags for suicide lie within the group's philosophy. The leaders and members are fanatics, he says, and the followers are the type of people who need something to worship, even to the point of self-annihilation. They willingly sacrifice whatever is necessary to a spiritual vision that they believe will enlarge them. It gives them a sense of purpose. Frustrated with the status quo, they seek a simple idealistic truth and they cherish inclusion in a likeminded community that shares their own spiritual goals.

Another cult of likeminded members willing to sacrifice themselves for ideals was known as Heaven's Gate. A peaceful and secretive group, members engaged in rigorous training for higher consciousness (Wessinger, 2000). Marshall Applewhite had joined Bonnie Lu Trousdale Nettles to present themselves as ancient aliens who were two witnesses mentioned in the Book of Revelation. The biblical "cloud" mentioned in scripture, they preached, was actually a spaceship. They attracted followers before Nettles died from cancer. Applewhite told the disciples that she was "away" to prepare the "mothership" but would soon be back to pick them up. Some disillusioned members left, but a devout few remained, waiting for their salvation.

In 1996, the group rented a mansion in California. There, they awaited the Hale-Bopp comet, with Nettles reportedly driving a spaceship in its tail. They had to be ready when she arrived. First, they had to depart from their physical forms. On Saturday, March 22, 1997, 39 members dressed identically to commit groupmind suicide. They took barbiturate phenobarbital mixed in pudding or applesauce before lying on their beds, under a purple shroud, with plastic bags over their heads.

COERCIVE SUICIDES

Among the most difficult situations to predict are those that involve depressed or angry individuals who are determined to kill others, and often quite a lot of people, before they die: the suicidal mass murderer. They commit what we call *coercive suicide*, or forcing others to die, too, as part of their demise. Typically, they have derived pleasure from imagining power over their targeted victims and from thinking about their moment of fame immortalized in international headlines. They think about all the deaths they will have caused. These killers tend to give signals about their intent, but the ability of police to try to stop them is restricted by conservative laws about danger to self or others. There must be highly convincing proof.

Elliot Rodger had an act of coercive suicide in mind. He had grievances. He posted long videos of himself on YouTube to let the world know how angry he was. The 22-year-old had failed to get the type of girlfriend he thought he deserved, so he armed himself and formed a deadly plan to ensure that everyone would know how the world had injured him. He put it into action on May 23, 2014. In Isla Vista, California, Rodger killed three men in his residence before uploading another video. Then, he set out on his suicidal mission (Beekman, 2014).

Rodger had planned to enter the Alpha Phi sorority house at the University of California at Santa Barbara and kill everyone there. He wanted these girls, with all their beauty and privilege, to pay for his misery and isolation. However, no one answered the door. Frustrated, he got in his car and drove down the street, shooting and ramming random people. He killed 6 and hurt 14 before he crashed. Sitting there, he shot himself. Could this massacre have been stopped? Possibly, with the right training and foresight.

Rodger had written a 107,000-word manuscript, "My Twisted World," which he had emailed to several people. Despite growing up in privilege, he failed to appreciate what he had. He believed he deserved more. He especially hated sorority-type college girls who would not respond to him. Twice, he had thrown hot coffee on women over ignoring him. He thought his anger was fully justified. It appeared that he had planned the Isla Vista attack for months. Yet, there *had* been an opportunity to stop him. At the request of his parents, police had come to his home to check on his welfare. To them, he had seemed calm and rational. Had they known about the videos and manifesto, they might have spent more time with him. He had named specific targets and expressed plenty of anger. Many killers can pass as normal for a brief discussion with police. To actually see if someone is a threat requires a more in-depth analysis of several sources.

The signals for suicidal mass murderers can be linked to factors that are statistically significant in the sophisticated field of risk assessments (Conroy & Murrie, 2008). The need for control, mixed with an attitude of entitlement and obsessive fantasies are all high on the list. These are evident in Rodger's videos. In addition, he made a clear and specific plan. His frustration had simmered for some time, and he had a rigid temperament. He dealt poorly with disappointment. He warned of revenge. Life had lost all meaning. He saw no reason to go on. He was checking out, mentally, but he wanted others to pay. He was not going alone.

Upon meeting with someone like this, investigators can evaluate the risk factors, especially for suicide. Even the shortcut mnemonic, IS PATH WARM, will help. Those who make welfare checks need to be trained in the kinds of questions to ask that could elicit more than is typically done. If individuals know important things about the potentially violent person, such as a ranting video or manifesto, they must convey this in specific terms to officers. Mental health experts are already aware of these requirements. Every state has laws that dictate what to do, but family and friends must also be forthcoming if they expect appropriate intervention (Ramsland, 2003).

Vague threats are of less concern than specific ones. Having a plan is more alarming than being aimless. Quite a few suicidal mass murderers wrote manifestos that contained their suicide message. A few had left suicide notes just before they went out to kill. These are among the notes that assist with understanding the suicidal mind.

SUICIDE NOTES

The following study was undertaken with Northampton County Coroner Zachary Lysek, along with input from forensic linguist Carole Chaski.

Death investigators tend to accept notes left at apparent suicide scenes as genuine, unless they find clear indications of a homicide. This practice can cause erroneous judgments about notes that are part of successful staging and about ambiguous texts in cases with manners of death other than suicide. They have no tool to assist with distinctions and no training on this aspect of suicide. A practical checklist of items that consistently show up in a majority of genuine suicide notes, based on valid protocol statements from extensive suicide note research, could increase the accuracy of death investigation decisions. This project involved using protocol statements from numerous studies that used content analysis on suicide notes. The goal was to develop a Suicide Note Authenticity Checklist (SNAC) as a testable device.

Although only about one in four suicidal people write notes (Joiner, 2005, 2010; Leenaars, 1988), these documents can offer clues about state of mind prior to death. "Suicide notes are windows to the mind of the deceased" (Leenaars, 1992, p. 338). Because they are often written hours to minutes before death, or because they have been written and revised over a longer period, they provide a starting point for trying to understand, even if the note offers no clear explanation (and most do not). Among the typical sentiments expressed are

- I can't figure out how to go on.
- What I'm doing is best for all concerned.
- Life sucks. I hate myself.
- I don't want to do this, but I've never been much use to anyone.
- I don't want to be a burden.
- Everything I do, fails.
- I hope you're happy now that I'm gone.
- I can't go on without him (or her).
- I can't live with this (condition, illness, and emptiness).
- I see no other way out.

A young man just out of a brief stint in jail wrote this one: "I took my life in the basement. Don't come down. I don't want you to see me like this, but I understand if you do. It wasn't depression. It was the stigma. I would always have to worry about getting a job, with possible imprisonment for doing the slightest thing wrong. That is not the life I want to live. No one is to blame. I'm sorry."

A divorced older woman wrote a note to the police, whom she expected would find her body: "People have always put obstacles in my way. One of the great ones is leaving this world when you want to and have nothing to live for ... My mind was never more clear."

Behavior can sometimes speak louder than words. For example, a college student who keeps a 3-year suicide journal shows chronic depression versus a 15-year-old at a train track who leaves an unsent text message one word long on his phone—"Goodbye"—before leaping. Those who make suicide pacts frequently leave notes (Fishbain, D'Achille, Barsky, & Aldrich, 1984). Most people do not.

Note-leavers often feel a need to "talk" to someone. Some spew anger, some apologize, some insist they're better off, some ask forgiveness, some give others their love, some hope their death will not harm anyone, some want to punish or blame, and some want to ensure that their final wishes are carried out. A few take the opportunity to be philosophical. A note might include a single word, multiple pages, or multiple notes to various different people. They might even take the form of a full diary, a text, a voice mail, a social media message, an inked tattoo, a poem, or an audio or video. Investigators might find a note near the body or left in a notebook, a car, a locker, or even placed in the mail.

One woman left a series of brief Post-it notes all over her house, and another created hers as a complex piece of needlework. Some include bills that must be paid, PIN numbers to bank accounts, or instructions for how to work the washing machine. Sometimes, they write on some part of their body. They might even post a suicide note on a social media site. One man wrote his as a wall-sized poster, penned in black marker ink. A few have slipped them into favorite books, hoping that someone who knows them well will discover it.

Although many researchers have performed and described psychological autopsies, the role of the suicide note has received little attention, especially in terms of how to distinguish a genuine note from a staged note written by someone else. Acinas, Robles, & Pelaez-Fernandez (2015) looked specifically at the role of suicide notes in psychological autopsies. They categorized the types of notes typically found, but they only mentioned the possibility of a fake note in a staged death event. Their classification includes farewell notes, instructions, accusations, requests for forgiveness, and justification. Even a brief note can shed some light, such as the one from a teenage boy that said, "I'm sorry for the lifes [sic] I have affected." A person who gives instructions ("I have signed over the car to you and I want you to pay a debt I owe to my friend") is different from one who cries out, "I have been alone too long and no longer wish to go on." The person who hides the note differs from the one who uses a lipstick tube to scrawl it on a mirror. Leenaars said, "Suicide notes offer us a living link to his or her ideation" (1992, p. 339). Putting a psychological autopsy together with a deeper grasp of genuine versus nongenuine suicide notes can assist with more accurate investigations. (We decided to use "genuine" versus "nongenuine" rather than "authentic" versus "inauthentic," due to written items found near decedents that were not actual notes but also were not staged notes.)

As described in Chapter 1, a study of suicide notes launched the formal field of suicidology. Shneidman and Faberow (1957) started the ball rolling. They set up experiments to learn about distinct features of genuine notes. Shneidman had originally believed that the content of suicide notes would be an invaluable source for state-of-mind determinations, but he found that most offered little to clarify their reasoning. Many notes were banal and some were too short to be meaningful. After a long career in suicidology, Shneidman ultimately decided that a suicide note had to be understood within the decedent's life context, a time-consuming endeavor (1993).

A few more attempts were made to study suicide notes, and Leenaars (1988) undertook an extensive qualitative analysis. He first reviewed the literature of suicide notes and diaries from the 1940s through the mid-1980s, including Shneidman and Faberow's experiment with genuine and simulated notes. With the aim of developing a standardized analysis protocol, Leenaars examined the note-writers' relationships, emotional states, cognitive states, and demographics. With 33 additional genuine notes from 1984–1985, also gathered from the Los Angeles Coroner's Office (now the Los Angeles County Department of Medical Examiner—Coroner), Leenaars found that most content items remained stable across time in the United States, despite significant social upheavals over this 40-year span. Ambivalence occurred *less* often in the 1980s sample, while a constricted mental state characterized by an inability to distinguish options was evident *more* often.

Narrative qualitative analysis is often criticized for its subjective approach and lack of rigor. Its goal is to "understand the relationship between a text and social reality" (Neuendorf, 2017, p. 11). This method makes inferences by objectively and systematically identifying specific elements in texts for developing protocol statements. The protocol statement is a text sampling manipulation that (1) searches for specific words and phrases or that (2) rephrases content into basic categorical units. The intent is to keep the expressions as natural as possible while also translating the items for collection and comparison (Neuendorf, 2017). Protocol statements interpret written expressions into flexible constructs so that researchers can gather seemingly diverse expressions from different documents into "meaning unit" categories. Manageable units allow for the measurement of phrase frequency, but researchers must also be alert to the loss of experiential richness. Quality control over maintaining original meaning enhances validity. Practical parameters can organize key items based on frequency and commonality (Neuendorf, 2017). This is true of the suicide note content analysis research (Bennell & Jones, 2007).

Objectivity increases with the intersubjective agreement of multiple qualified coders; that is, they can make judgments about variables that can be applied to message units and that will resemble coding by other judges. Reliability is based on their consistent agreement. To make this study scientific, Leenaars used several judges trained in psychology. Examples of protocol statements include the following: (1) a derogatory and hostile attitude is evident that is directed toward the self; (2) the person is preoccupied with a person he has lost; and (3) the person sees suicide as a solution to an urgent problem.

As Shneidman had defined it, genuine notes are authenticated notes written by people who committed suicide. Nongenuine notes include (1) simulated notes written by subjects in control groups, (2) computer-generated notes (yes, there are websites for this), (3) control documents for a note database, and (4) notes written to stage a death (usually a homicide or autoerotic accident) as a suicide. For example, a man who committed a murder–suicide wrote two notes to give the appearance that his girlfriend had participated in a suicide pact. There are also written items, such as a poem, that can be mistaken for a genuine note.

To create a research foundation, Leenaars derived protocol statements for his suicide note dataset based on 10 prominent theorists, listing 10 statements for each, which resulted in 100 protocol statements. Although deriving these categories from 10 experts provides interjudge reliability, Leenaars admitted that there were complications due to theoretical disagreements.

For the next step, he identified common elements across the statements. He found 23 that occurred in two-thirds of the statements, which yielded 23 protocol statements. Eighteen statements occurred significantly more often in the genuine notes, so they helped to differentiate these categories. Five statements proved to be both "highly predictive *and* differentiating" (p. 173), that is, present on both lists. Leenaars used them to form five organizing categories, seen in Table 3.1.

Leenaars (1992) continued to combine and expand upon his protocol statements until he had assembled 35 that either predict (P) suicide or discriminate (D) genuine from nongenuine notes, or do both (P&D). The clinically relevant factors for genuine suicides were found to be psychic tension, mental confusion, unfulfilled desires, hostility, futility, dependency, constriction, and fatalism.

No differences were found between males and females, or between attempters and completers, except that more attempters saw themselves as weak individuals who could not cope. Differences were noted in suicide notes written by younger people, in that some of the eight categories applied only later in the lifespan. Teenagers also tended to think in terms of "all or nothing" absolutes, such as "I will *never* have what I want" or "I *always* fail at what I try."

From his research, Leenaars developed the Thematic Guide for Suicide Prediction as a lengthy 35-item, 8-subscale "inferential guide" that can be applied to written or oral communications. It can help to analyze content as well as to predict behavior, specific to the constructs of *perturbation* and *lethality*. Each dimension can be rated low, medium, and high. Leenaars concluded that no single guide may be the answer for suicide prediction, and an accurate assessment could involve using several different types of evaluations.

Subsequent research has built on Leenaars' approach.

TABLE 3.1   Leenaars' Organizing Categories

1. The note reflects a communication about a *situation* for survivors and/or others.
2. The note highlights the importance of a *relationship*.
3. The note exhibits the presence of an *emotional state*.
4. The note exhibits language and reasoning suggestive of a *cognitive state*.
5. The note reflects a fragmented or narcissistic *ego development* (pp. 177–178).

Black (1993) used a different set of suicide notes, but rather than screening his subjects for specific matched traits as Shneidman and Faberow had done, he enlisted 77 unpaid community volunteers over the age of 18, including 23 females (which Shneidman and Faberow had not included). He extended the age range to 90. Black found that genuine notes were longer and contained more neutral content. In addition, these note-writers gave more instructions, stated more facts, discussed religious ideas, and tended to add a date to the note. Simulators, in contrast, gave reasons more often for the suicide (guessing that this was typical), described their ambivalence, used absolute terms, discussed morality, expressed depression, asked forgiveness, and reflected cultural ideas about suicide.

Gregory (1999) derived nine variables for differentiating genuine from nongenuine notes. He found that five variables applied to content and four to structure. The content variables revealed the degree to which an individual has internalized the decision to die. Gregory also analyzed 84 additional notes, 51 of which were genuine and 33 written by volunteers. He found that the nongenuine note-writers used longer sentences but fewer verbs and nouns. The genuine notes showed more practical aspects and the writers were less likely to blame themselves.

Callanan and Davis (2009) found that note-writers tend to live alone and to have made prior suicide threats. Joiner et al. (2002) examined the perception of being a burden. Coster and Lester (2013) evaluated common cognitive and emotional themes from cognitive behavioral therapy to identify the most frequent emotions expressed in suicide notes. Using a statistical frequency analysis on 86 notes, they identified two forms of depression, guilt, shame, hurt, and anger. Males expressed guilt, while females expressed hurt.

The current text opened with the suicide note written by Stephen Port to give the appearance that one of his victims had accidentally killed another and was sufficiently depressed to end his own life. The police had accepted the note as genuine and closed two cases. Other cases show similar assumptions, with killers nearly getting away with their crimes (more examples will be shown in Chapter 4). The importance of knowing when a note is genuine versus when it might be used to stage a crime cannot be underestimated.

If an estimated 20%–25% of suicidal people leave notes and the rate of note-leaving has remained constant, the ability to accurately evaluate note authenticity affects an estimated 8,000–10,000 cases each year (Leenaars, 1988; Shiori et al., 2005; Tavernise, 2016). First responding officers, who initially decide whether a text document at a death scene is a suicide note, show only average skill for evaluating genuine notes (Snook & Mercer, 2010). Even mental health professionals have shown only 50%–70% accuracy, because they accept cultural beliefs as fact.

Many of those beliefs are incorrect (Joiner, 2010; Leenaars & Balance, 1984; Pestian et al., 2008).

The potential for error during key stages of suicide note evaluation suggests a need for training among death investigators, especially for equivocal deaths that require a full psychological autopsy. A valid, standardized authenticity tool derived from research about suicide notes, which could be developed as a practical checklist for first responders, would benefit the investigative community. It could be used in training and on the scene for a quick analysis and decision about the need for further investigation. Research exists that offers the right material for developing a SNAC.

Chaski and Huddleston (2012) point out problems with the typical manner of suicide note interpretation, identifying three phases of assessment. First, factors such as death scene appearance and a prior acquaintance with the decedent can influence responding officers, who decide whether a text document at a scene is a suicide note. Second, specific types of bodily trauma can influence how forensic pathologists and medical examiners interpret such documents. A third phase might call on a forensic psychologist or psychiatrist, whose judgment is at, or slightly better than, chance (Leenaars & Lester, 1991; Pestian et al., 2008; Snook & Mercer, 2010).

After viewing Leenaars' note collection, Chaski, a forensic linguist, created the Suicide Note Assessment Research, or SNARE as part of the Automated Linguistic Identification and Assessment System. She hoped to devise a way to objectively compare questioned suicide notes against a database of genuine notes. SNARE uses computational linguistic analysis to identify and count linguistic features in the text. This results in quantifying each text so that it can be classified as either a suicide note or a control text (nongenuine). SNARE shows an accuracy rate of 80%–88%, with shorter notes on the higher end, because longer notes tend to include elements of control documents, such as lists, love letters, and directions. Nineteen percent of genuine suicide notes were misclassified as control documents when they included control-type items, and just 7% of nongenuine texts were misclassified as suicide notes. In sum, if SNARE classifies 100 new documents, it is expected to make errors on 14. (The error rate for the notes from this current study of 2 years of notes from the coroner's office—28 notes—was 71.4%, in part because SNARE does not correct for spelling errors, and many suicide notes contain them.)

Chaski has collected over 400 authenticated suicide notes, running from 2 to 1,500 words (in English), written by males and females, aged 18 to mid-60s. Of these, 133 notes are under 45 words and 231 are under 100 words. For comparison, Chaski developed a database of over 500 written control texts. The control texts include love letters, apologies, threats, complaints, lists, instructions, business letters, and other types of ordinary communication. SNARE uses only the note contents and no other forensic or medical information.

Besides the basic SNARE software, a more detailed analysis can be performed with SNARE-Quals, a database search that retrieves real notes with specific comparisons to a questioned note. Each genuine suicide note in the database has been classified according to specific themes. A search for a theme, such as "self-blame" or "hostility" results in a list of notes that contain it. The questioned note can then be compared to real suicide notes.

Results from the SNARE-Qual database allowed a comparison against the themes that Leenaars and other content analysts found in studied suicide notes. It also allowed comparison with the frequency distribution chart devised for the SNAC. Having access to this database provided a way to standardize the comparisons and rank the frequencies of specific themes.

The following case of a questioned suicide called on Chaski's approach. American computer engineer Shane Todd was found hanged in Singapore in June 2012. Law enforcement told his family he had killed himself, leaving suicide notes to explain it. They described him using an elaborate mechanism for hanging himself on his bathroom door. Todd's family refused to accept that he had composed the five typewritten notes found at the scene. In them, he had referenced activities with them that had never happened and the language and tone did not sound like him. Earlier, he had told his mother that he feared for his life and thought he might never see them again, due to the sensitive nature of a project he was working on for a Chinese company. He believed they were attempting to get him to breach US security. He stated that he would be returning to the States soon to take another job. He had seemed relieved. Shane's girlfriend confirmed that he had been frustrated and unhappy for 8 months. A psychiatrist had prescribed a mild dose of antidepressants. Neither thought that Shane had been suicidal (LaRosa, 2014).

His parents traveled to see his apartment and found no evidence that the story the police had told was true. Instead, they saw evidence that Sean had been packing, preparing to leave the country. The police then denied their own original narrative but maintained that the death was a suicide. There was no evidence of a thorough investigation at the scene. Caught exploring files on his computer 3 days after his death, they admitted it, but said it was part of the investigation. Still, the only files accessed were his work files. After being repeatedly thwarted in their attempt to get the facts, the Todds hired a medical examiner to examine the autopsy report and photographs they had taken of the body. He saw bruises on the hands and a bump on the forehead. He believed that Shane had been strangled with a cord (although he would later retract this finding). A 2-week coroners' inquiry turned up evidence on

Shane's computer that he had repeatedly accessed suicide websites, specifically seeking information about knots for hanging. There was no evidence that his computer had been hacked to upload fake suicide notes. The US Embassy affirmed the finding of suicide, with reports from two medical examiners, despite an employee who had stated that the original police report, now retracted, had been submitted. Then a test showed DNA from a person other than Shane on the noose. The Singapore government had it destroyed, claiming standard practices ("Spies, Lies and Secrets," 2014).

The family hired two linguistics experts, who performed a content analysis and found that Shane Todd was not the likely author (Todd & Villegas, 2014). Dr. Carole Chaski ran the notes through the SNARE software program. She claimed that the Singapore notes did not share characteristics of genuine suicide notes from her dataset of 400 notes and that nothing from Shane's computer from the months prior to his death bore resemblance to a suicide note. Because Chaski had cross-cultural linguistic capabilities in her program, she also stated that the phrasing in the notes was non-native English. The other expert, Dr. David Camp, stated that someone who did not share Shane's cultural background had written the notes. Specific phrasing, a lack of emotionality or individuality, an emphasis on certain values, and the types of passive sentences used suggested that the note-writer was of Asian or Middle Eastern origin (Camp, n.d.). These items also conflicted with the manner in which Shane ordinarily wrote. In addition, he thanked the company for which he worked, despite being at odds with them and ready to quit. (Recall the finding that killers are often mentioned in notes in a positive light.)

This case demonstrates a number of items specific to the investigation of a supposed suicide that might actually be a homicide. It also demonstrates the need for a practical tool that can be used by investigators in the field.

THE SUICIDE NOTE AUTHENTICITY CHECKLIST

Twenty-eight genuine notes from the Northampton County Coroner's office, 2015–2016, were added to the genuine notes available from studies mentioned above, including the 400 thematically analyzed notes in the SNARE database. Nongenuine notes include the 500 control documents in the SNARE database, plus 33 simulated notes from earlier studies and a dozen known false notes from homicides staged as suicides. This project used a univariate frequency distribution, focused on themes that show up most often in genuine notes in other studies. The lists for the SNAC would include characteristics that distinguished genuine suicide notes and characteristics that were found in nongenuine notes. Unlike with SNARE, this list derives from staged and simulated notes, not from neutral content documents. The purpose of the SNAC is to assist investigators with accurate identification of documents found at a death scene.

Elements from genuine notes are listed on one side of the SNAC. The frequency distribution provided items that occurred only rarely, which helped to identify items for the nongenuine notes column. That is, if certain items are hardly ever present in the majority of suicide notes but those items show up in a questioned note, it raises a red flag for the potential that it is a nongenuine suicide note. The same can be said for *behaviors* that cluster around suicidal note-leavers, and these were added as well.

To derive the tool, 63 elements were identified for Column 1. Because the nongenuine notes did not have as much analysis or as many elements, this chart is not bivariate. However, there were a sufficient number of items mentioned in the research about staged or nongenuine notes and about suicide myths (Black, 1993; Leenaars & Lester, 1991; Snook & Mercer, 2010) to fill in the other side of the SNAC. Further research can validate these items or support their removal. Measurement precision is higher for genuine notes, as this content has received greater research focus. The best information is found in the SNARE database.

After analyzing notes from research and the Northampton County Coroner's Office and comparing them with the thematic analyses from the SNAC, a numbered code was devised to differentiate items that should be on the SNAC from items that should not (Table 3.2).

Some notes had more than one theme. For those themes that showed up in less than 10% of the 94 genuine notes examined, a 0 was used. From 10%–30%, 1 was used. From 30% to 50%, 2 was used. For items that showed up more than 50% of the time, 3 was used. SNAC items for the "Genuine" column were selected from those items denoted by 2 and 3, up to the top 15. For the "Nongenuine" column, behaviors or content described in the research as raising red flags were added. In addition, those items that were rated 0 in genuine notes were considered for the "Nongenuine" SNAC column. That is, since they were rarely found in genuine notes, they could be red flags for nongenuine notes.

From this analysis, the results for the SNAC are listed in Table 3.3.

The notes from the coroner's office showed some differences from earlier research, such as little expression of hostility and more requests for forgiveness. SNAC items can now be compared against more confirmed genuine and nongenuine notes in the future and should be further validated. Items might still be replaced.

TABLE 3.2   Frequency Distribution Chart for the SNAC

Potential Emotional and Cognitive Items for Genuine Notes Column

Meaning Unit	Number	Frequency (%)	Code
1. Perception of trauma	59	63	3
2. Frustrated need	39	42	2
3. Unbearable anguish	35	37	2
4. Difficult adaptation	32	34	2
5. Suicide as only resolution	11	12	1
6. Values escape from situation above life	5	5	0
7. Intolerance for identified life disturbance	26	28	1
8. Sense of depletion	30	32	2
9. Obsession with lost or ideal person	25	27	1
10. Unrealistic needs	20	21	1
11. Extreme dependency	8	8.5	0
12. Broken relationship or lack of success in establishing a relationship	29	31	2
13. Insurmountable sense of injustice	6	6.3	0
14. Inability to foresee success	23	24	1
15. Disconnection from others	33	35	2
16. Forlorn, hopeless, helpless, and trapped	63	67	3
17. Perceives no other options	17	18	1
18. Inward anger, self-abasement, and self-punishment	22	23	1
19. Aggression, vengefulness, and hurt another	28	30	2
20. Ambivalence via content inconsistency	7	7.4	0
22. Emotions intoxicate	2	2	0
23. Feelings of weakness, limitation, and defeat	34	36	2
24. No justification for living	11	12	1
25. Perverted justification for suicide	8	8	0
26. Expressions of love	24	25	1
27. Requests for forgiveness	31	32	2
28. Expressed fear	21	22	1
29. Frustration/annoyance	40	42	2
30. Unwarranted entitlement	14	15	1
Behavioral Items			
31. Content consistent with life situation	85	90	3
32. Constricted thinking	71	76	3

(Continued)

TABLE 3.2 (Continued)   Frequency Distribution Chart for the SNAC

Potential Emotional and Cognitive Items for Genuine Notes Column

	Number	Frequency (%)	Code
33. Rigidity, fixation, and obsession	61	65	3
34. Inadequate maturity	24	26	1
35. Unrealistic needs	21	22	1
36. Lives alone		Unknown	
37. Prior suicide attempts	56	60	3
38. States facts	24	26	1
39. Gives instructions	61	65	3
40. Note is long	22	23	1
41. Makes religious comments	10	11	1
42. Presence of a serious disorder (schizophrenia, bipolar, and OCD)	25	27	1
43. Neutral content	52	55	3
44. Dates note		Unknown	

Potential Items for Nongenuine Notes Column[a]

Meaning Unit

	Number	Frequency (%)	Code
1. Gives reasons for suicide	17	18	1
2. Situation inconsistent with note contents	9	9.5	0
3. Expresses ambivalence	8	8	0
4. Specifically describes depression	17	18	1
5. Uses absolute words ("never" and "always")	15	16	1
6. Discusses morality of suicide	4	4	0
7. No neutral content	11	12	1
8. No instructions	14	15	1
9. No sense of cognitive constriction	7	7	0
10. Lives with others		Unknown	
11. Has significant emotional buffers		Unknown	
12. No prior suicide attempts	37	40	2
13. No sense of burdensomeness	5	5	0
14. No expressions of love	24	25	1
15. No date		Unknown	
16. No sense of fear	19	20	1
17. Uses uncharacteristic phrases	2	2	0
19. Expresses options/shows hope	3	3	0

Note: SNAC, Suicide Note Authenticity Checklist

[a] Based on identification in research as significant in simulated or fake notes. The count is for presence in genuine notes.

TABLE 3.3   The SNAC

Genuine Suicide Notes	Nongenuine Suicide Notes
1. Perception of trauma, distress, and loss	1. Circumstances inconsistent with note content
2. Frustrated need	2. Gives reasons for suicide
3. Forlorn, hopeless, helpless, trapped	3. Discusses morality of suicide
4. Content consistent with life situation	4. Expresses ambivalence
5. Constricted thinking/no options	5. Has emotional buffers, no sense of failure
6. Rigidity, fixation, and obsession	6. Note not signed
7. Prior suicide attempts	7. Speaks in absolute terms
8. Gives instructions/neutral content	8. Refers to a third person
9. Self-blame	9. Few verbs and nouns, long sentences
10. Unbearable anguish	10. Elaborate apology
11. Difficult adaptation	11. Note left close to body
12. Frustration	12. No neutral content or instructions
13. Aggression, vengefulness, and hurt another	13. No prior suicide attempts
14. Requests for forgiveness	14. No cognitive constriction
15. Disconnection from others	15. Uncharacteristic phrases

Death investigators who interpret suicide notes in the context of a death incident are generally coroners or medical examiners. In small jurisdictions, however, police officers might make the initial decisions, or even freelance death investigators. As noted earlier, Snook and Mercer (2010) found that officers' ability to evaluate whether a suicide note was authentic is equivalent to chance. They had 36 officers read 30 suicide notes, half of which were genuine and half of which were simulated. The subjects were accurate in their evaluations about 50% of the time. The officers focused on two items before concluding that a note was fake: the use of verbs like "I think" or "I feel" and the absence of an explanation. They were wrong on both counts. Some officers think that suicide notes will not contain positive affect; again, they would be wrong (and so would families who resist such notes as proof). This is a small subject group, but few officers are educated in the nuances of suicide, and uneducated judgment tends to mirror social notions (Leenaars & Lester, 1991). Arbeit and Blatt (1983) reported that few research subjects could distinguish genuine from simulated suicide notes. In the following case, a piece of writing near a decedent triggered a threshold diagnosis that led to a messy investigation.

Hughes de la Plaza was found stabbed to death in his San Francisco apartment on June 2, 2007. His body was discovered quickly, stabbed three times, but ambiguities at the scene caused confusion. Blood drops were found outside and in. Where the body lay, extensive blood smears and overturned furniture suggested a struggle. His watch, ripped from his wrist, lay beneath him. The back and front doors were locked. Only one set of bloody footprints was found inside, identified as made by the decedent (Ferenc, 2009; McKinley, 2009).

All blood that was tested was from the decedent. No bloody knife was found inside the apartment, but detectives found a piece of writing on the living room table. A notepad adjacent to the cell phone said, "Learn as if you were to live forever, live as if you were to die tomorrow." After seeing this note and the locked doors, officers began to investigate the incident as a suicide (Gellman, 2009). They reportedly ignored evidence to the contrary and did only a cursory investigation into the decedent's life.

There were no suicide indicators in the decedent's life. Acquaintances said that he had been celebrating a promotion that evening and had made plans for the following day. A former girlfriend who had not seen the decedent in 6 months told the police that he had been depressed over their breakup 4 years earlier, and the officers accepted this as sufficient reason for him to take his life that night. Yet she was certain it was not suicide. De la Plaza had been drinking, but there were no drugs in his system. Several people who lived next door said the detectives had decided it was a suicide before asking them questions and ignored their reports about noises and footsteps. Three independent investigators determined that the incident was a homicide and that the note was not a suicide note, but rather a common philosophical phrase from Mahatma Gandhi (Spicuzza, 2007). When Chief George Gascone asked an outside department to evaluate the case, they found that errors in the original investigation precluded a definitive determination of the manner of death (van Derberken, 2008). Had the original responders viewed the piece of writing on the tablet as just a possible and not a definitive suicide note, the investigation might have been more careful and the officers might have collected more details.

Similarly, in November 2015, a 14-year-old girl died. Officers found a number of poems that had dark tones and referred to a sense of a fragmented self. Investigators collected the poems as potential evidence of suicide, but the autopsy showed that the girl had died a natural death from cardiac arrest associated with a rare syndrome. This is an example of ambiguous writings that investigators initially thought supported a finding of suicide. Had the autopsy not been definitive, this death investigation might have been conducted as a suicide investigation, causing the parents greater grief.

SUMMARY

Psychological autopsies depend heavily on suicidology. Suicidologists must know the literature, including the unique and bizarre cases, in order to offer useful consulting to investigators. A better grasp of suicidal mindsets comes from studying the range of suicidal behavior, including clusters, groupmind suicides, and the decision to write a suicide note. Next, we look at one more twist: the staged scene.

REFERENCES

Acinas, P., Robles, J., & Pelaez-Fernandez, M. (2015). Suicide note and psychological autopsy: Associated behavioral aspects. *Actas Españolas de Psiquiatría, 43*(3), 69–79.

Arbeit, S., & Blatt, S. (1983). Differentiation of genuine and simulated suicide notes. *Psychological Reports, 33*, 283–293.

Beekman, D. (2014, May 26). Elliot Rodger wrote manifesto on his hate for women and his vindictive scheme prior to deadly rampage. *New York Daily News.* Retrieved from http://www.nydailynews.com/news/national/maniac-writes-manifesto-prior-deadly-rampage-article-1.1805474

Black, S. (1993). Comparing genuine and simulated suicide notes: A new perspective. *Journal of Consulting and Clinical Psychology, 61*(4), 699–702.

Callanan, V. J., & Davis, M. S. (2009). A comparison of suicide note writers with suicides who did not leave notes. *Suicide and Life-Threatening Behavior, 39*(5), 558–568.

Campman S.C., Springer, F.A., & Henrikson, D.M. (2000). The chain saw: an uncommon means of committing suicide. *Journal of Forensic Science, 45*, 471–3.

Chaski, C.E., & Huddle, D. (2012). *Is this a real suicide note? Authentication using statistical classifiers and computational linguistics.* Presentation, American Academy of Forensic Sciences, Atlanta, GA.

Chung, J. (2015, December). The Silicon Valley suicides. *The Atlantic.* Retrieved from https://www.theatlantic.com/magazine/archive/2015/12/the-silicon-valley-suicides/413140/

Conroy, M. A., & Murrie, D. C. (2008). *Forensic assessment of violence risk.* Hoboken, NJ: Wiley.

Constable, B. & Felis, L. (2015, November 23). Special report: Gliniewicz' final hours as he staged his 'hero' cop death. *Daily Herald.* Retrieved from http://www.dailyherald.com/article/20151122/news/151129722/

Coster, D., & Lester, D. (2013). Last words: Analysis of suicide notes from an RECBT perspective: An exploratory study. *Journal of Rational Emotive Cognitive-Behavioral Therapy, 31*, 136–151.

Ferenc, M. (2009, February 11). Review of death scene/autopsy findings of Mr. Hughes de la Plaza. SFPD case *070-557-605*.

Fishbain, D., D'Achille, L., Barsky, S., & Aldrich, T. (1984). A controlled study of suicide pacts. *Journal of Clinical Psychiatry, 45*, 154–157.

Freuchen, A., & Groholt, B. (2015). Characteristics of suicide notes of children and young adolescents: An examination of the notes of suicide victims 15 years and young. *Clinical Child Psychology and Psychiatry, 20*(2), 194–206.

Geberth, V. (2015). *Practical homicide investigation: Tactic, procedures and forensic techniques*, 5th ed. Boca Raton, FL: CRC Press.

Gellman, J. (Producer). (2010). A case for murder [Television series episode]. *48 Hours*, New York: CBS Broadcasting.

Gregory, A. (1999). The decision to die: The psychology of the suicide note. In D. Canter & J. A. Laurence (Eds.), *Interviewing and deception* (pp. 127–157). Dartmouth, England: Ashgate.

Hoffer, E. (1951). *The true believer: Thoughts on the nature of mass movement*. New York: Harper & Row.

Joiner, T. E. (2005). *Why people due by suicide*. Cambridge, MA: Harvard University Press.

Joiner, T. E. (2010). *Myths about suicide*. Cambridge, MA: Harvard University Press.

Joiner, T. E., Pettit, J. W., Walker, R. L., Voelz, Z. R., Cruz, J., Rudd, D., & Lester, D. (2002). Perceived burdensomeness and suicidality: Two studies on the suicide notes of those attempting and those completing suicide. *Journal of Social and Clinical Psychology, 21*(5), 531–545.

Jones, N. J., & Bennell, C. (2007). The development and validation of statistical prediction rules for discriminating between genuine and simulated notes. *Archives for Suicide Research, 11*, 219–233.

LaRosa, P. (2014, September 2). Experts: Engineer found dead didn't write suicide notes. *CBS News*, Retrieved from https://www.cbsnews.com/news/experts-engineer-found-dead-didnt-write-suicide-notes-2/.

Lee, J., Lee, W., Hwang, J., & Stack, S. J. (2014). To what extent does the reporting behavior of the media regarding a celebrity suicide influence subsequent suicides in South Korea? *Suicide and Life-Threatening Behavior, 44*(4), 457–472.

Leenaars, A. A. (1988). *Suicide notes: Predictive clues and patterns*. New York: Human Science Press.

Leenaars, A. A. (1992). Suicide notes, communication and ideation. In R. W. Maris, A. Berman, J. T. Maltsberger, & R. I. Yufit (Eds.), *Assessment and Prediction of Suicide* (pp. 337–361). New York: Guilford.

Leenaars, A. A., & Balance, W. (1984). A logical empirical approach to the study of suicide notes. *Canadian Journal of Behavioural Science, 16,* 249–256.

Leenaars, A. A., & Lester, D. (1991). Myths about suicide notes. *Death Studies, 15,* 303–308.

Ma-Kellams, C., Baek, J. H., & Or, F. (2016, April 21). Suicide contagion in response to widely publicized celebrity deaths: The role of depressed affect, death thought accessibility, and attitudes. *Psychology of Popular Media Culture.* Retrieved from http://psycnet.apa.org/?&fa=main.doiLanding&doi=10.1037/ppm0000115

McKinley, J. (2009, March 5). Gruesome San Francisco death becomes international mystery. *New York Times.* Retrieved from http://www.nytimes.com/2009/03/05/us/05murder.html

Mesoudi, A. (2009). The cultural dynamics of copycat suicide. *PLoS One* 4(9), e7252. DOI: 10.1371/journal.pone.0007252

Moran, S. (1999). *The secret world of cults.* Surrey, England: CLB International.

Neuendorf, K. A. (2017). *The content analysis guidebook* (2nd ed.). Los Angeles, CA: Sage.

Palmer, S. (1996). Purity and danger in the Solar Temple. *Journal of Contemporary Religion, 11*(3), 303–318.

Pestian, J. P., Matykiewicz, P., Grupp-Phelan, J., Lavanier, S., Arszman, C, & Kowatch, R. (2008). Using natural language process to classify suicide notes. *Current Trends in Biomedical Natural Language Processing, 208,* 96–97.

Ramsland, K. (2003). *Inside the minds of mass murderers: Why they kill.* Westport, CT: Praeger.

Shiori, T., Nishinura, A., Akazawa, K, Abe, R., Nushida, H., Ueno, Y., Kojika-Maruyama, M., & Someya, T. (2005). Incident of note-leaving remains constant dispute increasing suicide rates. *Psychiatry and Clinical Neuroscience, 59*(2), 226–228.

Shneidman, E. S. (1993) *Suicide as psychache: A clinical approach to self-destructive behavior.* Lanham, MD: Jason Aronson.

Shneidman, E. S., & Faberow, N. L. (1957a). Some comparisons between genuine and simulated suicide notes in terms of Mowrer's concepts of discomfort and relief. *Journal of General Psychology, 56,* 251–256.

Smith, B. (2012, June 18). The cluster conundrum: Copycat teen deaths in Lake Forest. *Chicago Magazine.* Retrieved from http://www.chicagomag.com/Chicago-Magazine/July-2012/Bryan-Smith-on-the-Challenges-of-Writing-The-Cluster-Conundrum/

Snook, B., & Mercer, J. (2010). Modelling police officers' judgments of the veracity of suicide notes. *Canadian Journal of Criminology and Criminal Justice*, 52(1), 79–95.

Spicuzza, M. (2007, July 18). Who killed Hugues de la Plaza? *San Francisco Weekly*. Retrieved from http://www.sfweekly.com/2007-07-18/news/who-killed-hugues-de-la-plaza/html

Spies, Lies, and Secrets. (2013, October 5) *CBSnews.com*. Retrieved from https://www.cbsnews.com/videos/spies-lies-secrets/

Tavernise, S. (2016, April 22). U. S. suicide rate surges to a 30-year high. *The New York Times*, pp. A1, A15.

Todd, M., & Villegas, M. (2014). *Hard drive: A family's fight against three countries*. New York: Morgan James Publishing.

Tournel, G., Dedouit, F., Balgaires, A., et al. (2008). Unusual suicide with a chainsaw. *Journal of Forensic Science*, 53(5), 1174–1177.

Van Derberken, J. (2008, April 1). Homicide or suicide? Man's death a mystery. *San Francisco Chronicle*. Retrieved from http://www.sfgate.com/news/article/Homicide-or-suicide-Man-s-death-a-mystery-3219748.php.

Visser, J. (2013, December 2). Ontario University working to remove disturbing video after student sets fire in apparent online suicide attempt. *National Post*. Retrieved from http://news.nationalpost.com/news/canada/ontario-university-dorm-evacuated-after-student-sets-himself-on-fire-in-apparent-online-suicide-attempt

Wessinger, C. (2000). *How the millennium comes violently*. New York: Seven Bridges Press.

CHAPTER 4

Staging

The body of a young woman was found in April 2000 under a New Jersey bridge. It looked like a suicide, but an investigation turned up more to the story. The victim was an exotic dancer, Rachel "Foxy Roxy" Siani, who worked in Philadelphia. There was no means of transportation parked near the bridge, she wore no shoes, and there was no dirt on her socks. Clearly, she had not driven or walked to the spot. A small patch of blood on the bridge supports and fibers caught on the bridge that matched what she was wearing suggested that someone had carried her there and shoved her over. Some of her fingernails were broken, as if in a struggle, and there were bruises on her neck. Further digging turned up no depression or suicidal ideation in her background. Friends said that Siani was dancing to pay her way through college and had looked forward to becoming a psychologist. She was close with her family, despite their disapproval of her dancing.

Now, it appeared that Siani had been murdered. Police went to question coworkers at Diva's International Gentleman's Club and discovered Siani's car parked there. A tip led them to a regular customer named John Denofa. Witnesses had seen him in a drunken state that night. Siani had helped him into his room, but no one had seen her leave. When questioned, Denofa insisted that she had not entered all the way, but a search of his truck turned up blood that matched hers. A surveillance video showed him driving the truck that night with something in the back that could have been a body.

A reconstruction based on Siani's injuries indicated that Denofa had strangled her into unconsciousness and pushed her out his second-floor window. He placed her into the back of his truck and drove her to the bridge. She had died from the fall off the bridge.

Confronted with the surveillance tape, Denofa claimed that someone had copied the keys to his truck and had used it to transport Siani. During that timeframe, he had been asleep in his room, too drunk to drive. His story did not fly. Denofa was convicted and sentenced to 30 years in prison (*State v. Denofa*, 2006).

TABLE 4.1   Staging Possibilities

Manner	Natural	Accident	Suicide	Homicide
Accident	X		X	
Suicide	X	X		X
Homicide	X	X	X	

After strangling Siani, Denofa had tried to make her death look like a suicide. This is one form of staging, an act that changes elements of a scene to deflect investigative focus away from the actual nature of an incident. The intent is to simulate a different scenario that will fool investigators.

Scenes can be staged in many ways. The most common are homicides staged as suicides or accidents, or one type of homicide staged as a different one or as a missing person case. However, there are also suicides staged as homicides, accidents, or natural deaths, and homicides staged as natural deaths. Even autoerotic accidents have been staged as something else, usually to avoid embarrassment. Because relatives typically do this, AEFs are not staged as homicides, as no one wants further investigation. (Some analysts say that this is not staging but is mere alteration to disguise the nature of a death.) In addition, some people fake their own deaths through staging mechanisms (called *pseudocide*) (Table 4.1).

Geberth (1996) surmised that the rise in staging in recent decades was related to the abundance of information available on television and online about investigations. He has privately investigated several staged homicides that were erroneously determined to be suicides and found that each investigation had lacked a detailed victimology. Red flags for staging often turn up in the details. Pettler (2016) offers cases as far back as 1514. Even the Bible contains staged incidents, and cases can be found in the legal documents from ancient Rome. Pettler provides a full review of literature on the topic and offers tips for recognizing staged events.

The aim is to learn how to spot a potentially staged incident. This chapter describes examples of staging a death scene. Case analyses demonstrate the kinds of behaviors that investigators should look for. Finally, we wrap up this section with psychological autopsies as forensic evidence.

HOMICIDE STAGED AS A NATURAL DEATH

Steve Robard was only 38 when he suffered from what appeared to be a cardiac arrest. He had experienced what he called stomach cramps during the evening of February 18, 1993, and they grew worse over the course of the evening. His girlfriend called 911, but by the time help arrived Robard was dead. He did not have a negative health history, but his heart appeared to be enlarged, which seemed to the coroner in Fort Worth, Texas, to be a contributing factor. A routine toxicology screen was run, but nothing out of the ordinary came up.

Robard had been the primary guardian of his 16-year-old daughter, Marie, who now had to live elsewhere. She had disliked her father's cramped apartment, but she also disliked her stepfather whom she had caught having an affair. Marie hoped to live with her mother, with whom she was quite close, but her mother was moving to Florida. Marie tried for a few months but could not tolerate her stepfather, whom her mother refused to divorce. To finish high school, she moved in with her paternal grandparents. A top student, Marie excelled in the sciences and aspired to become a pathologist. She graduated from high school and went on to college, always at the top of her class. To this point, no one had any idea that Robard's death was anything but natural.

However, Marie had a secret. She told it to her best friend, Stacey. She had killed her father with a rare poison, barium acetate, which she had stolen from her chemistry class. She begged Stacey to keep the secret. Stacey tried, but she had nightmares and a psychological breakdown. Finally, she told. Marie was arrested. She admitted that she had poisoned her father in order to be able to "go back home" to live with her mother. She said she had intended only to make her father ill, but while he was dying she had made no move to assist him. She also knew from her science classes that the poison she had used—in a very large dose—was not just lethal but so rare it would not come up on most toxicology screens. The jury was forgiving. She received a 28-year sentence, eligible for parole in seven (Hollandsworth, 1996).

Staging a homicide as a natural death is difficult to achieve and is probably rare. Even if the poison Marie used was not part of a typical toxicology screen, the mystery of this man's death might have expanded the search. Had she kept quiet, Marie would have gotten away with murder. However, there were some "tells" in her behavior. She did not want to live with her father, she was angry with both of her parents, she had not helped her father when he was in distress, and after the death she did not act like a typical grieving daughter. After going through more case examples, we collect behavioral tips below.

HOMICIDE STAGED AS AN ACCIDENT

A 911 call on August 16, 1999, from a distraught Michael Fletcher seemed genuine. His story initially made sense as well. He and his wife Leann had been to a shooting range to practice near their Michigan home and had come home for some time alone before picking up their daughter from Leann's parents. They were going to clean their guns and then get in bed. Fletcher said he was in the bathroom when he heard the gun discharge. He rushed into the bedroom to find Leann dead on the floor. She seemed to have been reloading a magazine and had shoved it into the weapon without taking precautions. Accidents while cleaning guns happen all the time. Fletcher was a criminal defense attorney. The police knew him. He had seemed happy about a recent announcement that he and his wife were expecting their second child. They had separated recently but had reconciled. There was no reason to suspect him.

Leann was transported to the morgue. The autopsy contradicted Fletcher's narrative. Blood on the Leann's palm meant she had not held the gun. Stippling on her face suggested that the muzzle had been 12–18 inches away when fired, and the horizontal trajectory meant that for her to have fired the fatal shot, her arm had to be 4 feet long. In addition, her body had been found on top of blood on the floor, as had the gun. Police confiscated Fletcher's shirt to test it for blood spatter. It was positive: he had been in the room, not far from Leann, when the gun went off.

Motive for murder was easy to find. Fletcher was having an affair with a judge, Susan Chrzanowski, who had sent him numerous cases over which she had presided. She claimed she thought that Fletcher was no longer sexually involved with his wife.

Research on 911 calls that distinguishes genuine calls from those made to stage an incident shows that Fletcher made some classic mistakes. Harpster et al. (2009) formulated linguistic attributes on 50 "innocent" versus 50 "guilty" 911 calls, crystallizing specific verbal indicators for each. They expanded this research to double that number and confirmed their tool, the Considering Offender Probability in Statements Scale (Harpster & Adams, 2016). Among guilty indicators are giving extraneous information, blaming the victim, offering conflicting facts, and accepting the victim's death. Fletcher had several behaviors from the "guilty" column. He had called his wife by pet names like "honey" during the call but not her actual name, and he included extraneous information that would exonerate him. It was as if he were setting up the scenario for the record, not expressing concern about his wife's condition. The jurors who convicted Fletcher said the call had seemed rehearsed (People v. Fletcher, 2004).

Hueske (2010) described another indicator that an incident was staged: failing to match physical evidence to one's narrative. A police officer called 911 to report the accidental death of his wife. He said that he had started to clean his Glock 9-mm pistol but interrupted the task to go out and complete an errand. When he returned, he found his wife dead. Next to her were the gun and cleaning materials. She would sometimes clean his guns for him, he stated, and he believed she had decided to finish the job that day. Investigators realized that the gun and magazine were coated in cleaning solvent, and they observed a bloodstain on the side of the solvent canister. The blood proved to be the victim's. However, no solvent was found on her hands or clothing, and there were no interruptions of the solvent on the gun. Clearly, she could not have handled it.

In another example, when 84-year-old Marina Calabro was found dead, on top of a bag of trash, at the foot of the stairs in her home in Quincy, Massachusetts, in 2001, detectives relied on stereotypes about the elderly to declare it an accident. The bruises on her body were believed to have come from tumbling down the steps. No one took photos. In fact, she had been murdered. Nearly a year later, an accomplice confessed to a friend that Calabro's grandnephew, Anthony Calabro, had staged the murder as an accident to get the inheritance. He had paid another man to carry it out. In preparation, they had studied crime shows like *Forensic Files*. While Calabro kept watch, the other man had bashed Marina with a frying pan and teakettle. As she lay screaming, terrified, and struggling to survive, he had strangled and then smothered her (Ellement, 2006).

As Geberth noted, crime TV provides plenty of instruction. If there is a reason to kill, such as an inheritance, assumptions that shortcut the investigative process should be dismissed.

HOMICIDE STAGED AS SUICIDE

In this age of CSI and DNA, people have the impression that no one can get away with murder anymore, but some crimes have no leads and some have deceptive ones. Forensic analysis is not foolproof, especially when there is enough information available to simulate a specific type of scenario. In those that we know about, mistakes were typically made.

Jocelyn Earnest was discovered on the floor in her home in 2007, shot in the head. Police found a suicide note that described her despair: "Mom, I just can't take it anymore. I've tried so hard to be strong but I just can't continue. The ups and downs are too much to deal with. I keep trying to appear as though I am doing fine but the days are so overwhelming and lonely. My new love will never leave the family. Wes has buried us in debt and starting over is too much. I am so sorry mom. I am so sorry everyone" (Fanning, 2014, p. 11).

Although she had been through a rough divorce, the note's sentiments were inconsistent with the facts of Jocelyn's life. Several items alerted officers to withhold judgment before performing a thorough investigation. They learned that Jocelyn had been terrified of her husband, Wesley (mentioned in the note), who was in desperate financial difficulty and whose fingerprints were on the note. He had disliked his divorce settlement and had been trying to force Jocelyn to make some changes. Since the unsigned note was typewritten and Jocelyn usually wrote by hand, police searched her computers and found no indication on any device she used that she had written it. Her beloved dog was crated and would have starved, and Jocelyn had been in the midst of texting a friend when she went silent. The friends reported that Wesley had shown up unexpectedly in the recent past, jumping out at her from the shadows. When investigators talked with Jocelyn's therapist, she said that Jocelyn was not in therapy for depression. She did not think that Jocelyn had been suicidal.

Investigators noted significant issues with the attempt to stage the death as a suicide. The thermostat had been turned up to an uncomfortably high temperature and it was clear from bloodstains that the body had been moved. Jocelyn's injury would have been instantly fatal, so she could not have moved herself. Someone else had been there, postmortem. Her friends said they had not entered the house.

Other items undermined Wesley Earnest's claim of innocence. The gun belonged to him and he had the box for it. He had borrowed a friend's truck on the day Jocelyn died, returning it with brand new tires, which he had purchased with cash under a false name. He said Jocelyn had been despondent over their shared house debt, but the judge had assigned the brunt of the debt to Wesley. His fingerprints were on the notepaper for the suicide note. Despite his claim that he could have touched the notepaper when he lived in the house, it seemed clear that Wesley had written the suicide note as part of a staging effort. He was convicted.

Besides the obvious errors at the scene, he had also neglected to simulate his victim's habits. He should have realized that a typed note would be suspicious, and court records would show that Jocelyn had no debt. In addition, she had no "new love." That phrase puzzled everyone who knew her. Also, she would not have left her dog in a cage to starve.

Although most crime scene processing books mention staging, Pettler (2012, 2016) focuses exclusively on it. She performed a content analysis of 18 staged homicides to identify the most common behaviors. Her initial sample contained 27 offenders and 19 victims. She identified 62 behaviors, which she categorized into six thematic typologies (see Table 4.2 below). These types, she found, were currently more helpful for theoretical considerations than for field use. These categories are not mutually exclusive and do overlap. Staging appears to be a function of the victim–offender relationship, since 16 of the 18 victims knew the perpetrator.

Among key problems for any investigator, and the reason why staging might succeed, is the cognitive error, threshold diagnosis,

TABLE 4.2 Pettler's Staging Typology (2016)

The cleaner: This is more alteration than staging, because this person cleans the scene to remove evidence.

The concealer: Hides or destroys items related to the incident to prevent discovery.

The creator: Adds items to the scene, or rearranges for a specific effect.

The fabricator: Relies on ability to verbally deceive as a means of deflection.

The inflictor: Might include self in incident, with self-wounding, or might claim self-defense.

The planner: Spends considerable time preparing the incident to appear as something else instead of reacting, postincident.

mentioned earlier. Making a decision too soon about what happened can quickly turn into tunnel vision. Investigators become oblivious to items that might discount their initial notions or change the investigative direction entirely. An inconsistency, such as Jocelyn Earnest's habit of writing by hand or the lack of any suicidal red flags, might be easily minimized and dismissed, so as to keep to the initial hypothesis.

Staging probably dates back as far as social or legal consequences for murder. Some have been elaborately planned and some were just staged as "the other guy did it." Pettler (2016) presents several historical cases. Richard Hunne's death in a jail cell in 1514 was called a suicide, despite the fact that his hands were tied behind his back. An investigation showed that his neck had been broken prior to the hanging, so he was acquitted of the charge of self-murder.

It would be difficult to know the true statistics about how many scenes are staged, because those that fool investigators are obviously not included in a count. Schlesinger, Gardenier, Jarvis, and Sheehan-Cook (2014) estimate the figure at 8%, but others have cited lower numbers.

There is little agreement in the literature on the most common type. Schlesinger et al. (2014) examined 79 staged homicide scenes and found arson to be the most common concealing behavior (one in four). Eight percent involved staging a homicide as a suicide. Three-fourths of the victims were related to the offenders. Ferguson (2014) examined 115 cases, with 188 offenders. She recommended paying particular attention to whoever reported the body. Offenders often "discover" it, and in one study that included three fake suicide notes, the killer was named in the note, usually in a positive light. Those without legitimate reasons to have been in that area should be persons of interest. In 67% of the cases, a single offender staged the scene. Males accounted for 79% of staging, and 14% were homicides staged to look like suicides. In 98% of the cases, the victim and offender had a prior relationship, mostly as intimate partners, with one in four being work associates or friends.

Some researchers believe that the most important aspect is wound analysis; others emphasize physical evidence, especially weapon arrangement, or a thorough victimology. Ferguson and Petherick (2016) describe staging as a "precautionary act" used by offenders to distance themselves from crimes. The stagers they studied had introduced something into a scene to deflect investigative focus, for example, a fake suicide note, evidence of a break-in, ransacking, or simulated self-injury. Most victims (75%) were discovered in their own homes. In half of the cases, the offender "discovered" the victim. In 56.3%, gunshot wounds were the cause of death, with 30% being some form of asphyxiation or strangulation. The most common elements of staging were weapon placement, simulated self-injury, body arrangement, and the addition of items such as drugs or a suicide note.

One case had a rather odd presentation. In November 2000, Kristen Rossum reported the suicide of her husband, Gregory de Villers, in their bedroom. Police found rose petals around de Villers' body, which Rossum said was his "romantic" suicide note. She was about to have the body cremated when suspicious behavior on her part reopened the investigation. Rossum was having an affair with her boss in the medical examiner's lab where she worked as a toxicologist. She had access to the potentially fatal pain killer, fentanyl. She had also purchased roses just before Gregory's death, and the death scene copied her favorite movie, *American Beauty*. A new analysis showed fentanyl poisoning. Rossum was convicted of murder (Glatt, 2007).

A more striking case of using a note to stage a suicide served another purpose as well: it implicated the near-victim in two homicides. Ashley Wallace revived from an alleged suicidal drug overdose in 2007 to identify her mother, Stacy Castor, as the person who had written a 750-word suicide note that implicated Ashley in the antifreeze poisoning deaths of her father and stepfather (Chambers & Meyersohn, 2009). Investigators found that Castor had poisoned both of her husbands for insurance money before poisoning her 20-year-old daughter to frame the girl for murder. A telltale detail was that "antifreeze" was misspelled four times in the note as "antifree," and Castor had also pronounced the word in this manner during her interrogation. Even if she had succeeded in a third murder, it seems unlikely that anyone would have believed that Stacy had killed her mother's two husbands. A comprehensive investigation would have turned up issues in the marriages that would have placed doubt on the daughter's supposed suicide. Ashley and her sister testified against their mother. Stacy Castor was found guilty of second-degree murder.

Albert Perez strangled his former girlfriend and her 5-year-old daughter in 2007 and then staged the scene to look as if the mother had hanged the daughter before hanging herself ("Prosecutors to seek," 2008).

A content analysis of the presumed suicide note, when compared with the idiosyncrasies of phrasing in known samples of writing from both Perez and his girlfriend, supported the FBI stylistics analysis that Perez was more likely to be the author than his ex-girlfriend.

But what if a note was typed on a computer? Forensic linguist Carole Chaski took on this task. A deceased individual was found dead in bed. His roommate had called 911. He had died from a mixture of drugs, including lidocaine. Yet no needle was found near the body. The roommate, with medical background, had access to lidocaine, but a suicide note was discovered on the decedent's computer. So, where was the needle? An investigation turned up an altercation between the decedent and his roommate. Chaski ran the note and writing samples from both parties through a software program of her design, which had been scientifically validated. Key syntactical items eliminated the decedent but not the roommate. He eventually confessed to writing the note after accidentally injecting the decedent with medication for a migraine (Chaski, 2005).

SUICIDE STAGED AS A HOMICIDE

The primary reason to set up a suicide as a homicide is to get the payout from an insurance policy that has a prohibitive suicide clause. However, it is best not to leave the insurance document in plain sight. A young man in North Carolina was found in his car in the garage, with his legs and arms bound and tied together. Inside the residence was a note that claimed he was being held hostage. His phone had been destroyed and the windows were calked shut. The car was rigged to appear that the victim had been subjected to carbon monoxide poisoning after being tied to the steering wheel. Yet, a toxicology analysis showed no trace of it. Insurance papers left on the kitchen table provided the probable scenario. He had attempted to make it appear that others had held him hostage and had then killed him. The death seemed more consistent with a suicide staged to simulate a murder in order to get the money.

When Bill Sparkman failed to show up at work in September 2009, a coworker at a day-care program was concerned. Sparkman was conscientious. He held three part-time jobs and was looking for something full-time. Two days after he was reported missing, Sparkman's body was discovered near a small family cemetery in Clay County, Kentucky. He was hanging from a tree, naked, bound, and gagged, but his feet touched the ground. Across his chest was scrawled the word, "Fed," as if some antigovernment group had lynched him for venturing into their area to get information for a census. His census

ID card was taped to his neck. Violence against census takers was rare but not unheard of. Many people blamed talk shows and blogs filled with angry antigovernment rhetoric. Others thought Sparkman had inadvertently walked into a secret illegal meth operation (Morello & O'Keefe, 2009).

Sparkman's son said that several items were missing from his father's car, including a laptop. He had noticed nothing in his father's demeanor that suggested depression or anxiety. Sparkman was unhappy about working three jobs but not distraught.

Yet there were no defensive wounds or bruises on Sparkman's body and his bound hands were mobile enough to have handled the noose and bound his hands himself. If he had been killed on the job, his family could receive $10,000 from the government. He also had a life insurance policy. In fact, he had two, both of which were recent purchases, and the payout would have totaled $600,000. His son, the beneficiary, was unemployed and in some financial trouble.

The investigation concluded that Sparkman's death was an elaborate attempt at insurance fraud. He had killed himself to make his son more financially secure. "Fed" had been written from the bottom up in a way that a person standing facing him would have a difficult time doing. There was no evidence that anyone else was involved. In addition, Sparkman could have taken the pressure from the noose off his neck just by standing straight. He had cancer. An acquaintance had told police that Sparkman had talked about ending his life and was aware of the perception about negative attitudes in certain parts of the country toward census workers. Sparkman had exploited the notions about fiercely protective backwoods people to manipulate the scene to look like he had been murdered (Jonsson, 2009).

PSEUDOCIDE

Madison Rutherford was an American financial advisor. In July 1998, he told people he was going to Mexico to acquire a rare breed of dog. He did not return. Reportedly, while out for a drive, he struck an embankment and died in a car fire. Nothing was left but some bone fragments. Because he had taken out a hefty life insurance policy, the Kemper Life Insurance Company sent investigators. Among them was a forensic anthropologist, Dr. Bill Bass, founder of the Forensic Anthropology Center, aka the Body Farm.

Bass sorted through the debris. He discovered the top of a skull. Its position in the car was suspicious. In addition, the car had little front-end damage and the fire had seemed inexplicably destructive. This incident looked like a staged accident for insurance fraud.

When Bass examined the intact teeth, he found them inconsistent with those of an affluent, 34-year-old Caucasian male. Instead, they were consistent with an older native of Mexico. Bass's report gave the insurance company what they needed to hire a private investigator. He found Rutherford alive and well. To stage his death, Rutherford had stolen a corpse from a Mexican mausoleum, placed it in the car, crashed the car, torched it, and walked away to collect on the life insurance policy. Rutherford went to prison (Bass & Jefferson, 2003; Kohn, 2002).

Some people fake their death to avoid jail or to get away with a crime; others want to escape debt, a stalker, or a burdensome relationship. For behavioral analysts, scenes involving body obliteration or missing-presumed-dead, the potential reason for disappearing must always be checked out. In her book, *Pseudocide*, Greenwood (2016) provides a comprehensive account of how people fake their own deaths.

MORE CASES WITH STRANGE ANGLES

Since investigators who must interpret behavior operate with probability analysis, they must also be aware that some cases are outliers on any probability scale. Generally, the staging will be discovered only with luck or a very sharp eye.

The body of Thomas Hickman was found near Santa Rosa, New Mexico, on March 15, 2008. His Jeep was nearby, out of gas, his mouth was taped shut, and he had been shot in the head. Since he was an executive for Red Lobster who lived in Texas, police believed he had been kidnapped and murdered. However, not far away was a bundle of helium balloons snagged on a cactus. Attached was a Smith and Wesson Airweight gun. The grip had been removed and the trigger guard was tampered with. The gun proved to be the weapon that had killed Hickman. It looked as if the gun was supposed to float away from the body. With no weapon present, investigators would had to have called it a homicide.

Back in Texas, evidence showed that Hickman had purchased the balloons and the gun and had worked on the gun to make it lighter. One investigator had seen this before: on television. An episode of *CSI: Crime Scene Investigation*, which had aired in October 2003, had shown the discovery of a gun and some helium balloons in someone's backyard. The gun was traced back to a death across town. Although they could not prove that Hickman had ever seen the show, a psychological autopsy turned up markers for depression. Hickman's wife was seriously ill and he had suffered significant financial losses in the stock market.

Police acknowledged the effort that Hickman had put into making his death look like a murder, possibly to spare his wife from learning that he would leave her like this on his own volition, but they closed the case as a suicide (Ellis, 2008).

In England in 2004, police responded to calls about a knife attack: a 15-year-old had stabbed his 14-year-old friend in the chest and stomach. As the story unraveled, it turned out that they had both been interested in a woman they met online—allegedly, a female spy. Supposedly, she had ordered the older boy to kill the younger boy. However, this woman did not actually exist. Computer analysis showed that the victim had created the entire scenario to get the older boy, with whom he was in love, to fatally stab him. He survived. It was an attempted suicide-by homicide ("Web friend conned," 2004).

Forensic pathologist Cyril Wecht was consulted on the strange death of motivational speaker Jeffrey B. Locker. The 52-year-old man, deep in debt, had applied for several life insurance policies, with collective payouts of $18 million. In July 2009, Locker was stabbed to death in his SUV, in East Harlem. When Kenneth Minor was arrested, he claimed it was an assisted suicide: Locker had wanted to ensure that his family received the insurance money, so he had looked for a random stranger in East Harlem who would accept money to kill him. Minor had initially resisted but then decided to do it. Wecht testified that Locker's wounds were consistent with Minor's narrative (Wecht & Kaufman, 2014).

What looked like a clear case of suicide in South Carolina had features that suggested staging. The decedent was lying facedown in his trailer, over his .22-caliber rifle. A bullet hole was found in his right temple and another through his mouth. There was a single bullet hole in the ceiling. He was shot twice and only two bullet casings were found. In addition, blood turned up in many different places: pooled on the front stairs, spattered in the living room near the TV remote control, dripped on various areas of the carpet, in a trail from the living room to the bathroom, on the bathroom walls and floor, on a raincoat draped over a chair, and in the kitchen. Some areas of blood indicated that the wounded victim had spent some time in that location.

This might have looked like a homicide or a suicide elaborately staged to appear as a homicide, except for the suicide note taped on the rifle. A homicide staged as a suicide made no sense, since the killer would have cleaned up some of the blood and removed bloody items. Based on blood patterns and spent cartridges, investigators decided that the decedent had shot himself through the mouth while sitting in a chair but had not died. He had walked around the house, perhaps watched TV, and sat on his porch, and smoked a cigarette while aspirating blood from his throat. Finally, he returned to the living room to end it with a second shot (Mayo, 2007).

MISREAD DEATH SCENES

Psychologist David Canter (2005) analyzed a suicide note for Paula Gilfoyle, who was found hanging in 1992 in her garage. She was 8 1/2 months pregnant. Because of the note, the scene was not fully investigated. Yet, those who knew Paula claimed she was happy and would not have committed suicide. Her husband, Eddie Gilfoyle, was eventually arrested and convicted of her murder. Since the note proved to be Paula's handwriting, police believed that Eddie had tricked Paula into writing it and had actually dictated it. He had also tricked her into getting onto a ladder and putting her head into a noose. He was presented in court as a fiendish manipulator who had told his wife he was studying suicide at his job in the medical field and needed her assistance with reconstruction. However, the rope was never tested for DNA, which could have proved if he had handled it.

At first, Canter agreed with the prosecution, but he pointed out that, contrary to claims made by some forensic linguists, there is no scientific proof that a certain word or phrase is definitively characteristic of an individual. He examined more samples of writing from Paula and Eddie and found themes in the note typical of both. When Canter had the opportunity to perform a more thorough victimology by questioning relatives on both sides, he concluded that Paula had been depressed and could have been suicidal. He also found that Eddie was not the deviously calculating person the prosecutor had described.

In Chapter 3, the duct-taped young man was believed to have been a homicide victim because it seemed impossible that he could have taped himself in this fashion. Several of the ends of the tape were beyond where he could have reached. In addition, it appeared that his arms were already bound before his legs. Only when other items were found at the scene, along with a computer record of the decedent's access to instructions of how a lone individual could successfully tape himself in this manner was it clear that this death was a sad accident in the pursuit of pleasure.

Janice Johnson, 36, was found dead at the bottom of the basement stairs in her home in Shelburne, Nova Scotia. She had been talking on a phone with a neighbor and quickly hung up, as if in a hurry to meet a friend who was coming over with his daughter. Her husband, Clayton, had gone to work, and the expected friend found her. She lay face up, with her car keys in her hands. There was blood and hair on a jutting piece of concrete wall and around her head. A high-heeled shoe nearby suggested that she had lost her balance at the top of the stairs. Once police closed the case as a freak accident, helpful neighbors cleaned up the blood. There were no photos.

A few months later, Clayton started dating a woman 20 years younger. This, and his insurance payout of $125,000, made police reopen the investigation. This time, investigators and the pathologist interpreted the evidence with a bias toward murder. They decided that the lacerations on Janice's head could not have happened if she had fallen face-first, which is the most common way for people to fall down steps. The various neighbors' stories had changed as well, with memories of more blood spattered on walls where none had been noted before. Clayton was arrested, tried, and convicted for his wife's murder. He spent 6 years in jail before he won a new trial, with a powerful defense team of scientific experts.

They were able to show that the lacerations made sense if Janice had fallen down the steps backwards (a scenario no one had reconstructed during the original investigation). A reconstruction with a model matched Janice's wounds, and she did not have the defensive wounds she should have had if someone were trying to beat her to death. Clayton had been at a gas station at the time the neighbor found her. He would not have had time to get back home to kill his wife. During his hearing before the Nova Scotia Court of Appeal, Clayton was acquitted (Makin, 2002).

This is a case that shows the dangers of probability analysis. Since most people who fall down stairs go down face-first, it made sense to reenact this scenario. However, it did not match the initial reports. Using the less likely scenario (but still possible), all of the evidence worked for a finding of accident. This case also shows the effect of bias. At first, the accident was accepted. Then Bill dated a much younger woman, which made people suspicious. They now viewed the entire incident in a darker way, willing to accept inexplicable additions to witness accounts that fit their new ideas rather than doubt witness memory that had become infected with bias. Clayton Johnson's story is a good one for demonstrating cognitive distortion in investigations.

If writing is present that might be interpreted as a suicide note, death scenes are vulnerable to being misread and quickly closed as suicides. In 2001, police in Ottawa, Canada, told the parents of John Connelly that their son had killed himself (Guilli, 2010). The content of the note confirmed it: "Best of luck in the future," it said. "To my family my love will always be with you." The decedent's initials were scribbled under this message. But the family did not believe that this was a suicide note. Their son would not have been so formal or vague, they said. Yet they could not get officials to yield and rethink the case.

By examining cases for behavioral interpretation of a death incident, we can form a list of tips for investigators (Table 4.3).

TABLE 4.3   Tips for Investigators to Evaluate for Staging

- Beware of personal assumptions, especially those that attract investigative shortcuts.
- Remember that the majority of stagers (except for suicides) had a relationship with the decedent.
- The relationship is most likely intimate, past or present.
- Stagers often discover the body or report the person missing.
- The reason a body discoverer is at the scene should be legitimate.
- Stagers might inject themselves into an investigation to "be helpful."
- Stagers often "find" a suicide note or other evidence they want police to see.
- 911 calls from stagers will have unique elements common to "guilty" versus "innocent" callers.
- Besides manipulating the scene, stagers will reinforce it with verbal manipulation.
- Their efforts to deflect might include an explanation for the incident.
- The staging will probably feature mistaken notions about how such incidents occur, such as suicide notes that have more nongenuine indicators than genuine.
- Learn the items that characterize genuine notes, rather than make assumptions.
- Look for items that copy media reports or narratives.
- Look for scene behavior uncharacteristic of decedent.
- If a suicide note mentions a close associate, consider them a person of interest.
- Stagers are most likely to be male.
- Staging a suicide most often involves firearms.
- Suspicious indicators are weapons positioned too perfectly, or positions do not match where blood spatter or shell casings are found.
- Staged scenes are most often in a place familiar to the decedent, such as their home.
- Watch for unexpected behaviors during interviews.
- Match narratives about the incident against evidence.
- Develop competing hypothesis to help highlight issues of concern.

FORENSIC VALUE

Some of these cases will end up in court. The method of psychological autopsy lacks certain characteristics that are required for methodologies that claim to be based on scientific analysis. We look first at the decisions that affect admissibility before noting those cases in which the method has been allowed for support. Admissibility issues will also apply to behavioral analysis used in profiling, on which the next section focuses.

The first case in a US court to form a standard for scientific admissibility occurred in 1923. Convicted murderer James T. Frye said in his appeal that the court had not admitted evidence from a lie detector that registered blood pressure. The District of Columbia Court of Appeals upheld the conviction and articulated the standard: "The thing from which the deduction is made must be sufficiently established to have gained general acceptance in the particular field in which it belongs" (*Frye v. U.S.*, 1923).

There were several attempts to reword *Frye*, including the Federal Rules of Evidence 702, which focused on expert knowledge, training, skill, and experience. The *Frye* standard remained dominant in courts throughout the United States until 1993. A liability case demanded that determinants for admissibility be clarified. The dispute involved a drug produced by Merrell Dow Pharmaceuticals. Both sides had experts to address whether this drug caused birth defects. The plaintiffs lost, so they went to the US Supreme Court, which spelled out admissibility conditions for federal jurisdictions: "scientific" means having a grounding in the methods and procedures of science that are sufficiently established as to have general acceptance in the field.

As the designated "gatekeepers," trial court judges would focus on the methodology, not on conclusions. Judges would decide if (1) the theory could be scientifically tested for reliability, (2) the error rate (or potential error rate) was known, (3) peers in the relevant scientific community had reviewed and accepted the method, (4) there are known standards and methods, and (5) the testimony was relevant to the issue in dispute. Some *Daubert* analysts add another condition: standards controlling the discipline's operation are maintained (*Daubert v. Merrell Dow Pharmaceuticals*, 1993). *Daubert* became the federal standard and replaced the *Frye* standard in many states. Some states have formed a combination of both, but about 75% use *Daubert* (Bernstein & Jackson, 2004).

Two related cases, *General Electric Co. v. Joiner* (1997) and *Kumho Tire Co. v. Carmichael* (1999), clarified the trial judge's role. They also applied the *Daubert* criteria to other types of specialized knowledge, including technical expertise. In truth, guidelines are slippery and judges are selective. As long as the practitioner has credentials, is experienced, and seems unbiased, judges tend to view the results as trustworthy. Many judges have little training in science and are stymied by how error rates are calculated. Some ignore this part of their duties altogether (Shelton, 2009, 2011).

The lack of reliability and validity studies for psychological autopsy is a concern in the field, along with the lack of a standard definition, textbook, or methodology. The AAS offers a training and certification program, but even this has been challenged in court. In *State v. Guthrie*, the judge restricted the use of one of the program's suicidologists, who had performed a psychological autopsy.

Sharon Guthrie's husband, Bill, had found her dead in her bathtub in May 1999. Prescription medications had caused her death. One of them, temazepam, was prescribed for Bill. She had taken 20 capsules, which had made her lose consciousness and drown. Bill had an explanation: he thought it was an accidental overdose during sleep-walking. Further investigation was needed, which uncovered Bill's secrets: he had a mistress and he had filled his prescription at two different pharmacies shortly before his wife had died. He had also done several computer searches on the effects of drug overdoses. Curious mishaps in the home for a few months prior to the death looked as if someone was trying to stage a serious accident. Investigators were also aware of odd things at the scene. Bill had told them that he had dragged Sharon from the tub, and yet his clothing was dry. He said he had just come in from work, yet he was barefoot. He had assured investigators that the marriage was fine, but his daughter said that Bill had pledged to get a divorce.

Under pressure, Bill provided a typed, unsigned suicide note from Sharon that he said he found between the pages of a liturgy book. He claimed that he had given the note to his attorney in June. Analysts did not find it on Bill's or the church's computer, but investigators discovered a second computer. This one showed the note. It was written 3 months after Sharon's death, as was a second note, listing Sharon as the author. Guthrie admitted he wrote them but said it was just an exercise to work through his trauma.

Bill was arrested. At his trial, a psychological autopsy was used for the prosecution to evaluate Sharon for her potential for killing herself. The clinician was Dr. Alan Berman, a member of the AAS. A *Daubert* hearing evaluated Berman's credentials. Because he had impressive experience, the judge admitted his testimony. Berman had reviewed the death records, police interviews, and grand jury testimony. As per protocols that he had helped to design, he had also interviewed several family members. In court, he described characteristics of suicidal people and said that Sharon had minimal predisposing factors for suicide and several good reasons not to do it, especially in a bathtub. Less than 2% of women kill themselves in this manner. Berman concluded that Sharon was an unlikely candidate for suicide. He stated that her manner of death was not suicide. The defense offered a psychologist to attack Berman's method as unscientific, based on a lack of validity studies.

On appeal, Guthrie challenged the admission of Berman's testimony, claiming that he had improperly addressed the ultimate issue. The court found that providing typical suicide characteristics was acceptable, but applying these items specifically to the decedent had overreached. This part of the testimony was inadmissible but did not rise to being prejudicial. The conviction was affirmed (*State v. Guthrie*, 2001).

Psychological autopsies are based largely on clinical assessment, but there is no universally authoritative body. Still, over the past decade, quite a few researchers around the world have begun to take it seriously. It is moving in the right direction. Examples of psychological autopsy can be found in case law dating back to the 1930s, mostly in civil proceedings. However, courts have rejected or restricted it in several criminal proceedings.

In *Jackson v. Florida* in 1989, an appellate court upheld a decision to admit a psychological autopsy. Tina Mancini, a teenage girl, had fatally shot herself in 1986. Her mother had pressured her to become a topless exotic dancer for "rent money," altering her birth certificate to make it appear that she was 18. Tina wished to quit, but her mother would not allow it. They frequently argued over it. Dr. Douglas Jacobs had performed a psychological autopsy, reviewing school records, medical records, the autopsy photos, an incident report from an earlier suicide attempt at age 13, and witness testimony from her friends, finding that the mother's mental abuse had been a strong factor in the suicide. The mother, Andrea Hicks Jackson, was found guilty of child abuse. The verdict was challenged on appeal, stating that the method of psychological autopsy was not reliable. However, the appellate court, using the *Frye* criteria, found that there was general acceptance in the relevant professional community and that the psychologist had experience with suicide evaluations. The justices considered the process to be similar to a clinical sanity evaluation. The court decided that the issue of reliability was best left to the jury and affirmed the verdict (*Jackson v. State*, 1989).

Some death scenes literally beg for a psychological autopsy, because without it no sense can be made of the death incident. For example, a psychological autopsy might be undertaken in the following case. A 16-year-old girl allegedly decided to commit suicide in Utah, so her friend, Tyerell Przybcien, purchased a rope and an aerosol spray can to get high on. Because he was interested in watching someone die, he did nothing to stop or help her as she stood on a rock and let the rope asphyxiate her. He recorded it on his cellphone and even recorded himself checking her to ensure she was dead. When hunters called police, Przybcien freely told them what he had done. They arrested him for murder (Folley, 2017).

Bullis (2012) took a different approach. Instead of fine-tuning the method, he looked at the narratives that already exist in the court system. In fact, he stated, narratives form the basis of every part of the legal system, from confessions to attorney arguments, to witness statements, to instructions from the judge. In that case, qualitative analysis, which has been done extensively in various areas of psychological autopsy, should be accepted if it has been subjected to inter-rater reliability checks. This has long been an accepted method for social science data analysis. The real issue is the lack of a certifying body for developing standards, but experts in this field already look for internal consistency, protocol adherence, completeness, and plausibility.

Ormerod (2001) provided an overview of other legal cases, although most took place in England. He notes that emphasis on being sensitive during the collection of information from survivors poses a problem for specificity of data. Despite the development of interview protocols, this aspect of deriving information remains an issue. As such, evidence that might serve a death investigator might not be adequate for legal proceedings. Yet, despite defects, the method has general peer acceptance and meets ethical requirements. The two categories in which psychological autopsies would be of most benefit in a legal context, Ormerod stated, are deciding whether a death meets criteria for suicide and understanding its cause. Such information would be relevant for life insurance claims, testamentary disputes, health-care negligence, and breach of duty in a corrections situation, as well as for criminal trials and decisions made in coroner's inquests.

SUMMARY

The value of specialized information from suicidologists has already been established for investigations. Staged incidents pose a particular challenge, especially as viewers and readers of true crime investigations grow more sophisticated. Whether this assistance will eventually reach the level of widespread admissibility remains to be seen. The legal arena poses many challenges to the method. However, as organizations such as the AAS continue to collect and analyze data about mental states and suicidal candidacy, the discipline will be able to reduce error rates in opinions rendered by certified experts and provide more accurate consulting.

REFERENCES

Bass, B., & Jefferson, J. (2003). *Death's Acre: Inside the legendary forensics lab, the Body Farm, where the dead do tell tales.* New York: Putman.

Bernstein, D. E., & Jackson, J. D. (2004). The Daubert trilogy and the states. *Jurimetrics,* p. 44. Retrieved from https://www.researchgate.net/profile/David_Bernstein9/publication/228158634_The_Daubert_Trilogy_in_the_States/links/56603a6908aefe619b28cb6d.pdf

Bullis, R. K. (2012). Narrative approaches in psychological autopsies: Suggestions for methodologies. *Journal of Forensic Psychology Practice, 12,* 124–146.

Canter, D. (2005). Suicide or murder? Implicit narratives in the Eddie Gilfoyle case. In L. Alison (Ed.), *The forensic psychologist's casebook: Psychological profiling and criminal investigation* (pp. 315–333). Devon, UK: Willan Publishing.

Chambers, A., & Meyersohn, J. (2009, April 23). Exhumed body reveals Stacy Castor's first husband 'didn't just die': Exclusive look inside anti-freeze murder mystery. *ABC News*. Retrieved from http://abcnews.go.com/2020/story?id=7394363

Chaski, C. E. (2005) Who's at the keyboard? Recent results in authorship attribution. *International Journal of Digital Evidence, 4*(1). Retrieved from www.ijde.org

Daubert v. Merrell Dow Pharmaceuticals, Inc. 113 S. Ct 2786 (1993).

Ellement, J. (2006, March 10). Witnesses tell of grisly Quincy murder. *Boston Globe*. Retrieved from http://archive.boston.com/news/local/articles/2006/03/10/witness_tells_of_grisly_quincy_murder/

Ellis, T. M. (2008, July 18). CSI-like suicide ruled in death of Red Lobster exec Thomas Hickman. *Dallas Morning News*. Retrieved from http://articles.orlandosentinel.com/2008-07-18/news/hickman18_1_lisa-hickman-thomas-hickman-anglada

Fanning, D. (2014). *Under cover of the night*. New York: Berkley.

Ferguson, C. E. (2014). Staged crime scenes: Literature and types. In W. Petherick (Ed.), *Serial crime: Theoretical and practical issues in behavioural profiling*, 3rd ed., (pp. 141–164). Boston, MA: Andersen.

Ferguson, C. E., & Petherick, W. (2016). Getting away with murder: An examination of detected homicides stages as suicides. *Homicide Studies, 20*(1), 3–24.

Folley, A. (2017, May 9). *Utah man arrested for murder of teen girl after filming her suicide*. Retrieved from https://www.aol.com/article/news/2017/05/09/utah-man-arrested-for-murder-of-teen-girl-after-filming-suicide-hanging-from-tree/22078436/

Frye v. U. S. DC Circuit. 293 F. 1013. No. 3968. (DC Cir. 1923).

Geberth, V. (1996). The staged crime scene. *Law and Order Magazine, 44*(2), 45–49.

General Electric Co. V. Joiner, 522 U.S. 136 (1997).

Glatt, J. (2007). *Deadly American beauty*. New York: MacMillan.

Greenwood, E. (2016). *Playing dead: A journey through the world of death fraud*. New York: Simon & Schuster.

Guilli, K. (2010). What if it wasn't really suicide? *Maclean's, 123*(21), 60–61.

Harpster, T., & Adams, S. (2016). *Analyzing 911 homicide calls: Practical aspects and applications*. Boca Raton, FL: CRC Press.

Harpster, T., Adams, S., & Jarvis, J. P. (2009). Analyzing 911 homicide calls for indicators of guilt or innocence: An exploratory analysis. *Homicide Studies*, *13*(1), 69–93.

Hollandsworth, S. (1996, July). Poisoning Daddy. *Texas Monthly*. Retrieved from http://www.texasmonthly.com/articles/poisoning-daddy/

Hueske, E. E. (2010, September). An unusual indicator of scene staging. *Evidence Technology Magazine*, pp. 22–24.

Jackson v. State. (1989). *So. 2d*. Vol. 553; 719.

Jonsson, P. (2009, November 24). Census worker Bill Sparkman staged his suicide. *The Christian Science Monitor*. Retrieved from https://www.csmonitor.com/USA/Society/2009/1125/p02s05-ussc.html

Kohn, D. [Correspondent] (2002, March 13). Dead men talking. *CBS*. news.com. Retrieved from http://www.cbsnews.com/news/dead-men-talking/

Kumho Tire Co. v. Carmichael, 526 U.S. 137 (1999).

Makin, K. (2002, February 19) Wrongly convicted man cleared in wife's death. *Globe and Mail*. Retrieved from http://www.theglobeandmail.com/news/national/wrongly-convicted-man-cleared-in-wifes-death/article25292029/

Mayo, K. (2007). It's suicide...isn't it? *Evidence Technology Magazine*, *5*(1), 12–15.

Morello, C., & O'Keefe, E. (2009, September 26). Slain census taker warned of job dangers. *The Washington Post*, p. A3.

Ormerod, D. (2001). Psychological autopsies: Legal implications and admissibility. *The International Journal of Evidence and proof*, *5*(1), 1–31.

People v. Fletcher (2004). 229092. Retrieved from http://caselaw.findlaw.com/mi-court-of-appeals/1354865.html

Pettler, L. G. (2012). *Crime scene behaviors of crime scene stagers* (Doctoral dissertation). Retrieved from Proquest (2251577601).

Pettler, L. (2016). *Crime scene staging dynamics in homicide cases*. Boca Raton, FL: CRC Press.

Prosecutors to seek death penalty for Bernville killing. (2008, June 20). *Reading Eagle*, p. 1.

Schlesinger, L., Gardenier, A., Jarvis, J., & Sheehan-Cook, J. (2014). Crime scene staging in homicide. *Journal of Police and Criminal Psychology*, *29*(1), 44–51.

Shelton, D. E. (2009). Twenty-first century forensic science challenges for trial judges in criminal cases: Where the "Polybutadiene" meets the "Bitumen." *Widener Law Journal 18*(2), 309–396.

Shelton, D. E. (2011). *Forensic science in court: Challenges in the 21st century*. New York: Rowman & Littlefield.

State of New Jersey v. Denofa. (2006). Retrieved from http://caselaw.findlaw.com/nj-supreme-court/1101897.html

State v. Guthrie. (2001). *SD 61, 627 NW 2d. 401.*

Web friend conned into murder bid. (2004, May 28). *BBC News.* Retrieved from http://news.bbc.co.uk/2/hi/uk_news/england/ manchester/3758209.stm

Wecht, C & Kaufman, D. (2014). *Final exams. Seattle*, WA: Rule Publications.

SECTION II

Behavioral Profiling

CHAPTER 5

History and Purpose

On August 31, 1888, Mary Ann "Polly" Nichols went out to earn some money. She was 45, living in an eastern neighborhood of London known as Whitechapel. Many women in her circumstances sold themselves to earn enough for a bed or a drink. Nichols's body was found in the street, violated. She had deep cuts across her throat and abdomen. Three weeks earlier, another prostitute, Martha Tabram, had been slashed to death not far away, but there seemed to be no link. It was a dangerous place, especially at night.

When Annie Chapman's throat was cut a week later on September 8, the killer went a bit further. Presuming he was male, he disemboweled her, removing her bladder and uterus. These crimes were disturbing, but police had no leads. They took witness reports, but nothing suggested that the same person had killed these women. It was 3 weeks before a "double event," in which two prostitutes were killed on the same night, woke up the media to a serious danger in Whitechapel. Elizabeth Stride's throat was cut like Polly Nichols, but Catherine Eddowes' mutilation resembled Annie Chapman's. Eddowes' intestines were removed and placed over her shoulder. Her uterus and kidney were cut out and her face was oddly mutilated. All of the women had been subjected to a knife attack and all had been left where they were killed, in a tight geographic area that came to be called the "Wicked Quarter Mile." All were prostitutes out on the street at night.

Soon, a letter, "from Hell," came to the head of the Whitechapel vigilante organization, enclosed with half of an alcohol-preserved kidney that appeared to have been cut from someone afflicted with an alcohol-related disorder. The letter's author swore that there would be more. However, the sender of this bloody missive remained unidentified. Unfortunately, dozens of letters poured in to police and media, especially after someone signed "Jack the Ripper" to one of them. The name caught on and a fad was born. It was difficult to know which letter was from the killer—if any. Plenty of correspondents also gave the police advice about catching him.

The police increased their Whitechapel patrols, anticipating a pattern, with their sights set on October 8. But nothing happened. Similarly, the end of the month passed quietly. Then, on November 8, a fifth victim, Mary Kelly, was slain, brutally mutilated, and gruesomely disemboweled inside a rented room. Parts of her were everywhere, as if cut and flung in a frenzy. If this was the same offender as in the other murders, he had grown exponentially worse. Here, there was a severed breast, and over there, the contents of her stomach. Pieces were sliced from her legs, and her heart was gone. A doctor who arrived at the scene estimated that this mad man had spent around 2 hours, slicing and mutilating before leaving. It was a stunning display of savagery, which increased the pressure to find this killer before he struck again.

The police investigated many suspects, but in the end no one was arrested. Jack the Ripper, whoever he was, still inspires people today to figure out if the five crimes were related, if there might have been more, and the type of person who would do this. Even FBI profilers have tried their hand at this murder mystery (Evans & Rumbelow, 2006). Suspects range from psychotic sex maniacs to doctors to poets and artists.

This is where criminal profiling seemed to begin. There was no FBI at the time, and it did not even start with someone in law enforcement. The creation of a postcrime psychological portrait of an offender formally began with the suppositions of a surgeon. Later in this chapter, we will come back to his work, as well as another profile that focused on behavioral linkage only a few years later. Several professionals focused on behavioral analysis as a tool for solving crime before the FBI got up and rolling with its own methodology.

Criminal profiling is not limited to the FBI, but the agency's methods have gained the most visibility. This is partly due to the celebrity status that certain serial killers have achieved who were the subject of an investigative profile. This chapter provides a comprehensive account of how behavioral analysis for criminal profiling evolved over the past century, how the FBI's Behavioral Science Unit (BSU) formed, who its founding personnel were, and how it developed into an elite investigative support team that consulted on serial murder.

A BRIEF OVERVIEW OF SERIAL MURDER BEFORE CRIMINAL PROFILING

Jack the Ripper was not the world's first serial killer, nor even the first to draw the attention of law enforcement. Although behavioral profiling is not exclusive to serial crimes or to murder, it is used more often for linkage analysis than any other aspect of behavioral interpretation of a crime scene.

The earliest documented serial killers are found in the records of ancient Rome, mostly as poisoners (Ramsland, 2005). This includes a prominent female who ran poisoning schools under the protection of an emperor. In later centuries, a few aristocrats used their wealth and influence to protect their spate of crimes. Some were arrested, tried, and sentenced. Between 1573 and 1600 several men and their families were prosecuted for "lycanthropy"—killing as a werewolf. Some people even viewed themselves as being cursed with an animal compulsion, and it was not uncommon to have cases that involved cannibalism, vampirism, or necrophilia.

Poisoning was in vogue during medieval times and in Italy during the seventeenth century, Giulia Tofana was reportedly implicated in several hundred deaths. There were probably many more serial poisoners who were never caught or documented, because some people worked for wealthy people who wanted to kill those people who were hurdles to their power or inheritance. Then, during the nineteenth century, forensic toxicologists developed a technique to detect arsenic in human tissue, which helped to identify and lock up serial poisoners.

With the growing sophistication of scientific inventions, industrial technology, and medical discoveries occurring parallel to the waning dominance of religion, physicians needed cadavers to advance their knowledge about disease and to teach human anatomy to medical students, so they encouraged grave robbing. Some of these necro-entrepreneurs became serial killers. In Scotland, William Burke and William Hare would grab their victims in an arm-lock around the throat or sit on their chests while holding their noses closed, which provided the most valuable bodies that had no marks of trauma. They killed 16 before they were caught in 1828.

Even children were becoming cold-blooded killers. In America, 14-year-old Jesse Pomeroy, the "Boston Boy Fiend" killed and mutilated two other children, while church sexton Thomas Piper confessed to four brutal sex murders. He said that opium had made him do it.

In 1885, 3 years before the Ripper's spree, the "Servant Girl Annihilator" caused a sensation in Austin, Texas. This killer, too, went unidentified (Ramsland, 2005). Some officials wondered if there was a connection between Austin's killer and London's, but the killer's approach and victim type was quite different. Dismissing a connection involved a bit of linkage analysis before it became a method.

DEFINING THE TERM

The FBI today prefers to use the term *criminal investigative analysis* (CIA), in part because *profiling* has receded from popularity and has been criticized by serious researchers. However, CIA covers more law enforcement activities than criminal profiling, so for this chapter we stick with the history and development of profiling. The term itself is confusing, in part due to the different ways it has been used.

During the 1990s, several of the early members of the BSU published accounts of their investigations, such as the book by former BSU chief John Douglas, *Mindhunter*. His formula, *how* plus *why* equals *who*, meant that profilers assume that personality dictates behavior, so offenders will leave clues that show patterns that reveal their unique traits and behaviors. Who they are will stay consistent from one activity to another. So, an investigator can *profile* (a verb) to develop a *profile* (a noun). The point is to interpret behavior at a scene to help reduce the potential pool of suspects. Profilers "read" crime scene behavior.

However, media began to discuss "the profile of a serial killer" as if it were a blueprint for a criminal type. This, too, was a noun, but it was different from the development of a behavioral portrait devised specifically from criminal acts. The FBI did not offer generic portraits of a serial killer, and the agency resisted this trend, but it was not difficult to develop a *prospective* profile, because the FBI's profiles about loner white male offenders between 25 and 40 who lived with a female relative began to sound generic.

Prospective blueprints work for only categories of offenders who operate in similar ways, such as disgruntled middle-aged mass murderers who commit workplace violence, or health-care serial killers who share common traits. We will discuss this in Chapter 8. However, there are too many differences from case to case for most serial killers, especially in other countries, to use a checklist-based profile. In other words, while a prospective profile has its place, its use for an active serial crime investigation is significantly limited.

Another misunderstanding was to use *profile* as a form of risk evaluation. Although behavioral profiling does involve assessments of the risk for future violence by an unknown offender, it is not inherently a prognostication tool.

The fifth notion is that profiling means "reading" people, like Sherlock Holmes would do whenever he first met someone. Profilers supposedly have the keen ability not just to "scent" behavior at a crime scene but also to fully understand individuals at a glance. In one popular televisions series about FBI profilers, the characters reprimand each other, "Don't profile me."

Although these activities are related in that they seek to interpret behavior to devise a portrait, offering hypotheses about a known person is quite different from describing an "UNSUB" (the FBI's term for an *unknown subject*).

For example, some narratives about profiling describe an analysis done on Adolf Hitler during World War II to evaluate his likelihood of suicide. Dr. Walter C. Langer, a psychoanalyst, offered a "long range" estimate of what would happen if Hitler believed he was going to lose the war. Langer thought Hitler would end his life rather than surrender. However, Langer's analysis bears little similarity to trying to figure out who Jack the Ripper was.

For this book, we use *profile* as a retrospective analysis of behavior at a crime scene or series of scenes, to devise a portrait of traits and projected behaviors of an UNSUB. The only deviation will be in Chapter 8.

EARLIEST PROFILES

Back to the Ripper. Dr. Thomas Bond had studied the incident reports or participated in the autopsies of victims attributed to an unknown offender in Whitechapel (Evans & Rumbelow, 2006). He was curious about the type of person who would commit such crimes, especially after Mary Kelly was killed. Bond had an interest in early psychiatry, and by this time medical journals had been published over the past few decades to discuss such things as the mind of the criminally insane.

No one at the time was undertaking the activity of linkage analysis, and these were not the only prostitutes who had been attacked in the area. A behavioral analysis might have even eliminated Mary Kelly, who was attacked inside and much more viciously than any of the others. An analysis might have included Martha Tabram, whose murder on August 8 went along with the pattern. Perhaps, Elizabeth Stride would be removed from the list, as she had just a cut to the throat. However, the police had decided to link just these five. They are known as the "canonical five."

Just after the murder of Mary Kelly, Bond offered his profile of the type of person who would commit such crimes. "In each case," he wrote, "the mutilation was inflicted by a person who had no scientific nor anatomical knowledge ...." He thought the man was physically strong, as well as calm and bold. He worked alone. "He must, in my opinion, be a man subject to periodic attacks of homicidal and erotic mania ... The murderer in external appearance is quite likely to be a quiet inoffensive looking man, probably middle-aged, and neatly and respectably dressed ... He would probably be solitary and eccentric in his habits, also he is most likely to be a man without regular occupation" (Evans & Rumbelow, 2006, p. 187).

Bond suggested that the police offer a reward, which would attract information from people who knew the man. Surely, someone would notice a person like this! Bond thought that the same offender was responsible for the 1889 murder of another victim, Alice McKenzie. Even *he* did not entirely agree with Scotland Yard. Since no one was ever arrested, it is not possible to know how accurate his profile was.

A prominent Scottish surgeon, Joseph Bell, also gave his opinion after examining the police and autopsy reports, but his analysis was sealed, sent, and subsequently lost in the mail. Reportedly, he favored a young doctor who had committed suicide after the Kelly murder.

Six years later, two magistrates in France devised the next known profile. A series of rape–murders began in 1894, but because the incidents occurred in different districts around the country they were not linked at first. Most had been in rural areas and there was no news coverage. The killer had different victims as well. He targeted young men and women who were walking alone or alone with their sheep. Some journalists who heard about the mutilations proposed that Jack the Ripper had come across the English Channel (Starr, 2010).

In 1895, Magistrate Louis-Albert Fonfrède investigated the assault and murder of a 17-year-old girl in his district. With his report, he compiled a dossier of similar incidents that he learned about from other areas. Witnesses, he knew, had reported a vagabond near several crime scenes. No one had identified him or even offered descriptions similar enough that a single offender could be linked to all of the incidents.

Magistrate Émile Fourquet heard about murders near Lyon. He acquired Fonfrède's dossier and spotted common behaviors: All of the victims were young, all had been alone, many were shepherds, all were mutilated with a sharp implement, like a knife, and all had been sodomized as they died. He dismissed the Ripper connection. This was a different killer altogether. The neck wounds showed the killer's approach: he came up from behind. Witnesses had noted a twisted lip on the vagabond they saw, a droopy eye, and strange mannerisms, as if he were mentally unbalanced (Starr, 2010).

Fourquet created two charts. One was for victimology, including how they were handled. Eight of the incidents seemed clearly linked by wound pattern, circumstances of the crime, and body disposition. On the second chart, Fourquet devised a profile. He used witness reports, but he knew something about criminal behavior as well. This offender had a specific sexual ritual. He had a "signature." He watched for an opportunity to find a young person alone. He attacked quickly, from behind. He stabbed them in the neck to kill them fast, so he was after the body. He wanted to feel the person dying as he had anal sex. He then mutilated the body and tried to hide it. Fourquet suspected that they had not yet found all of the victims. Whoever this person was, he was careful but also suffered from a compelling need to keep doing what he was doing. The addictive aspect was apparent.

Using these charts, Fourquet developed a report with charts and maps and sent it to magistrates all over France. He urged them to watch for a stranger traveling alone, thirtyish, with dark hair and eyes.

He would have a menacing manner and a disturbing grimace. He tended to walk around where he could find young people alone.

A few more victims turned up before the unsub targeted a woman in the town of Adrèche. He approached her, but she fought him off and screamed. Her husband came running and was able to grab the vagabond before he got away. Local police arrested him and learned his name: Joseph Vacher. He was 29, he wore rags, and he had a droopy eye and twisted lip. He seemed surly. Fourquet arrived to interview him. In the process, he elicited a confession. As he had suspected, there were more victims.

A discharged soldier with a sordid history, including shooting himself in the head, Vacher admitted to the murders on Fourquet's list and added one that he had tossed down a well. He had suffered since the age of 14 from irresistible urges to kill. He seemed to be laying the foundation for claiming insanity. However, the "French Ripper" was convicted of multiple murders and duly executed (Starr, 2010).

OBSERVANT PATHOLOGIST

On February 9, 1929, in Düsseldorf, Germany, men on their way to work discovered a dead girl, bloody from knife wounds and partially burned. Dr. Karl Berg performed the autopsy and noticed a strange behavior. He counted 13 oddly parallel stab wounds to her left breast, 5 of which had penetrated the heart. The wounds appeared to have been made by something dull and thick, like scissor blades (Berg, 1945). He wondered if this death was related to an assault 5 days earlier. A man had come up to an elderly woman and stabbed her. Her wounds looked the same. Within a week, an intoxicated mechanic fell to a killer who stabbed him with a similar implement. Berg started a file. He noted the blitz approach, usually from behind. He wrote down the geographical locations, the modus operandi, the time of day, the suspected weapon, and the lack of an obvious motive, like robbery. Each victim had been stabbed in the temple, an odd place to aim. This attacker was after something other than outright murder.

On the night of August 21, someone stabbed three different people, once each. They all survived. Berg thought this weapon was different, which suggested a second stabber. Or, their killer had changed his weapon. Berg thought that the new weapon was a dagger.

Not long afterward, the bodies of two girls turned up in a garden near a public market. Berg found that the youngest child, just 5 years old, was nearly beheaded. The older one, age 14, had suffered stab wounds to her back. Later that same day, an adult woman was stabbed, but she survived. This presented an opportunity. Berg had a witness.

She said the man had flirted with her. He was good-looking and seemed harmless. But then he had tried to rape her before stabbing her three times in the temple and twice in the neck. A piece of the knife had broken off, stuck in her back. It was from a dagger, just as Berg had surmised.

Then the attacks stopped for two months, as if the killer wanted to lie low after his failure. The next body discovered was that of a servant girl. She had been raped, dragged 100 feet, and sexually posed. A circle of wounds was present around the crown of her head. When Berg autopsied her, he discovered they now had another weapon: a square-faced hammer. Within 2 weeks, he had another victim, another girl similarly treated. Then a 5-year-old girl was found in a patch of weeds near an abandoned property. She was strangled, as well as stabbed 36 times. There were wounds to her skull.

The escalation of these attacks was worrisome to the community. Police had no leads, despite victim descriptions. Berg did not know the word *signature*, but he believed they had a single offender switching his weapons, times of day, and victim type. The head wounds were a significant signal, because they were so odd.

Then, a letter arrived to a local newspaper. Apparently, this killer wanted attention. He gave directions to this body and another. When the victim was exhumed from her shallow grave, Berg saw the telltale stab wounds to the left temple and neck, apparently with a pair of scissors. The killer's attempt to communicate was a positive sign. It wasn't long before he made a mistake: he took a victim to his house and then let her leave. She returned with the police to the home of Peter Kürten.

After the arrest, Berg met with Kürten in his cell. He had seen what this killer had done as intimately as anyone could. He wanted to hear the details of motive, especially for the odd features of these crimes. Kürten confessed. He was willing to give Berg all the details. Berg achieved an intimate form of validation and correction, offering one of the most insightful portraits of early criminology.

Kürten reeled off the numerous crimes he had perpetrated, culminating in a list of 79 incidents. Thirteen were murders. The first one had happened years earlier, in 1931. In a bedroom he had entered with the intention of burglary, he had seen a sleeping girl. He used a knife to slice open her throat. When her blood spurted forth, he had caught it in his mouth. This had given him an orgasm. Afterward, he developed a thirst for more. He served some time in prison, but once released, he started his assaults. He had learned that a blow to the temple produced a lot of blood. He would drink it, satisfying himself sexually. After his conviction on multiple counts, Kürten was executed in 1931 (Berg, 1945). Berg wrote up his account, producing the longest and most detailed work to date on paraphilic signature murder.

PSYCHIATRIST ASSISTANCE

Less than a decade later, an American psychiatrist provided a profile for a sensational triple homicide. He was the first known psychiatrist to become involved with this aspect of law enforcement. Most people have heard of James Brussel, whom we address shortly, but Dr. J. Paul de River came well before him. De River was head of the LAPD's Sex Offense Bureau, which he had formed, and he consulted on crime scenes with a sexual component (King, 1949). He was asked to assist on a case on June 26, 1937, when three missing girls from Inglewood, California, were found murdered. Madeline and Melba Everett were 7 and 9. Their friend was 8-year-old Jeannette Stephens. They were seen talking to a man in Centinela Park and leaving with him. Their bodies were found in a gully in Baldwin Hills. They had been strangled and sexually assaulted.

De River viewed the crime scene area, crime scene photos, and the bodies in the morgue. After the girls were killed, they were placed close together, facedown, with their dresses pulled up, and their shoes taken off. The shoes were side by side in a row. De River drew up a profile so police would know the type of person to seek: a sadistic pedophile in his twenties who was single, meticulous, religious, and remorseful. He might have a past arrest record, especially involving children. This crime had been planned. He looked safe, because he had easily approached the girls and led them away. They might even have known him (King, 1949).

This description seemed to fit a school crossing guard, Albert Dyer, who had come to help with the search. He had presented himself, unsolicited, at the station to find out why police wanted to question him. They brought him in. De River assisted with the interview and Dyer soon confessed. Yet he did not really fit the profile. He was 32, he had a wife, he had no record, and he seemed to suffer no remorse. Dyer described how he had lured the girls with a fake story about rabbits. He had separated them before strangling them with a clothesline one at a time. As their bodies lay still in the gully, he had sex with them. Finally, Dyer had removed the girls' shoes, placed them in a row, and prayed. Whatever accolades de River won for this case resolution were eventually eclipsed by scandals in his own life (Ramsland, 2010).

After him, two decades later, Dr. James Brussel would profile a case that influenced the development of the FBI's approach. In 1956, detectives approached Dr. James Brussel to help with a psychological analysis of New York's unidentified Mad Bomber. Since 1940, this angry man had placed innocuous bombs around Manhattan and written rants to various public agencies. The officers handed over the letters and crime reports to Brussel. He studied photos of the bomb scenes and analyzed the content and handwriting in the letters, moving from first to last. He called on his clinical experience and provided details about the kind of person they were look-ing for: since the first letter had been sent to Consolidated Edison, Brussel surmised that the offender was a former employee who had a grudge. He thought he had not been treated right. Because bombs were the sole weapon of choice, Brussel said the perpetrator was a male European immi-grant, which also meant he was most likely Roman Catholic. His paranoid messages placed his age between 40 and 50 and suggested that he was single and fastidious. This meant he probably had a female relative looking after his needs. Since the letters were often mailed in Westchester County, he probably resided in an ethnic community near the city He would be miserly, wearing old-fashioned clothing, probably a double-breasted suit. And because he was fastidious, as many paranoid people are in their desire to maintain control, he would button it (Brussel, 1968).

Brussel thought that his profile should be published in newspapers, because it would elicit a response. This could gain more information. He was right that publication sparked new information, but most of it was false leads and tips that wasted resources. However, the bomber also responded, because he wanted to correct some errors. He inadvertently revealed the date of the incident that had so angered him. With this, a clerk for Consolidated Edison went through their files and matched unique phrases the Bomber had used to phrases in complaints to the company. When the police arrested George Metesky, age 54, in Waterbury, Connecticut, many profile points matched, including the buttoned double-breasted suit.

Brussel wrote a memoir to describe this experience. He had also pro-filed the Boston Strangler in 1964 and had interviewed Albert DeSalvo, the man arrested. He said that he used a mix of science and intuition, along with clinical experience. He checked his hunches against research data and probability analysis. He also used mental immersion to acquire a sense of the offender's thoughts. "When you think about an unknown criminal long enough," he stated, "when you've assembled all the known facts about him and poked at them and stirred them about in your mind, you begin to see the man" (Brussel, 1968, p. 39).

Howard Teten read the memoir. At the FBI, he was already thinking about linkage analysis and psychological factors that can assist inves-tigators at crime scenes. He made an appointment to discuss Brussel's methods with him.

THE FBI'S PROFILING PROGRAM

The BSU formed in May 1972 in response to rising murder rates, espe-cially crimes committed by strangers to the victims. There were also more serial murders. It required special training. The first publications about criminal profiling from the FBI featured the special agents who were the first members of the BSU, which most people now know as the Behavioral Analysis Unit (BAU). Howard Teten was the program's founder. Prior to his stint with the FBI, he had begun his own research to make homicide investigation more systematic. He wanted to be able to look at a scene or a series of potentially linked scenes and offer an accurate sense of the kind of person they were looking for. Before anyone had used the word *profiling*, Teten was engaged in it.

Teten had enrolled in the School of Criminology at the University of California at Berkeley, which was known to be among the most progressive in the nation for criminalistics. He was fascinated with criminal psychology and began to compare what he was learning about to what he saw when he responded to crime scenes as a police officer. He studied books on the subject, including Karl Berg's in-depth treatise. He read Bond's writing about Jack the Ripper, along with the work of August Vollmer, Hans Gross, and Walter Langer. He developed several hypotheses about the method of profiling and he wanted to test them. He collected homicide cases from local police agencies and members of the California Identification Officers Association so he could set up an experiment. He placed crime scene information on one side, separate from offender information. From the crime scene data, he prepared a description of the kind of person he thought was responsible for the homicide. With the information about the person who was convicted, he checked himself. He got pretty good at it, but he consulted with two psychiatrists to learn from experts about various mental illnesses and personality disorders. Along the way, he joined the FBI (Personal interview, 2010).

In 1969, Teten taught Police Management (DeNevi & Campbell, 2004). When he was transferred to DC headquarters, he joined a teaching team that went to different police jurisdictions. He included his own research in his course. Then in 1970, Teten put in a request to teach a course on Applied Criminology. He included his unique approach to analyzing a crime scene. Officers were impressed. He asked for cases and offered good suggestions. He even helped to solve some, which enhanced his reputation. Patrick Mullany, with a graduate degree in psychology, joined him. Teten would describe the crime to participants, while Mullany supplied the mental disorder. Applied Criminology became a core course for the newly formed BSU. Eventually, it became Psychological Criminology, or Psychological Profiling.

Eventually, Teten read Dr. Brussel's memoir, *Casebook of a Crime Psychiatrist*. He read about the profiles made for the Mad Bomber and Boston Strangler cases. Teten arranged a meeting. Brussel was pleased to help. They discussed their methods, seeing the overlap and the places where they diverged. It was clear to Teten that, while psychological insight was valuable, it did not replace experience with homicide investigation. "Brussel's approach was to seek specific areas of psychiatric potential,"

Teten recalled, "and then to combine them to form a profile. This was different from my approach, which was to derive an overall impression of the gross mental status based on the crime scene as a whole" (Personal interview, 2010).

Among the early cases that tested Teten's approach to profiling was the 1974 kidnapping of 7-year-old Susan Jaeger (Campbell & DeNevi, 2004), who disappeared in Montana while on a camping trip with her family. No ransom was demanded, which was bad news. It meant her killer wanted her for himself. Investigators feared the worst. When they called the FBI, Mullany told them that the perpetrator was likely a local Caucasian male. The girl was probably dead. They needed to find the offender, because he would do it again.

An anonymous tip led to David Meirhofer, but local investigators dismissed this polite 23-year-old Vietnam veteran as a viable suspect. He was cooperative and educated. They believed they were looking for someone rougher, less educated. Yet Teten and Mullany said that Meierhofer was exactly the type of person they should consider.

Soon, the burnt remains of a young woman associated with Meirhofer were discovered in an old barrel on his property. Yet even under the influence of truth serum he denied any wrongdoing. He also passed a polygraph. Again, the local police struck him off their list, but Mullany and Teten remained convinced. They knew that psychopaths can lie with ease. They predicted that he would call on the anniversary of the kidnapping because it had emotional meaning to him. They urged the Jaegers to keep a tape recorder by their phone.

Exactly as predicted, a man called and said that Susan was with him. Mrs. Jaeger surprised him when she forgave him. He started to cry and hung up. Mullany encouraged Mrs. Jaeger to return to Montana and confront Meirhofer. She decided to follow his advice. In an attorney's office, she was face to face with the man the FBI believed had killed her daughter. It was a tense moment. Meirhofer did not break down, but the Jaegers received another call. When Mrs. Jaeger said she knew his voice, it was sufficient for a search warrant. In Meirhofer's home, the police discovered body parts from Susan and other victims. Before Meirhofer committed suicide, he admitted to the murder of a missing boy.

The profilers had been correct. Teten felt vindicated. No matter how nice and respectable people look, they can still be cold-hearted killers. It was an important lesson, because around this time, Ted Bundy was on the loose.

Teten knew that his training in a homicide unit had been invaluable. He believed that every agent selected for the BSU should do a 6-month internship with a big city crime scene unit. However, the bureau thought otherwise, and agents came in with little or no crime scene investigation experience.

The new agents began to research specialized areas of crime. They wrote articles, many of which are collected in the anthology *Profilers* (Cambell & DeNevi, 2004). Robert R. Hazelwood and Richard Ault described how law enforcement had to incorporate more advances from the behavioral sciences. With John Douglas, Hazelwood created the distinction still used today between the "organized" and "disorganized" offender (Douglas & Olshaker, 1995), which will be more fully described in the next chapter. Initially, the BSU had 11 members, with Jack Kirsch as chief. The hiring committee handpicked agents who appeared to have a knack for behavioral analysis (Jeffers, 1991).

By 1977, the BSU had a distinct set of goals: crime scene analysis, criminal profiling, and the analysis of threatening letters. This became the Crime Analysis and Criminal Personality Profiling Program, which was taken on the road. The early profilers were pioneering a unique approach that they would have to introduce carefully to law enforcement agencies. They came to be regarded as an elite unit of specialists who could help others to better understand the most brutal and extreme forms of human behavior. The BSU eventually became the BAU, spreading out into an investigative or field unit that could actively assist local jurisdictions. It was one thing to brainstorm over a case in a classroom, but they knew they could be more helpful if they went to scenes and looked at what offenders did up close.

SUMMARY

Like detectives who looked for physical clues at a crime scene, members of the BSU viewed a crime scene's appearance and the way the crime was committed as symptomatic of an offender's unique aberration. They emphasized the analysis of *behavior* at a scene, to coordinate with the physical evidence. The goals were to devise a list of traits and behaviors for the kind of person (or people) who would commit the crime, to predict if they might commit future violence, and to assist in other capacities. The method of profiling became part of a larger mission, but it retains its original purpose. We now turn to the methods, critiques, and improvements over the years.

REFERENCES

Berg, K. (1945). *The sadist: An account of the crimes of serial killer Peter Kürten: A study in sadism.* London: Heineman.

Brussel, J. (1968). *Casebook of a crime psychiatrist.* New York: Grove Press.

Campbell, J. H., & DeNevi, D. (2004). *Profilers: Leading investigators take you inside the criminal mind.* Amherst, New York: Prometheus.

DeNevi, D., & Campbell, J. H. (2004). *Into the minds of madmen: How the FBI Behavioral Science Unit revolutionized crime investigation.* Amherst, NY: Prometheus Books.

Douglas, J., & Olshaker, M. (1995). *Mindhunter: Inside the FBI's elite serial crime unit.* New York: Scribner.

Evans, S., & Rumbelow, D. (2006). *Jack the Ripper: Scotland Yard investigates.* Phoenix Hill, England: Sutton.

Jeffers, H. P. (1991). *Who killed Precious?* New York: Dell.

King, B. (1949). The strange case of Dr. de River. In B. King (Ed.), *The Sexual Criminal* (pp. xxxii–xxxix). Springfield, IL: Charles C. Thomas; reprinted by Bloat Books, 2000.

Ramsland, K. (2005). *The human predator: A historical chronicle of serial murder and forensic investigation.* New York: Berkley.

Ramsland, K. (2010). *The mind of a murderer: Privileged access to the demons that drive Extreme violence.* Santa Barbara, CA: Praeger.

Starr, D. (2010). *The killer of little shepherds: A true crime story and the birth of forensic science.* New York: Knopf.

CHAPTER **6**

Methodology

Near Sacramento, California, in 1986, a fisherman came across a murdered young woman submerged in an irrigation ditch. It was clear to investigators that she had been dragged to the spot and hit several times before she was strangled with a ligature. The presence of semen showed that this had been sexual. The victim was 19-year-old Stephanie Brown. People she knew were located, and her boyfriend said she had been on her way to his house but had never arrived. Her abandoned car, with no evident mechanical problems, showed that she had taken a wrong turn on I-5. The driver-side window was rolled down. Stephanie's parents insisted she would not have done this at night if a stranger had approached. The armrest was broken, as if she had grabbed it to prevent being taken from the car (Henderson, 1998).

When an investigator saw pictures of Stephanie, he realized something was different. The body had short hair, but Stephanie's was long. Her parents said she had not cut it. This suggested a signature: her killer had cut it. There was more. A blue tank top was cut through the shoulder straps as well for no apparent reason. A search of the area around the scene produced a pair of shears. This suggested two important behaviors: the killer had a "hit kit" and he had a paraphilia. He was a predator with an addiction that required a victim. He would have others, past or in the future.

A month later, Charmaine Sabrah, 26, and her mother, Carmen Anselmi, broke down on a lonely stretch of I-5. A man approached and offered to help. Driving a two-seater sports car, he could take only one. He promised to return. Charmaine went with him. The man never returned and Charmaine disappeared. Her body was found 50 miles away. Like Stephanie Brown, she had been strangled with a ligature, the straps of her bra had been cut, a section was cut from her panties, and clumps of her hair had been pulled out. Investigators figured it was the same guy.

Then the remains of another victim turned up near where Stephanie Brown's body had been left. Lora Heedick had been similarly strangled and her tank top bore the same nonfunctional cutting. A witness had seen her enter a small sports car like the one Carmen Anselmi had described. Three linked victims matched the FBI's definition of a serial killer at the time: at least three victims in three incidents in three locations, with a "cooling off" period. Some people called him the "I-5 Strangler." Like other sexual predators, he was sure to keep killing until he was caught.

By this time, serial murder was well known. Among those who had been arrested were Ted Bundy, John Wayne Gacy, the Hillside Stranglers, the Son of Sam, the Atlanta Child Killer, "Candy Man" Dean Corll, and Henry Lee Lucas. A barrage of media usually accompanied such cases (Ramsland, 2005). They had to catch this guy.

Soon patrol officers pulled over Roger Kibbe, 47, for a traffic violation and noticed that he resembled the composite drawing from Carmen Anselmi. Oddly, Kibbe's brother was a homicide detective on the I-5 investigations. Under questioning, Kibbe admitted only to soliciting prostitutes and to being in several places that could have put him close to the victims. Yet they could not hold him.

The I-5 Strangler struck again. In June 1987, Karen Finch's car was found abandoned near I-5. When her body turned up, her clothing had been oddly cut. The next victim, Debra Guffie, survived. Her screams had attracted the attention of a patrol officer. The man who had attacked her was Kibbe (Smith, 2008). His murder kit was in his car: a pair of scissors, duct tape, handcuffs, rubber hair bands, pieces of a wooden dowel, and cut lengths of white nylon cord. Besides fiber evidence, investigators learned enough about Kibbe to link him behaviorally to these crimes. It was no surprise to learn that he had queried his brother several times about the progress of the investigation (Lindeloff, 2008).

Kibbe had a fetish. He had started cutting up female clothing when he was young. He had been arrested at age 15 for stealing clothing from a clothesline. He said that stealing clothes excited him. The signature behavior that had linked these murders was the nonfunctional scissor damage to the clothing.

Evidence supported a conviction. Afterward, Kibbe revealed his MO: he would drive the remote I-5 interstate on a regular basis, looking for a woman that caught his attention. Once he had his eye on a potential victim, he drove ahead of her and parked on the side of the road to pretend to need help. These women usually stopped. He knew the areas around the interstate where he could take the victim without being discovered in the act. Yet because police were now more vigilant in that area, he had been caught (Henderson, 1998).

A retrospective criminal profile—also called a *behavioral* or *psychological profile*—is developed for a criminal incident or for a series of incidents that have already occurred and that appear to share a pattern. The purpose is to examine key items such as modus operandi, physical evidence, and signature behavior that can reveal offender traits and link the incidents to one another and to an offender. A full evaluation, based on prior experience and on database evaluation, provides law enforcement agencies with information meant to reduce the potential suspect pool, as well as to identify areas for investigative advice. Criminal profiling is meant to make a complex investigation more manageable by providing expertise on behavioral interpretation. It is informed speculation about the type of person who might have committed the crime(s) (Douglas & Olshaker, 1995; McCrary & Ramsland, 2003; Ressler & Shachtman, 1992; Scherer & Jarvis, 2014a). This chapter shows how a profiling consultation is initiated, the type of information needed to develop it, how it is developed, how it assists an investigation, what a geographical analysis adds, and the role of profiling methods in several types of scenarios.

INFERENTIAL ANALYSIS

Profiling led to, and is now just one area under the umbrella of, CIA. Three types of profiling are described in the current literature (Scherer & Jarvis, 2014b): criminal investigative, clinical practitioner, and statistical or empirical. The first two rely heavily on experience and a focus on case details; the criminal investigative approach derives from methods described in Chapter 5. The third approach focuses on global patterns and trend analysis via statistical calculations. Profiling currently incorporates all three, with emphasis on the first type. Because detailed death investigation is not routinely taught in police agencies, especially the behavioral manifestations of mental conditions, qualified personnel are generally sought to consult. The FBI supplies this assistance, but psychological practitioners who are familiar with investigation can help as well. Behavioral experts will enhance task forces as long as they understand the investigative needs.

CIA unfolds in stages (McCrary & Ramsland, 2003; Scherer & Jarvis, 2014a). Agents must first determine whether a crime has actually been committed. Sometimes crimes are falsely reported or an incident is misread. This is Stage 1. If the answer is affirmative that a crime has been committed, they go to Stage 2, which defines the type of crime. Most often, this would be murder, rape, arson, bombing, or hostage-taking. Once it is clear that the incident(s) can benefit from behavioral analysis, they enter Stage 3 to examine behavioral evidence and offer ideas about the kind of offender that is likely involved. Psychological autopsy is also now part of CIA, as are indirect personality assessment, interview strategies, investigative advice, search warrant support, and critical incident analysis. If necessary, the agents might become part of legal proceedings (Stage 4) by offering testimony or advice on strategy.

Scherer and Jarvis (2014a) note problems with the lack of a standard universal definition of profiling and offer an example of CIA, based on current best practices. Since 2005, the FBI has changed its definition of *serial murder*, reducing the victim toll and offering a simplified definition: at least two victims in two separate incidents. The requirement for different locations was dropped, because some killers take victims to their home (single location). The notion of a "cooling off period" was too vague to be useful, so this part of the earlier definition disappeared as well (Morton & Hilts, 2005). However, the briefer definition has not been universally adopted, in part because it appears to be too simplistic and too broad, and it fails to identify anything that links the two murders to a distinct motivation. Although "serial murderer" is not a type of offender, because the motives, ages, and personalities involved are too diverse, there does appear to be something about the predatory nature of such offenders that should be captured in a definition.

Scherer and Jarvis (2014b) focus on a case from the 1980s to show how an FBI team performed a victimology and linkage analysis between the murders of two unrelated hitchhikers. They also offered a threat assessment on the likelihood of another victim. The FBI analysts listed characteristics of the type of person who would commit these crimes. For example, he would be local and familiar with the route. Since they thought the public should be warned, they provided suggestions about handling the media coverage. Later, they offered advice about a decoy operation (which worked) and provided data to support probable cause for a search warrant. When a suspect was arrested after killing a fourth woman, the FBI team provided an indirect personality evaluation and suggested interview strategies. For the prosecutor, they recreated scenes, described motive, and suggested trial strategies.

To become proficient as a profiler requires an in-depth education in law enforcement, experience with investigation, and knowledge of several subdisciplines of psychology, especially personality theories, legal psychology, and clinical psychology or psychiatry (Campbell & DeNevi, 2004). To assess motive, one needs to understand psychopathology that manifests in criminal behavior, specifically how mental illness and personality disorders influence behaviors that can be detected at crime scenes. Profilers must also be experienced with past crimes and crime scenes, including signals to a scene being staged (Douglas, Burgess, Burgess, & Ressler, 1992; Scherer & Jarvis, 2014b). They must be able to perform a full victimology relevant to behavior leading up to an incident. In the FBI, agents who go into the BAU have plenty of investigative experience, and they take many classes that offer in-depth training and information. They also keep updated on developments in criminology (DeNevi & Campbell, 2004).

Scherer and Jarvis (2014b) provide a research study based on 40 individuals (87% male) who had practiced CIA or been trained by the FBI to perform these analyses. All subjects had at least 15 years of law enforcement experience. They were given a semi-structured interview that evaluated their understanding of CIA. The results showed a wide variety of interpretations and a lack of standard definitions for several distinct areas. This makes it difficult to determine how successful it is as a method. Nevertheless, it has shown anecdotal utility.

Another issue to consider, which was also true for psychological autopsies, is that interpretations of human behavior are based on probability analysis, that is, specific behaviors are weighed for their frequency or likelihood of occurring and for making inferences from them. Because human behavior is complex and not always what it seems, there is room for error (Cresswell, 2009). Statistical analysis based on data can offer a measured error rate, or the quantified likelihood that a hypothesis about data is incorrect. In simple terms, one type of error is rejecting a true hypothesis and the other is accepting a false one. A profile developed from behavioral data is a sort of null hypothesis, which offers a statement about facts that one seeks to nullify with data (e.g., the person who killed this victim in this manner will not kill again). Any tentative inference is prone to one error or the other. They result from flaws in reasoning or from an inability to include all possible members of a class (e.g., all rapists). Reducing one type of error increases the chances of making the other (Cox, 2006). The ideal is to make neither.

For accuracy, the smaller the potential for error for either option, the better. Statistical conclusion validity is the degree to which statements made about the relationship of variables are accurate, or at least reasonable. It generally relies on qualitative inference. In part, interpretations are based on adequate sampling and reliable research measures (Cozby, 2009). In this regard, profiling has been somewhat negligent. Only recently did the FBI publish a monograph based on empirical research for investigators (Morton et al., 2014). The intent was to analyze situational factors in how serial killers approach victims and treat the bodies. Whether this approach was actually beneficial for investigators was not tested.

Details from a victimology can affect the analysis. For example, if a missing woman's car is found backed into a parking spot, this would not necessarily seem unusual. However, if her husband insists that she hated to back up her car, this would raise the likelihood that someone else maneuvered the car or forced her to. In profiling, victimology comes first.

Bias is another potentially negative influence. Criminologist Kim Rossmo (2008, 2011) indicates that investigative failures typically arise from three areas: cognitive biases, organizational traps, and probability errors.

Specifically, Rossmo discusses threshold diagnosis, tunnel vision, and assumptions from familiarity (gut instinct). He has drawn his insights from social cognition research, which focuses on how people organize and process information. We mentioned this in earlier chapters, and it can be especially acute when the pressure is on for a series of frightening incidents to be stopped. Because mental capacities are limited, humans use efficient mental shorthand, called *heuristics*. These are cognitive shortcuts that reduce complex problems into simple rules (Kebbell, Muller, & Martin, 2010). Heuristics form automatically while processing information. This is usually beneficial, but mental shortcutting can lead to serious errors.

A perceptual set is the readiness to perceive something in accordance with expectations, which can cause a threshold diagnosis and confirmation bias. Investigators' past experience, culture, education, and social context influence these expectations, making them vulnerable to selectively focusing on certain aspects of a stimulus that will then block other aspects (Gilovich & Griffin, 2002; Stelfox & Pease, 2005). They arrive at scenes prepared for action, knowing they have little time to make decisions, and this involves a specific perceptual set. With all the pressure and excitement, it can be difficult to make the effort to critically examine their ideas, because the human brain is not wired for uncertainty (Rossmo, 2009). They seek to know what happened and who did it, as quickly as possible.

Kebbell et al. (2010) list common cognitive shortcuts, any of which can derail an investigation. Judging the likelihood of an event because it is easy to envision is the *availability heuristic*. The *representative heuristic* occurs from a perceived similarity between an individual and a class to which he or she seems to belong. The *anchoring heuristic* focuses on how we "anchor" in initial judgments and fail to adjust with new information. There are many more. The mind is efficient. It will form quick decisions automatically, but this ability can cause errors. (A good idea for investigative teams is to include someone who can make quick judgments and someone who is more cautious and analytical. It might result in arguments, but others will be forced to at least consider their own thinking process.)

In addition, narrative force plays a role. Pennington and Hastie (1992) demonstrated how the mere structure of a story facilitates shortcutting to get to the story's gist. People respond well to stories. They remember details better in a story format. From story frames, they form expectations of how the narrative will develop and how it will (or should) end. A narrative with holes is vulnerable. Listeners will add details that make the story make better sense (Kahneman, 2013). This is a natural human process, but it can present problems for investigators. They need training in how to consider alternate scenarios and examine their automatic thinking processes.

TABLE 6.1   Myths about Serial Killers

1. Serial killers are all dysfunctional loners.
2. Serial killers are all white males.
3. Serial killers are only motivated by sex.
4. All serial murderers travel and operate interstate.
5. All serial killers are insane or are evil geniuses.
6. Serial killers want to get caught.

Besides typical human cognition, cultural narratives can also cause problems, especially when presented through news, social media, and entertainment venues that relate to behavioral profiling (Scherer & Jarvis, 2014b). In 2005, Morton and Hilts from the FBI published a monograph based on an international symposium dedicated to serial murder. They identified several cultural myths that had developed, which are listed in Table 6.1.

In addition, several movies and television series portray criminal profiling erroneously, and even the methodology can be mentally misrepresented. Notably, the intent of a profile is not to solve a case. Profilers are consultants to investigations, not the primary detective. The use of behavioral analysis should be kept in perspective. There is no "one size fits all" profile for any type of offender, including serial killers (Morton & Hilts, 2005). Those fictional detectives who yell, "He doesn't fit the profile," do not understand what the process and product are.

Profiling is also limited to the type and quality of the information that the analysts receive from task forces. In the case of the Baton Rouge serial killer who was identified via DNA as African-American Derrick Todd Lee, the officers who supplied crime information to the FBI for profiling had an unconscious bias. Although they had reports in their files about a black man loitering near a victim's home shortly before she disappeared, they reportedly believed that all serial killers were white, so they excluded these reports. Thus, the resulting profile was inaccurate.

VICTIMOLOGY

As with psychological autopsies, background on victims is vital to devising an accurate and helpful profile. This includes aspects of their personality and their behavior. Victim risk factors must be identified, as well as any potential relationship the victim had with the offender, even just a brief encounter. When and where a person was assaulted, abducted, and/or killed helps to identify their degree of risk, as does their age and occupation. Low-risk victims tend to live normal lives and be inside their homes when assaulted. High-risk victims include those engaged in marginal behavior, such as substance abuse, prostitution, sexual role-playing, memberships in risky clubs, and exotic dancing. The victimology involves a timeline of known movements prior to the incident. This will include an analysis of as many of the sources listed in Table 6.2 as possible (Douglas & Olshaker, 1995; McCrary & Ramsland, 2003; Michaud & Hazelwood, 1998; Ressler & Shachtman, 1992).

Among the most significant are communications that establish the victim's frame of mind, such as expressing fear of someone, being stalked, or breaking up with someone.

Once victim details are known and a timeline devised with as much information as possible, the crime scene and offenders' methodology are evaluated for how best to categorize them. Based on the idea that personality has a considerable influence on what people do and the decisions they make (Douglas & Munn, 1992), investigators can assess whether the person planned and arranged a crime or instead spotted an opportunity and acted impulsively. (Some researchers dispute that the relationship between behavior and personality traits is as consistent as this approach assumes; others accept the basic concept but view it as too simplistic.)

An example of a victimology is that of a 17-year-old boy who told his mother he was going to speak with a man about a summer job but

TABLE 6.2   Sources for Victimology

- Social media activity
- Journals, emails, or letters they wrote
- Phone records (land line and cell)
- Texts sent or received
- Images on cameras
- Items the individual is reading
- Current occupations, including hobbies
- GPS records, use of cell phone maps, E-Z Pass records
- Police and autopsy reports
- Witness statements (especially last sighting)
- Employment records
- Recent purchases
- Club memberships
- Acquaintance reports
- Reports of altercations
- Potential police reports or arrest records
- Analysis of tattoos (if present)
- Mental health history
- Surveillance videos near where victim was
- Trash

would be home shortly. He never came home. Someone had seen him sitting in the truck of the man he had mentioned he wanted to see. An analysis showed that he had a job and a girlfriend, was doing well in school, had applied to colleges, and got along well with his family. He had no police record and no known drug abuse. He had a solid network of friends and no known enemies. It was his mother's birthday and she had expected him home for a party. He had been eager to get home. The man he was going to see had been questioned in association with several other missing young men who had worked for him. The chance that something had happened to the missing boy was far greater than that he had suddenly decided to run away. (He was, indeed, the victim of a serial killer, who had used the job as bait to get him into the truck.)

THE METHOD

Profiling involves offsite and onsite procedures. Both require data from police and autopsy reports and from the crime scene, such as physical evidence, photographs, witness statements, location maps, body position, patterns of evidence, and whether or not a weapon was picked up from the scene (such as an electrical cord or a kitchen knife) or left at the scene (e.g., a dropped revolver). Wound analysis involves knowing the types and seriousness of wounds, their locations, how many, and a reconstruction of how they occurred (if more than one). There are ways to view much of this material remotely, but an onsite visit offers the best perspective. McCrary and Ramsland (2003) described how being in a Toronto neighborhood where serial rapes were occurring suggested that the rapist most likely lived there with his parents. He was not old enough to own such an upscale house, but he did not stand out to the victims or witnesses as a stranger. (This observation proved to be correct.)

Significant factors must be gathered from and about the incident and crime scene, as detailed in Table 6.3.

FBI profilers checked the neighborhood of a rape–murder in Texas and discovered quite a few reported rapes within a square mile, including one that closely resembled the incident being profiled. The offender, once caught, turned out to have committed quite a few of them (Michaud & Hazelwood, 1998).

Certain factors at a scene help to clarify how offenders think—how they entered, why they chose that specific time or domicile, whether they had access to a surveillance perch, and whom they targeted. The type of weapon (or lack of one), the wounds made, and evidence of unusual or ritual behavior offer many clues. Ressler and Shachtman (1992) describe a man who disemboweled a pregnant woman and drank her blood

TABLE 6.3   Crime Scene Factors for Profiling

- Approximate time the incident occurred
- How long it went on
- Why it stopped
- Whether the offender arrived prepared
- Whether something or someone at the scene facilitated offender behavior
- Whether the incident was inside or outside
- How many victims at each scene
- How many other potentially connected scenes
- Whether there is one primary scene per incident or several associated scenes
- Weather conditions at the time
- The time of day
- Details about if and how a body was moved
- The environment around the crime scene
- Whether similar incidents have been reported nearby
- Neighborhood demographics
- Geophysical features

from a used yogurt cup he took from her trash. The "Eyeball Killer" in Texas always surgically removed the eyes of women he murdered (Matthews & Wicker, 1996).

Profilers do not want extraneous information to influence their evaluations. They will also rate each item according to how confident they are about its accuracy. To a great extent, profiling is subjective, but the BSU agents also had meetings to brainstorm together, which offered a form of peer review and inter-rater reliability.

Suspects under consideration for linkage attributes are evaluated for modus operandi, rituals, signature, and victim approach style. These items are compared against the victimology and crime scene factors. The analysts will consider body location and how it was treated; incident timeframes; victim and offender risk levels; the crime scene dynamics and how each acted and interacted; the means of entry (where relevant); weapon(s) used; degree of planning evident; and any type of ante-, peri-, and postmortem activity.

With rituals, the core behavior does not change very much, but it can evolve into more developed or complex forms. Binding, for example, can become more elaborate. This type of behavior assists to show the offender's age and experience. Although rituals will elevate the risk of being caught, they are generally part of an addiction. The longer the victim and offender interact and the more aberrant the offender is (short of being obsessive-compulsive about cleaning up), the more behavioral markers will likely be present (McCrary & Ramsland, 2003).

From scene elements, profilers can deduce aspects of offender behavior that could inspire crime: whether they have a set routine, specific hours for committing offenses, a vehicle, a military history, and part- or full-time employment (Douglas & Olshaker, 1995). For the aforementioned serial killer operating in Baton Rouge from 1992 until 2003, the profile estimated his age, body size and strength, socio-economic situation, behavior around women, ease of mobility, potential vehicle, approach to his victims, and appearance of normalcy. Women who had interacted with him, the profilers stated, would not view him as dangerous, yet he would grow angry, even enraged, over rejection. He would also take risks by entering homes of those whom he had targeted. He liked to feel in control, and people who were close to him would have seen his rage during moments when he felt off-balance. He was mission-oriented and would be arrogant and openly dismissive of police efforts. He would "know better" how to investigate. The observation that he felt comfortable in the areas where he dumped victim bodies was from the risks he had taken transporting them there. If he discussed news of a body being found, he would be agitated and without empathy. Given the apparent addictive aspect of his behavior, it seemed likely that he would make a mistake ("Serial Killer," n.d.). He did.

Each aspect of the crimes is scrutinized to envision how the offender had experienced it and why. If a killer removes the eyes, what could this mean? If she attacks only elderly victims, what might they symbolize? Who might be next? Profilers look for indicators that the offender approaches victims by cunning and manipulation, a surprise blitz, or as the result of opportunity. Although Ted Bundy had specific methods of approach, such as pretending to need assistance or posing as a cop, he also acted on opportunity, such as grabbing a girl walking alone down an alley. The offender's method of controlling this person is also important: perhaps he invites victims to his home, as Herb Baumeister did, for premurder sex. Or, he drugs them, as Jeffrey Dahmer did. He might bind them, keep them captive for a while, or kill them immediately. Maybe he is a truck driver who discards them along the road or drags them for a while first. Perhaps he enters the homes of couples, kills the husband, and rapes the wife.

Douglas and Hazelwood (1980) described behavioral distinctions between organized and disorganized offenders. At the time, it seemed groundbreaking, but now it serves as just one of many possible guidelines. Most offenders are "mixed," that is, they show elements of both poles of this continuum. Organized offenders tend to be educated, social, aware of law enforcement methods and evidence handling, narcissistic, controlled, and prepared. They clean up their scenes and often hide a victim's body. They might take a trophy to relive the pleasure of their crime, which is generally a piece of jewelry or an item of clothing. Unremorseful, they pay attention to media reports.

On the other end of the behavioral continuum, disorganized offenders tend to suffer from a mental illness—especially psychosis—or be
criminally inexperienced. They are unprepared, using a weapon or binding that they find at the scene, rather than bringing one. They are either
uneducated about evidence or oblivious. They might experience remorse.
They participate in postmortem mutilation and their form of trophy can
be a body part. Both types have addictions that can cause them to be
careless, but the more mentally ill someone is, the more disorganized
they typically are. They are more likely to leave a distinct signature or
to have bodies or body parts in their possession. Psychotic Ed Gein had
a body eviscerated, beheaded, and slung up like a deer carcass when
he was arrested. Many more body parts were in his home. However,
there are outliers: Eyeball Killer Charles Albright was organized and
smart, but he collected eyes. (However, if he kept them, he had a secret
place that was never discovered.) No matter where on the continuum the
killer is, profiles are easiest to work up when offenders have ritual habits
(Douglas & Munn, 1992; Keppel, 2000). This includes biting, pinching,
chewing, positioning, piquerism, binding, body part removal, defeca-
tion, the theft of specific items of clothing, and mutilation.

Profiling offers basic facts about offenders, seen in Table 6.4.

These items are based on inferences from research. Profiles can
also estimate the likelihood of future attacks and probable target dates
(Douglas & Olshaker, 1995; Michaud & Hazelwood, 1998).

Skilled profilers develop an eye for patterns, an ability to synthe-
size different types of information, the ability to operate as part of a
team, and knowledge about the methods and technology of investigation. They know about cognitive biases and they endeavor to minimize
their impact. Open-mindedness and communication skills are a plus.

TABLE 6.4   Offender Information on a Basic Profile

- Approximate age
- Sex
- Race
- Typical MO
- Geographic comfort zone
- Probable living situation, including approximate location
- Education level
- Likelihood of full-time work
- Work hours
- Evidence of military experience
- Travel patterns
- Likelihood of a criminal or psychiatric record
- Psychological traits or disorders
- Fantasy scenario that compels

They must be focused, able to listen, and able to spot signals of deception. Computers can perform some types of linkage, but initial estimates in the field derive from experience and the ability to be analytical. In the previously mentioned survey of 40 professionals, most emphasized the need for experience with the investigation of violent crime. They should also be familiar with criminology, forensic science methods, and the nuances of interviewing (Scherer & Jarvis, 2014b).

LINKAGE ANALYSIS: FIRST STEPS

Behavioral linkage examines specific types of behaviors, such as the MO and signature, along with details from victimology. McCrary and Ramsland (2003) used a case to demonstrate how McCrary approached the task. In Rochester, New York, in 1989, Captain Lynde Johnston had nearly 20 cases of prostitute murders. He wanted to know if they had a serial killer in their midst. He spoke with McCrary at the BSU, and McCrary invited New York State Trooper Lieutenant Ed Grant, a graduate of the FBI's National Academy, to join him. Their first goal was to filter the case reports to acquire a preliminary sense of a pattern. They read and reread case materials and discussed the details. Their three qualifying categories for each were (1) definitely in a series attributable to a lone killer, (2) possibly in the series, and (3) not in the series. They identified a distinct pattern for seven cases, with a few in the second category. They were able to eliminate others.

Once they had a group that they believed were linked, they determined from the body dumpsites that the killer knew the Genesee River Gorge area well, so it was likely that he went there to hunt or fish. He could have been a jogger or hiker, but this seemed unlikely, given his other characteristics. He was ordinary and did not scare the women, despite knowledge of a local killer picking them off. He was probably a regular customer and he would continue to kill. In fact, he appeared to be getting bolder. Based on the race of the victims, he was likely white. If he worked, it would be a job that did not require skill, and he probably had a criminal record for assault, since he seemed to brutalize the women. McCrary and Grant agreed that law enforcement had already encountered him in some capacity. He returned to some of the bodies, so they suggested putting surveillance on the next one to be found. When officers spotted a body from a helicopter, the killer (Arthur Shawcross) was also there, eating lunch. He was arrested. It did not take long to get a confession and he was convicted (McCrary & Ramsland, 2003).

From a systematic analysis of behavior, this case was closed and successfully prosecuted. Often, victims of serial killers have no association with one another, so a careful analysis of behavior from one case to another is essential. The cases will have both similarities and dissimilarities. Linking them results from deciding how the similarities compare against the dissimilarities. Linkage blindness results when investigators exaggerate the dissimilarities, sometimes to minimize the idea that they might be looking for a serial killer. There is no formula that clarifies which behaviors to link, especially when there is no obvious signature (such as removing eyeballs). This skill generally improves with experience.

PROFILING BY LOCATION

Sometimes, serial offenders remain in a fairly tight location to commit their crimes, which draws on a more specialized method: geographic profiling. This approach focuses on locations where victims were selected and the murders committed, the routes that offenders probably traveled, and geographical features of dumpsite locations. This type of analysis can supply information about a suspect's travel habits, range and degree of mobility, method and means of transportation, and attitude about crossing physical boundaries such as rivers or country demarcations. Most such offenders stay within their psychological comfort zone, where they feel safe and know escape routes, unless an investigation forces them out. The profiler then tries to determine what the offenders generally do in the area besides seek out victims: reside, work, attend meetings, hunt, fish, or participate in regular athletic activities. Whatever it is, they will do it there on a fairly regular basis. "BTK" killer Dennis Rader tended to stick with houses in particular neighborhoods in Wichita, Kansas, that were close to the interstate that led directly to his home to the north, although he did break his own rules to kill a neighbor (Ramsland, 2016). Ted Bundy preferred university communities, even if he went to different states (Dekle, 2011).

Although several investigators have developed geographical analysis, former Vancouver detective inspector Kim Rossmo is the most visible and offers the most sophisticated tools. The director of the Center for Geospatial Intelligence and Investigation at Texas State University, he created a software program, Criminal Geographic Targeting, and tested it on numerous cases. Rossmo requires at minimum five similar crimes, so typically others have completed the linkage analysis. Should more crimes occur that can be linked, the analysis can be modified (Rossmo, 2000).

Investigators with data from a series of crimes feed the relevant geographical markers into Rossmo's computer program. Onto a map of the area that shows roads and natural physical boundaries such as rivers and bridges, the crime locations are placed. This generates a 3D color-coded image that suggests the primary areas that the killer frequents.

The psychological component derives from the notion of mental maps or perceptual sets, which we have already discussed. Different people will have different perceptions about a location. Some people experience 200 miles as a great distance, while others view it as a mere 3-hour drive. Their perception, their ability and willingness to travel, their travel habits, and their familiarity with an area define their mental maps. Whether a rapist, arsonist, bomber, or killer travels in widening circles, zigzags, or moves along a linear path, much can be learned from the choices that he or she made.

Rossmo once applied his program to what was known about the murders attributed to Jack the Ripper in London's tight Whitechapel neighborhood. The five official murders were within a mile of one another and the total hunting ground was about half a square mile. The result of his analysis pinpointed an area that today lies between Commercial Street and Brick Lane, just north of Whitechapel Road. Because this area had a high concentration of lodging houses, which were filled with transients, it was difficult to pinpoint a specific residence, but it seemed likely that the killer had traveled the main drags, Commercial Street and Whitechapel Road. Examining where the fourth victim's apron was dropped relative to her body suggests a route to the killer's home (Rossmo, 2000). Some of the key suspects did live in this area.

Geographic profilers also want to determine the offender's degree of sophistication, evidence of planning, and the risk level of the victim(s). In addition, there might be evidence that offenders have changed their pattern and shifted out of their comfort zone, perhaps due to media coverage that has them concerned. Some offenders are more transient, or more mobile, than others. Some have a car; others do not. Some have local roots; others are unconnected and able to go longer distances. Some are truckers with specific routes.

For any analysis, important question center on distance and time traveled (if known), time of day incidents occurred, weather around the dumpsites for murders, amount of time that passed between crimes, victim type and where encountered, and the offender's hunting method. This latter point is categorized as one of Rossmo's four patterns, seen in Table 6.5.

TABLE 6.5   Rossmo's Four Behavioral
Killing Patterns

A hunter goes out searching in his comfort zone.
A poacher travels into outlying territory.
A troller is opportunistic.
A trapper lures victims to a specific place.

Analyzing potential settings for victim stalking helps to narrow the focus to the most promising places, and in this area investigators might then locate witnesses or possible survivors of a similar attack who might not have reported it. The places where offenders shop, work, live, hang out, and do recreational activities play a role in defining the parameters of what Rossmo calls their "crime awareness space."

DEFLECTING A PROFILE

The more the method of profiling has gained visibility via media reports and books, the more likely it is that a sophisticated offender will be alert to the speculations about him or her. Some have attempted to throw off investigators by purposely changing their behavior or by having no identifiable pattern. Dennis "BTK" Rader in Wichita, Kansas, and Gary "Green River Killer" Ridgway in Seattle, Washington, purposely shifted their MOs to throw off investigations (Ramsland, 2016; Smith, 2001). Ridgway posed one victim with odd items like a fish, and Rader took two victims out of their homes, dumping them outside rather than leaving them inside where he had killed them.

A serial killer who went to elaborate efforts to avoid leaving a pattern or having a victim type was Israel Keyes (Ramsland, 2014). A 34-year-old construction worker from Alaska, he committed suicide in jail in 2012 as he awaited trial for the murder of Samantha Koenig. He had also admitted to killing Bill and Lorraine Currier in Vermont, and said he had killed as many as eight others. Keyes had studied Ted Bundy, but he wanted to avoid Bundy's mistakes, such as paying for gas with credit cards. Keyes had *rented* cars in parts of the country that had no association with him, used false ID, robbed banks, and buried cash and murder kits in places to which he would return up to 2 years later to kill the first person he saw. Thus, he had no identifiable victim type or any association with his victims. He killed just to kill. But he then broke his own rules and got caught.

Profilers must keep in mind that with greater sophistication, there is more chance that serial offenders are aware of profiling methods and will make some effort to prevent being identified by their MO or signature. This will complicate a linkage analysis considerably.

MISSING PERSON PROFILING

Besides physical crime scenes, it is also possible to profile the scene of where someone went missing, because their last known behavior can assist to determine whether it is likely that a crime occurred, as well as the type of person who would take the risks associated with abduction.

On February 9, 1978, Kimberly Leach was at her junior high school in Lake City, Florida. The 12-year-old was excited to have been elected to the Valentine Queen's court (Dekle, 2011). She had forgotten her purse in a classroom and received a note to retrieve it. She went outside to cross campus. That was the last time anyone saw her. It was not until she failed to come home that it was clear that something had happened to her. Someone found her books, which meant she had left them behind. This was highly unusual behavior for her. Kimberly's parents called the police. They searched the school, school grounds, and nearby woods. They did not find her.

This case, like many missing persons cases, began with pressure to identify leads quickly. This meant getting possible witness reports, as well as questioning friends and family about plans the 12-year-old might have made. State of mind can be a factor, particularly with respect to running away. However, Kimberly was an unlikely runaway. Sometimes such cases get sorted out and the person is located. Those that remain unsolved need immediate professional resources. In this case, it seemed most likely that someone had grabbed her.

The question for behavioral profiling is the same for a potentially kidnapped child as for a discovered crime: what sort of person would do this? Was the girl a target or had the act been spontaneous? Did the family have enemies or potentially dangerous relatives? Did a pedophile live in the area? Kim had broken up with her boyfriend: did he carry a grudge? Was a vehicle involved?

If the abductor turned out to be a stranger to the girl and the community, the situation would be dire, as leads could be difficult to identify. Several students described Kim getting into a car, but descriptions differed and each lead failed to find her. One teacher recalled a brown-haired man standing across the street around the time Kimberly was last seen. The crossing guard had seen a white van driving slowly on a street near the school. The driver had looked at the school, returning twice in an hour.

The local news put out an appeal. A reporter noticed that a man had been arrested on February 15 for recent fatal attacks in a sorority house in Tallahassee, 100 miles west of Lake City. He was on the FBI's Most Wanted list: Ted Bundy. On the night before Kimberly vanished, records showed that Bundy had stayed at a nearby motel. A witness described a man who resembled Bundy trying to grab another young girl not far from Kimberly's school. He had been unsuccessful.

Investigators interviewed Bundy, but he offered no help. Still, they analyzed his MO: he targeted young women, but his suspected victims were older than Kimberly. Yet Bundy was bold enough to grab a girl in the middle of the day. He was suspected in abductions in other states, including a girl as young as Kimberly.

Bundy's photo was flashed on the news. A woman who had driven on Interstate 90 said she had seen a man driving a white van who resembled Bundy. Investigators knew about a white van that had been stolen from Tallahassee. They linked it to Bundy. Hotel towels from where Bundy had stayed were found off I-90, near Lake City. Planes went out with infrared cameras that could detect heat from buried decomposing forms. Even buzzard experts gave advice, as did numerous psychics. The more investigators pieced together, the more they believed that Bundy was their suspect. Since he was a suspected serial killer, it was likely that the missing girl was dead.

The van's odometer reading assisted with the search area radius. It had been driven 789 miles. Bundy was known to cover a lot of territory when he trolled for victims. With calculations, the farthest distance that he could have driven beyond Lake City offered an enormous search area of nearly 100,000 square miles. A geographical analysis of sand from the van's carpet narrowed the area to the Suwanee Valley, a flood plain. This led to a pile of cigarette butts.

The focus shifted from victimology to probability analysis of the suspected abductor. Eventually, Bundy vaguely admitted involvement but would not disclose a body location. The investigators studied his habits to identify a pattern. He tended to stay within a few miles of an interstate, and he had avoided agricultural inspection stations, so he had stayed on Interstates 10 and 90. Cigarette butts from the van were matched against those from the flood plain, including how the butts were bitten and the cigarettes extinguished. This behavioral similarity sent investigators back to where the butts were found. When they searched the area, they located a collapsed hog shed. Underneath was Kimberly Leach's body (Dekle, 2011).

The case was solved with the assistance of profiling methods that were coordinated with physical evidence. The behavioral analysis included Bundy's smoking habits, his abduction and body dump habits, and the type of victims he preferred, as well as the type of killer he was.

LINKING A COLD CASE

Besides missing persons, cold cases can also benefit from behavioral analysis that might link them to a series of crimes that were not considered at the time. Over the past decade, quite a few cold cases have been reexamined in light of their similarities to those of a convicted killer. Some resolutions have even freed people who were falsely convicted. DNA has played a role in some, so we will examine a case in which DNA analysis was not yet known in order to focus more fully on the behavioral angle.

An early member of the BSU, Supervisory Special Agent Robert Ressler was invited into a case in 1983 in Nebraska to assist with the murder of 13-year-old paper delivery boy Danny Eberle (Ressler & Shachtman, 1992). His body was found 4 miles from his bike. He had been gagged, bound, and stabbed nine times. He wore only his underwear and his ankles were bound with an unusual type of rope. He had also been hit in the face and bitten on the shoulder. The killer had attempted to obliterate the bite mark by slashing it with a knife.

Ressler thought the offender had wanted the body to be found or he had failed to carefully plan what to do with it. This suggested a young offender, probably early twenties. Picking Danny up when he could have been seen was high-risk behavior that indicated sexual compulsion. Ressler's profile placed this white UNSUB in his late teens or early twenties. He seemed harmless to Danny, and he was inexperienced with murder but was familiar with the area. He was employed in a job that required few skills. He was probably single and had a deep-rooted emotional problem. He was a loner with homosexual tendencies who worked in some capacity that let him get near boys, such as a Boy Scout leader or volunteer.

Then another boy around the same age was murdered in a similar manner. He had gotten into a tan-colored car while on his way to school, as if he knew the driver. This told investigators that the person was targeting boys and would likely try again (Petit, 1990).

Ressler looked at the crime scene behavior and thought this offender was angry with himself and possibly hated his attraction to boys. He directed police to an enlisted man who would do mechanical work. His instincts were accurate. When the offender trolled for a third victim, his license number for a tan car was given to police, who arrested John Joubert, a 20-year-old enlisted man at the Offutt Air Force Base. In his quarters was rope of the same type that had bound the boys. He was also an assistant scoutmaster. Joubert confessed and said he could not stop himself. It was a compulsion. Evaluations showed that he had a schizoid personality disorder, as well as a paraphilia that involved ropes and biting. As a boy, he had enjoyed stabbing other kids with pencils, razor blades, and knives.

The case seemed to be over, but when Ressler presented it to police in Maine, officers from Joubert's hometown thought the Nebraska crimes were similar to an unsolved murder they had from 1982. The body of 11-year-old Ricky Stetson was found on the side of the road. He had been stabbed, his jogging pants were pulled over his hips, and his sweatshirt had been removed and put back on. The boy had been strangled, bitten, and stabbed. Notably, the bite marks had been slashed with a knife. This was signature behavior. This bite mark impression was matched to Joubert, and it helped to convict him of this third murder (Petit, 1990).

In Ressler's interview with Joubert, he learned that the young offender had drawn quite a few renditions of his violent fantasies. He liked to bind children, boys or girls, and stab them. Joubert told him that he had experienced stress just before committing each murder. To explain the biting, he described long-term fantasies of cannibalism and admitted to trying to obliterate the bite marks. He had not realized that, far from removing this identifier, he had left a distinct behavioral brand. Joubert said that detective magazines had inspired him at an early age, and they had also taught him about how to avoid getting caught.

SUMMARY

Behavioral profiling of criminal incidents, whether a series of crimes, a missing person, or a cold case, relies on the ability to understand how offenders behave, which is partly based on understanding certain facets of personality. Whether or not it is true that personality dictates behavior, as early FBI profilers had claimed, it benefits profilers to understand such disorders as sadistic paraphilias, strange rituals, psychotic conditions, and the organized offender who plans versus the one who acts on opportunity. Data from many crimes and offender interviews have gone into databases, the better to analyze future offenders for behavioral prediction and apprehension. In the next chapter, we look at detailed analysis of methods and motives for these databases.

REFERENCES

Campbell, J.H., & DeNevi, D. (2004). *Profilers: Leading investigators take you inside the criminal mind.* Amherst, New York: Prometheus.
Cox, D. R. (2006). *Principles of statistical inference.* Cambridge, UK: Cambridge University Press.
Cozby, P. C. (2009). *Methods in behavioral research* (10th ed.). Boston, MA: McGraw-Hill Higher Education.
Cresswell, J. W. (2009). *Research design: Qualitative, quantitative, and mixed methods approaches.* (3rd ed.). Los Angeles, CA: Sage.
Dekle, G. R. (2011). *The last murder: The investigation, prosecution, and execution of Ted Bundy.* Santa Barbara, CA: Praeger.
DeNevi, D., & Campbell, J. H. (2004). *Into the minds of madmen: How the FBI Behavioral Science Unit revolutionized crime investigation.* Amherst, NY: Prometheus.
Douglas, J., Burgess, A., Burgess, A., & Ressler, R. K. (1992). *Crime classification manual.* San Francisco, CA: Jossey-Bass.

Douglas, J., & Hazelwood, R. R. (1980). The lust murderer. *FBI Law Enforcement Bulletin*, 49, 18–20.

Douglas, J. E., & Munn, C. (1992). Modus operandi and the signature aspects of violent crime. *Crime Classification Manual*. New York: Lexington.

Douglas, J., & Olshaker, M. (1995). *Mindhunter: Inside the FBI's elite serial crime unit*. New York: Scribner.

Gilovich, T., & Griffin, D. (2002). Heuristics and biases: Then and now. In T. Gilovich, D. Griffin, & D. Kahneman (Eds.), *Heuristics and biases: The psychology of intuitive imagination* (pp. 1–18). Cambridge, UK: Cambridge University Press.

Henderson, B. (1998). *Trace evidence: The hunt for an elusive serial killer*. New York: Scribner.

Kahneman, D. (2013). *Thinking fast, and slow*. New York: Farrar, Straus, & Giroux.

Kebbell, M. R., Muller, D., & Martin, K. (2010). *Understanding and managing bias*. Canberra, Australia: ANU Press.

Keppel, R. D. (2000). Investigation of the serial offender: Linking cases through modus operandi and signature. In L. B. Schlesinger (Ed.), *Serial offenders: Current thoughts, recent findings*. (pp. 121–133) Boca Raton, FL: CRC Press.

Lindelof, B. (2008, March 8). Murderer indicted as I-5 Strangler. *Sacramento Bee*, p. A1.

Matthews, J., & Wicker, C. (1996). *The eyeball killer*. New York: Pinnacle.

McCrary, G. (2003, October 31). Are criminal profiles a reliable way to find serial killers? *Congressional Quarterly*.

McCrary, G., & Ramsland K. (2003). *The unknown darkness: Profiling the predators among us*. New York: Morrow.

Michaud, S. G., & Hazelwood, R. (1998). *The evil that men do*. New York: St. Martin's.

Morton, R. J., & Hilts, M. A. (2005). *Serial murder: Multi-disciplinary perspectives for investigators*. Retrieved from https://www.fbi.gov/stats-services/publications/serial-murder.

Morton, R. J., Tillman, J. M, & Gaines, S. J. (2014). *Serial murder: Pathways for investigations*. Retrieved from https://www.fbi.gov/file-repository/serialmurder-pathwaysforinvestigations.pdf/view.

Pennington, N., & Hastie, R. (1992). Explaining the evidence: Tests of the story model for juror decision making. *Journal of Personality and Social Psychology*, 62, 189–206.

Petit, M. (1990). *A need to kill*. New York: Ivy.

Ramsland, K. (2005). *The human predator: A historical chronicle of serial murder and forensic investigation*. New York, NY: Berkley.

Ramsland, K. (2014). Building a mystery: Israel Keyes. *Serial Killer Quarterly*, 1(1), 48–61.

Ramsland, K. (2016). *Confession of a serial killer: The untold story of Dennis Rader, the BTK serial killer.* Lebanon, NH: University of New England Press.

Ressler, R. K., & Shachtman, T. (1992). *Whoever fights monsters: My twenty years of tracking serial killers for the FBI* New York: St. Martin's Press.

Rossmo, K. D. (2000). *Geographic profiling.* Boca Raton, FL: CRC Press.

Rossmo, K. D. (2008). Cognitive biases: Perception, intuition, and tunnel vision. In K. D. Rossmo (Ed.), *Criminal investigative failures* (pp. 9–21). Boca Raton, FL: CRC Press.

Rossmo, K. D. (2009, October). Failures in criminal investigation. *Police Chief Magazine,* 44–50.

Scherer, A., & Jarvis, J. (2014a). Criminal Investigative Analysis: Practitioner perspectives (Part One). *FBI Law Enforcement Bulletin.* https://leb.fbi.gov/2014/june/criminal-investigative-analysis-practicioner-perspectives-part-one-of-four

Scherer, A., & Jarvis, J. (2014b). Criminal Investigative Analysis: Skills, expertise, and training (Part Two). *FBI Law Enforcement Bulletin.* https://leb.fbi.gov/2014/june/criminal-investigative-analysis-practicioner-perspectives-part-two-of-four

Serial killer: Revised profile (n.d.). WAFB, Retrieved from http://www.wafb.com/story/1065571/serial-killer-revised-fbi-profile

Smith, C. (2001, December 16). Green River suspect fits FBI profile. *Seattle Times.* Retrieved from http://community.seattletimes.nwsource.com/archive/?date=20011216&slug=profiles16m

Smith, S. (2008, March 8). Believed to be 'I-5 Strangler,' Kibbe could face death penalty. *The Record,* Retrieved from http://www.recordnet.com/article/20080308/A_NEWS/803080327

Stelfox, P., & Pease, K. (2005). Cognition and detection: Reluctant bedfellows? In M. Smith & N. Tilley (Eds.), *Crime science: New approaches to preventing and detecting crime* (pp. 194–210). Cullompton, UK: Willan Publishing.

CHAPTER 7

Criminal Analyses

During the early 1970s, three different murderers grabbed headlines in Santa Cruz, California, which was quickly dubbed the world's murder capital. First, John Linley Frazier, the "Killer Prophet," climbed up the hill to the Victor Ohta house and murdered five people. It was his mission from God, he believed, to stop people from using up resources. Frazier had been diagnosed with paranoid schizophrenia, but he also took hallucinogenic drugs. Then, in 1972, another psychotic individual, Herbert Mullin, murdered 13 people over the course of 4 months, also on a mission. He had been assigned, according to him, to save California from a major natural catastrophe. This could be accomplished only with the sacrifice of lives. While Mullin was active, Edmund Kemper picked up hitchhiking coeds from around the university and killed them, sometimes two at a time. He admitted to necrophilia and cannibalism. When he was 15, he had murdered his grandparents. His final victims were his mother and her best friend.

Psychiatrist Donald Lunde (1976) was involved to some degree with all three cases. He made a distinction among the three types of killing sprees and offered a unique means of interpreting them according to developmental factors and personal narratives.

A pathologist in France, Alexandre Lacassagne, had developed this approach, which he called *criminal autobiographies*. They focused on the self-reflections of extreme offenders who willingly offered details about their lives and motives. Lacassagne visited regularly to collect these musings, discovering that incarcerated offenders appreciated a listening ear. Some were liars or attention-grabbers, but many took the process seriously. For Lunde, Kemper and Mullin were especially forthcoming, and Mullin provides extensive details about his important mission to restore the Earth's balance (Ramsland, 2011). We have mentioned Berg's analysis of Peter Kürten, another criminal autobiography, but these detailed accounts were rare until the 1970s. They became the basis of the earliest databases for assisting with the investigations of serial murder.

This chapter outlines how the Violent Criminal Apprehension Program (ViCAP), a national network used for linking crimes with similar signatures and MOs, identifies John Does who died violently and links offenders with victims. Investigators will learn more about how to work effectively with this resource, as well as learning about other databases that have developed with better digital resources, such as NamUs.

EARLY NARRATIVES

Asylum director Richard von Krafft-Ebing (1879/1928) gathered criminal narratives for *A Textbook of Insanity* and *Psychopathia Sexualis with Especial Reference to the Antipathic Sexual Instinct: A Medico-Forensic Study*. Mental health experts like him who took the time to sort through the life narratives of the most shocking offenders provided valuable information for the field of criminology. His study included the most offenders, but the research that focused on an individual offender provided a better examination of developmental details.

The more data that were gathered, the better the foundation for what the profilers would need (although some were clouded with speculative theory). There was an in-depth study during the late 1950s on spree killer Charles Starkweather. A prison psychiatrist made weekly visits to the cell of mass murderer Richard Speck, and Dr. Fredric Wertham had studied child killer Albert Fish. As the BSU emerged, they looked for such accounts. More were added as they came along. Ted Bundy, caught in 1978, offered different versions of his story to a variety of interviewers, including Detective Robert Keppel and psychologist Al Carlisle (Ramsland, 2011). Among the most revealing was a series of correspondences and interviews with Supervisory Special Agent William Hagmaier, from the BSU. Bundy hoped to prove his worth as a "scientific specimen." Hagmaier maintained this connection over 4 years, until Bundy's execution in 1989.

By this time, some BSU members had started visiting prisons to interview extreme offenders (Ressler & Shachtman, 1992). For the Crime Personality Research Project, they focused on offender thoughts and behavior prior to, during, and after committing their crimes. This information also went into a database. Included were items about how offenders look for victims, approach them, minimize risk, feel about their crimes, and dispose of a body. The agents also designed a protocol for these interviews, in an attempt to standardize them, and looked up details about 118 victims. Yet some interviews failed from the start, due to an offender's inability to remember much or to speak coherently, or to a lack of cooperation. The goal to acquire 100 such interviews fell far short of the mark. Fewer than 30 of those interviewed were serial killers (Petherick, 2013).

Among the initial interview, subjects were Frasier, Mullin, and Kemper, but only Kemper made any sense. They also interviewed Jerome Brudos, a fetishist who had killed women and removed body parts like breasts and feet for self-gratification; William Heirens, the "Lipstick Killer," who had begged to be caught; and Charles Manson, who had sent out his followers to commit the 1969 Tate–LaBianca murders. The sample was unrepresentative and far from scientific, but they continued to work on it. The agents realized that self-report interviews with killers and psychopaths had unique problems. They liked to talk but did not necessarily tell the truth. Some preferred to play games or brag and exaggerate their notoriety.

Although the project was based on a small, unrepresentative sample, the agents published articles that provided criminologists with statistically analyzed data. This looked pretty good and led to some myths and misconceptions in the field, especially that serial killers were smarter than the average person. (If one chooses the most articulate subjects from a specific population, one will probably get the smartest ones for the study.) In addition, by the 1970s, offenders had already learned how to manipulate by discussing their difficult lives, so some of the interview subjects could have added or exaggerated details of abuse. One-third of the subjects were white, all were males, nearly half had been raised by a single parent, three-fourths reported abuse or severe neglect, a majority had a psychiatric diagnosis, and three-fourths admitted to a sexual deviance.

Several agents used this data, with other records, to write a comprehensive manual for law enforcement, *The Crime Classification Manual*. They devised categories for murder, arson, and sexual assault, describing typical motivations and behavior for each. The more they collected, the more they realized that they would need a sophisticated way to file and organize it all. They needed a computer. By the mid-1980s, the pressure was on for funding and better data management.

THE NATIONAL CENTER FOR
THE ANALYSIS OF VIOLENT CRIME

It was one detective's persistence, and a few fortuitous meetings, that resulted in the FBI's current database. During the late 1950s, Pierce Brooks, commander of the Robbery–Homicide Division in Los Angeles, had two different homicides on his hands, and in both cases he believed the offenders had killed before (DeNevi & Campbell, 2004). However, trying to sort through numerous crime reports in different cities was tedious and required a great deal of time. Brooks spent his off-hours looking through library and teletype records for similar incidents, analyzed by behavior. The daunting task seemed hopeless at times, but he finally found a murder to link to one of his. His intuition had been correct; a fingerprint matched in both cases. Then, he got another case in Los Angeles.

In 1957, Harvey Glatman was arrested for attempted murder. A patrol officer had assisted a woman who told them that Glatman had threatened to kill her the way he had killed others. Glatman was brought in. Brooks got a detailed confession about the three women that Glatman had bound, killed, and buried in shallow graves in the desert. The killer had posed as a photographer for true crime magazines, so aspiring models consented to being tied up.

From these cases, Brooks realized how easy it was to overlook such connections, so he asked for a department computer. His chief denied the request, citing insufficient funds and space for an expensive mainframe. Yet Brooks knew that investigators around the country would benefit from a centralized database. He kept looking for ways to make it happen. He met Special Agent Robert Ressler, who listened to his ideas and thought the FBI was the perfect agency for it (DeNevi & Cambell, 2004).

In 1983, as the murder rate rose and stranger murders became more common, politicians knew that people wanted them to take a hard stance on crime: more punishment, longer sentences. The BSU exploited this zeitgeist to provide some disturbing numbers: 5,000 people had been victims of strangers in just the previous year and most of these cases were still unsolved. They estimated that there could be as many as 35–50 serial killers in the United States alone. These were disturbing figures. BSU chief Roger Depue stated that there was no reliable means for connecting the crimes of mobile serial killers, like Ted Bundy, who had moved from one coast to the other. He had heard about Brooks' idea for a national computerized database and had established a task force to evaluate it. Once the benefits were clear, they had to apply for funding.

At a Senate subcommittee meeting for the US Congress, Brooks and others presented a case for a computerized system. Brooks said that his own method of looking up linked crimes had remained the same for 25 years. The computerized ViCAP received funding. In May 1985, under the auspices of the National Center for the Analysis of Violent Crime (NCAVC), Pierce Brooks was named the first ViCAP director. His vision was finally a reality. He fed into this computer data from as many unsolved homicides as he could acquire from the 17,000 police departments at that time around the country. Case-matching on this grand scale had not been attempted before. It was a slow and frustrating process (DeNevi & Campbell, 2004).

To be effective, the data had to be analyzed into patterns. The analysts were aware that offenders did not precisely replicate their crimes,

TABLE 7.1   Brooks' ViCAP Process for Law Enforcement

1. Enter the facts of an unsolved homicide into the computer to compare MO against all other cases in the database.
2. Provide the analyst with a computerized summary ranking the top 10 best matches.
3. Employ a crime pattern analysis technique to the new data.
4. Produce a management information system report that monitored case activity geographically.

even when ritual was involved, but they generally followed the pattern of their chosen MO. The process required collaboration from several areas of specialty: investigators, computer programmers, computer analysts, and major case specialists. Test cities were identified for trial runs.

Brooks viewed the use of ViCAP as a four-step process (Table 7.1).

Subunits included profiling techniques from the FBI's program and psycholinguistics analysis. The program successfully linked homicides across jurisdictions, as it was intended to do. Yet, there were also problems. Local law enforcement needed access, and this was achieved by providing computers. Still, the programs used were sophisticated and expensive, and the 50-page, 300-question ViCAP Crime Report Forms were arduous to fill out. Unsurprisingly, the program received fewer cases than anticipated. The form was revised to 186 questions, sexual assault incidents were added, and the items were grouped into the sections listed in Table 7.2. More cases came in, but the program remained underutilized.

TABLE 7.2   ViCAP Section Headings

1. General Administration
2. Victim Information
3. Offender/Suspect Information
4. Offender Timeline Information
5. Offender's Approach to Victim
6. Dates and Exact Geographic Locations
7. Specific Event Sites
8. Crime Scene Information
9. Clothing and Property of Victim
10. Types of Trauma Inflicted on Victim
11. Weapon Information
12. Sexual Activity
13. Offender's Sexual Interaction
14. Vehicle Information
15. Additional Case Information
16. Narrative and Hold Back Information

The form comes with instructions. Investigators collect data from police departments around the country on solved, unsolved, and attempted homicides; unidentified bodies in which the manner of death is suspected to be homicide; missing-persons cases in which foul play appears to have been involved; and sexual assaults and attempts. Investigators are urged to let experience guide them in how to answer and to check as many boxes for items of information as they think apply to their cases. There is also a place to describe items that fail to fit standard categories. In addition, investigators can supplement or change past reports submitted. A phone number is provided for guidance and advice. Separate forms are completed for multiple victims and cases, and a single form is used for multiple offenders with a single victim. Examples are offered to assist with understanding the form.

When the Critical Incident Response Group was formed in 1994, ViCAP became part of it (DeNevi & Campbell, 2004). The ViCAP form underwent a redesign to serve as a platform for a new software application. When a man died in a drive-by shooting, for example, the software connected him as a witness in three other homicides. They could see from the results that his death had not been random. Leads then led to a suspect and a successful arrest.

By 1997, the database held details from over 17,000 homicide cases and was being used regularly in 23 states, with 1,500 cases submitted annually—a low percentage of actual homicides around the country. The goal was to increase participation, especially in larger cities. By 1998, Canada had a similar system in place, the Violent Crime Linkage Analysis System, or ViCLAS. A shortcoming for ViCAP was understaffing and poor promotion, so the FBI brainstormed ways to get higher levels of compliance. ViCAP is still in place, improving with new developments.

The website https://www.fbi.gov/wanted/vicap is searchable by category and year. Investigators should check with the FBI for requirements for using the program, which is now more widely available to law enforcement agencies via a secure Internet link. With ViCAP Web, they can get real-time access to enter information, and they can extract it for their own searches. The original algorithm was updated to accommodate more sophisticated access and comparisons. FBI analysts still review incoming cases for quality and consistency of the data and prepare reports for specific requests.

Case referrals from Oklahoma in 2004 eventually led to the development of the Highway Serial Killings Initiative, which officially launched in 2009. This program involved coordinating cases of murder along known trucking routes, especially after a serial killer is identified. Many of the victims are hitchhikers or prostitutes who sought clients at truck stops. ViCAP analysts have mapped a matrix across the country that includes more than 500 murder victims from along or near highways, as well as a list of 200 potential suspects.

(The map can be seen here: https://archives.fbi.gov/archives/news/ stories/2009/april/highwayserial_040609.) Law enforcement agencies assisted with suspect data, and several offenders have been charged. ViCAP analysts say that it is difficult to estimate from the database how many serial killers might be at large.

Long-haul trucker Robert Ben Rhoades is an example. Rhoades loved the book *Games People Play*, because he enjoyed matching his wits against others. He also had a sexual fetish for keeping women captive and torturing them. He was arrested in Casa Grande, AZ, in 1990. The state trooper who stopped him found his torture chamber and a live woman chained inside his truck. Had the highway program been active then, investigators estimate that they might have linked Rhoades to at least 50 murdered women who had been chained, whipped, raped, and beaten before being discarded along or near trucking routes (Michaud & Hazelwood, 1998).

Years later, when the highway initiative was in place, FBI agents contacted Rhoades for an interview, but he refused to talk. Yet law enforcement presentations on the case drew the interest of other investigators. One murder victim, hitchhiker Regina Walters, had been found in a barn in Utah. Her murder timing and location coincided with Rhoades' travel schedule. Collaboration between two agencies linked Rhoades to this unsolved cold case. Regina was featured in pictures that had been in his possession, including one that showed her standing next to the barn in which her body was found. She looked terrified. Her boyfriend was also missing. His body was found later in Mississippi.

Had the Utah investigators put their data into the system, the link would have been made more quickly. Regina, from Texas, had been dumped in Utah. Without a database, solving a case like this could happen only with random luck (as it did). Rhoades was eventually convicted of three murders, including a hitchhiking couple from Texas (Busch, 1996).

Speaking of databases, in 2014, the NCAVC issued a report, *Serial Murder: Pathways to Investigation*. This is an extensive, multifactor study of how offenders treat victims, so as to standardize specific items for investigative purposes. The monograph presents empirical research on criminal motivation and behavior for serial killers that correlates suspects with crime scenes. It covers 92 offenders and 480 cases, with items such as travel routes and body dumpsites. In each case, a male offender acted alone and killed at least two in separate events at different times. They ranged in age from 15 to 45 at the time of their first known murder. About one-third had served in the military and 30% were married. About the same percentage had been diagnosed with a psychiatric disorder. Less than one out of four had no prior arrest record. Half were white, 38% were black, nearly 8% were Hispanic, and 2% were "other." The cases were legally resolved with a plea or conviction or with a preponderance of evidence indicating guilt. The cases derive from a time span of 46 years, between 1960 and 2006, and all are from the United States. Only cases in which the FBI was involved were included (Morton, Tillman, & Gaines, 2014).

The goal for this report was to provide investigators with situational factors that have been associated with past serial murder, based on specific behaviors gleaned from dumpsites. The factors include offender approach to victims, evidence of sexual activity, treatment of the body, the nature of the relationship between offenders and victims, and offender characteristics and motivations. For example, the relationship in about 41% of these cases was one of client or customer (mostly through prostitution). One-third were random stranger murders. Two-thirds of offenders had used a ruse to get close to a victim and 60% had killed two to four victims. Only 12% had more than ten. About seven out of ten killers had a limited hunting area. Eight out of ten were sexually motivated (the kind of case usually referred to the FBI).

The monograph is divided into different sections for ease of use, and comparisons are offered among known killers. Subcategories cover sexually motivated serial murders, serial murders involving prostitutes, same-sex murders, and multiple motivations. The incidents are classified by specific behaviors, not by motivational categories, which the researchers found to be problematic if the subject is unknown.

With the history of criminal profiling from Chapter 5, the basic methods from Chapter 6, and the above description of the ViCAP database, we can put it all together in a case. This one came to Supervisory Special Agent Gregg McCrary, a member of the BSU, and was fully detailed in his casebook (McCrary & Ramsland, 2003). It presents a good example of how ViCAP assisted to organize and match a lot of complex information in an international case.

PROFILING PRACTICUM

Since the raw data from this investigation was not initially exposed to profiling methods, it can be assessed for what it yields in terms of behavioral clues. Questions are posed as a way to think through the case like an investigative consultant, followed by a discussion of which option is best. For maximum benefit, consider the options and the reasons for your selection before reading the discussion.

It started in 1990 in Czechoslovakia when the nude body of a young woman was found along the bank of the Vltava River. She lay on her back in a suggestive position, stabbed and strangled with a pair of stockings. She wore only a ring. She was also covered with leaves, grass, and twigs. Police saw no identification on her but discovered it not far away. This victim was Blanka Bockova. Questions in town produced more information.

Bockova had worked at a butcher shop in Prague. She had been there the day before and was seen that evening drinking with a middle-aged man. No one knew who he was, but he had been respectably dressed (Leake, 2007).

Bockova had met this man that night, so it was unlikely she would have calls on her phone record. However, if he had killed before in the area, the police could compare earlier crimes and possibly make a link.

If you were to advise the police to look for earlier crimes that were similar, which of the following might they seek that could be helpful in identifying Bockova's murderer?

1. Victims who were strangled
2. Victims left outside who had been covered with something
3. Victims with their socks left on
4. Victims who had been in that area of town

Killers who take the time to cover someone generally have a psychological need to do so. It is a ritual, and they will continue to repeat their pattern. Leaving the socks on may be incidental, and strangulation alone is too common. However, investigators might look for strangulation with an item of clothing, which itself could be part of the signature. Trying to determine if there were other victims who may have been picked up in that part of town could be more difficult, and it could also be true that the man was just passing through the area and met his victim by chance. The correct response is number 2, since that behavior is closer to a signature element of a crime than the MO (strangulation) or the items of clothing left on.

About 5 weeks later, in Graz, Austria, about 300 miles south of Prague, a prostitute named Brunhilde Masser vanished. She was last seen on October 26, 1990. Prostitution is legal in Austria and was not considered a high-risk activity. Austria saw only about one prostitute murder per year. Thus, there was reason for concern, which increased in December when Heidemarie Hammerer, an experienced prostitute, disappeared from Bregenz, Austria. Hikers discovered her body a month later in the woods. She was fully clothed, on her back, and partly covered with dead leaves. It appeared that she was redressed postmortem and dragged through the woods. She still wore her jewelry. She had been beaten and a piece of her slip was stuffed into her mouth. Pantyhose had been used as a ligature around her neck and bruises on her wrists suggested restraints. Several red fibers on her clothing did not come from items she wore.

Five days later, hikers stumbled across badly decomposed remains in an isolated forest north of Graz. The dead female lay in a streambed, covered with leaves. She had been stabbed and possibly strangled with her pantyhose, but it was difficult to tell. She still wore her jewelry. She was eventually identified as the missing Brunhilde Masser.

Two months later, Elfriede Schrempf vanished from her usual corner in Graz on March 7, 1991. Two days later, a man called her family twice to harass them. He mentioned her by name and made threatening comments.

The Austrian police did not know about Bockova in Prague, but they had two murders and a missing person that bore some similar associations. What factor from this list would most strongly suggest that at least two of the three Austrian cases were related?

1. Two were from the same city.
2. Two were found in the woods, with natural debris on top of them.
3. There are too many differences among them to clearly associate them.
4. A shared profession of prostitution.

Being from the same city or in the same profession does not usually provide sufficient detail to accept that there is a link between two murders. Linkage analysis gathers specific behavioral factors that stand out in ways that point to a killer's personality and the choices he or she makes. This person took prostitutes to remote areas. After he killed them, he seemed to have wanted to cover them but not hide them. The act of covering them indicates a psychological factor, possibly shame. There were behavioral differences that might keep the last one out of the series, since phone calls were made, and in those that were found, one was nude and one was clothed. However, there were sufficient similarities between two of the crimes to suggest the possibility of a common killer: two prostitutes found in the woods, covered with debris, with their jewelry intact. The one who was clothed appears to have been redressed. Although they were from different cities, the killer might have an occupation in which he travels. The correct answer is number 2.

Several months passed before hikers discovered a set of skeletonized remains in a forested area outside Graz on October 5. The only clothing found near the remains was a pair of socks. This victim was identified as Elfriede Schrempf.

In less than a month, Silvia Zagler, Regina Prem, Sabine Moitzi, and Karin Eroglu all vanished from Vienna, Austria.

At this point, what kind of information would best assist investigators in such a situation?

1. What prostitutes know about their actual risk factors
2. Information about the red fibers found on the second body
3. Risk assessment statistics about serial killers
4. The brand of socks Schrempf wore

Knowing something about how vulnerable these women perceive themselves to be does not contribute much to discovering who might approach them with hostile intent. Perhaps the killer's anger builds afterward in a way that might not be obvious upon initial approach. Perhaps he only kills in a specific context. Likewise, knowing the potential origin of the fibers only helps when the police have something to which to compare them. Sock brands and fibers are "class evidence," meaning that even if they could be narrowed down to fiber from a car or carpet used in a business, any number of places might be their source. Since only one of the victims had such fibers on her person, they are not as helpful as evidence that has been found across several crimes. Thus far, only certain circumstances link them, with nothing yet known about the missing prostitutes outside their occupation.

However, when several crime scenes suggest a single serial perpetrator as the source, which indicates that a serial killer is operating in the area, investigators can educate themselves about the potential motives and future behavior of such killers, based on what has been gathered in prior similar cases. For example, sexually compelled serial killers often start to kill more frequently, so extra patrols can be assigned to vulnerable areas. The correct response is number 3.

It appears that this killer had selected a victim group in which sex is an expected part of the association, but there is no evidence of sexual violation or ejaculation on or near the bodies. While it is true that lust killers may use handcuffs and engage in torture, they tend to leave some evidence of sexual violation as well. The fact that the victims have bruises indicates anger, which suggests that this man might have been unable to achieve an erection, so he possibly killed from intense frustration.

Given how spare the evidence is, with no one able to identify a specific person, he would be considered an organized killer, in terms of taking the body to a remote place and removing whatever evidence he might see.

The man who killed these victims appears to have been very careful, which indicates some degree of control over his violence, despite the level of anger exhibited.

Austria had no system at the time for linking crimes to make a sophisticated analysis. The official conclusion was based mostly on instinct, emphasizing the differences among the crimes and crime scenes, not examining the meaning of the similarities.

In May, Moitizi's and Ergolu's bodies were discovered in forested areas outside of town. Both had been strangled with an article of their own clothing. Ergolu had her jewelry but nothing else. Moitizi wore a jersey. Her clothing and purse were near her body.

The press named this killer the "Vienna Courier." Reporters were more eager than police to publicize the details. This proved to be fortuitous (McCrary & Ramsland, 2003).

When former Salzburg investigator August Schenner read the media coverage, he had a vague impression that he had seen this behavior before. Something about this killer's approach to women reminded him of Jack Unterweger, a brutal young man who was convicted of a 1974 murder, also committed in the woods. Schenner had tried unsuccessfully to get him to confess to a similar murder. In court, Unterweger had begged for mercy, claiming that he had been angry at his mother, a prostitute, for her neglect of him. The forensic psychologist who examined him at the time had said he was a dangerous sadistic psychopath with rage issues.

Schenner had thought that Unterweger, with a life sentence, would be locked up for a long stretch. However, something odd had happened and this killer was now free. Because Unterweger had published several acclaimed pieces of writing, he had persuaded the cultural community that he was a redeemed person. They had been sufficiently impressed to pressure politicians for his release. It had worked. In fact, Schenner discovered, Unterweger was a celebrity. He was on talk shows and at premiers for his own plays. Dressing flamboyantly in white suits with red scarves, he could now afford a lavish lifestyle. He seemed to revel in his new role.

What should be the next step for investigators?

1. Contact the suspect and bring him in for questioning.
2. Put obvious surveillance on the suspect to pressure him.
3. Get more information about the suspect's whereabouts on those dates linked to the crimes.
4. Ask the families of victims if the victim might have known the suspect.

Because Unterweger is a celebrity and any movement toward him could risk unwanted publicity, it would be best to quietly develop a file on him until they have a good circumstantial case. After that, they might question or watch him. Until it is clear that Schenner's tip is correct, they must approach this high-profile "person of interest" with caution. The correct response is number 3.

How can they develop a good circumstantial case but not alert the suspect to their interest?

1. Develop a timeline of Unterweger's whereabouts to see if he might have been where the victims were.
2. Get a warrant to search his residence.
3. Ask the prison psychiatrist about Unterweger's criminal potential.
4. Read Unterweger's publications to see if he let any clues slip about his intent to kill should he ever get out of prison.

The first task is to ensure *actus reus*—that it was physically possible for Unterweger to have committed any of the crimes. If he were in another city when a woman was killed in Graz, then he is not her killer. A warrant must show probable cause and thus far they have no case against the suspect. The last two options, numbers 3 and 4, rely on subjective interpretation that can be faulty. A psychiatrist can miss things, especially with a clever psychopath bent on getting out, and Unterweger might have hidden his intent by writing in such a way that he deflected attention to other things. Even if he did suggest that he might kill, this does not build a case against him that would be useful in court. The correct response is number 1.

Ernst Geiger from the Austrian Federal Police took charge of the investigation. He assigned officers to watch Unterweger. They were aware that he had gone to Los Angeles, California, "on assignment" for a magazine, and during his 5-week absence from Vienna, the murders had stopped. That was just one interesting behavior. Geiger knew he needed to build a solid case.

If you were to make a case thus far about the likelihood that Unterweger was a viable suspect, and you wanted to do that with behavioral evidence, which aspects of his past behavior would you consider *most* important to proving patterns that could be associated with the current crimes?

1. The remote sites, the MO of strangulation, and the means of pick-up
2. The remote sites, the MO of strangulation, and the fact that the victims were prostitutes
3. The fact that they all still had their jewelry, the killer's apparent mobility, the angry phone call
4. The remote sites, the fact that most of the victims were asphyxiated with their underwear, and the way they were left partially covered

The more specific the detail, the stronger the link. Both numbers 1 and 2 are vague and general. Number 3 includes a detail that is significantly different from the other crimes (the phone call), especially the first one in 1974. The correct response is number 4.

With Unterweger's credit card receipts from hotels, restaurants, and rental car agencies, investigators began to piece together his movements. They placed him in Graz in October when Brunhilde Masser was murdered and again in March when Elfriede Schrempf disappeared. He was in Bregenz in December when Heidemarie Hammerer was taken, and a witness said that Unterweger resembled the man who was seen with Hammerer. He had worn a red knit scarf—red fibers! When receipts placed Unterweger in Prague, investigators learned about Blanca Bockova's unsolved murder. It resembled theirs. She was found in the woods, covered in dirt and leaves, and wearing only socks and jewelry. She was strangled with an undergarment. There was one more circumstantial piece to the puzzle: Unterweger was in Vienna during the dates when the women went missing there.

Officers in Vienna questioned him about the Austrian murders. He admitted seeing hookers, but he denied knowing the victims. Yet now he knew he was a suspect. This put pressure on him, and he reacted. He published articles now about investigative failures and drew on the support of his allies. He wanted to insult the police but also protect himself. He had plenty of friends.

Around this time, the husband of Regina Prem received telephone calls from a man who claimed to be her killer. He said God had ordered her execution. She had been left in "a place of sacrifice" with her face "turned toward hell." He added that he had done the same to 11 others. Three months later, five empty cigarette packs of the brand that Prem smoked were stashed into the family's mailbox. They had no fingerprints.

Geiger tracked down the BMW that Unterweger had purchased when initially released, finding the man to whom he had sold it. The new owner allowed the police to go through it and they found hair fragments, including one with a root. This proved fortuitous. It matched Bockova's DNA (Leake, 2007).

What is the significance of this finding?

1. It means that Unterweger killed her.
2. It means that she was in Unterweger's car.
3. It means that Unterweger had some contact with her.
4. It means nothing to investigators.

At best, it means he had contact with her. He could have spoken to her in a bar or even sat where she had shed some hair and picked it up on his clothing. However, the police hoped that it could be added to other evidence to eventually help prove with a totality of circumstances that Unterweger had been with her on the night she died and that she had gotten into his car. The correct response is number 3.

Do you think this discovery will help to move the investigation forward?

1. Yes, it is sufficient for probable cause for a search warrant.
2. No, because he already admitted to being with prostitutes.
3. No, because it only indicates that Unterweger had encountered the victim, and he may have been one of several men who did.
4. It probably will not, because as evidence it cannot stand alone.

A strand of hair with useful DNA found in Unterweger's former vehicle that was linked to a murdered woman was sufficient to establish cause for an expanded search. The correct response is number 1.

The DNA match helped to acquire a warrant to search Unterweger's apartment in Vienna. When investigators arrived, he was not at home. They discovered a menu and receipts from a seafood restaurant in Malibu, California, as well as photographs of Unterweger posing with members of the Los Angeles Police Department. They also found a brown leather jacket and red knit scarf, which they seized.

How can the receipts from Los Angeles best assist the investigation?

1. They can call the hotel to see if he was really there.
2. They can call the LAPD to learn if they have any unsolved murders with a similar MO.
3. They can use the receipts to confront Unterweger with his whereabouts.
4. They can find out more about why he was in Los Angeles.

Contacting the LAPD to learn about possible murders in that location with a similar MO could provide further evidence, including direct physical evidence. They already knew from receipts that Unterweger was at the hotel but confronting him could have made him flee, and learning more about his purpose in LA would not have added anything. The answer is number 2.

Geiger contacted the LAPD. He asked about unsolved murders and learned that the authorities in Los Angeles were investigating three seemingly linked prostitute murders. All victims were left out in the open, all were strangled with their bras, and all had been killed during Unterweger's stay in Los Angeles. Geiger told them what he suspected. Detectives Jim Harper and Fred Miller discovered that Unterweger had requested a police escort to where the prostitutes walked the streets, telling them that he was covering the seedy side of Los Angeles for a German magazine.

Using the recovered receipts from Unterweger's apartment, Geiger learned that the places where each victim was last seen alive were near one of the hotels in which Unterweger had stayed. This gave the LAPD a viable suspect. They joined the German efforts.

By this time, analysts had examined the leather jacket and red scarf confiscated from Unterweger's apartment. Fibers from both were consistent with those found on the body of Heidemarie Hammerer. This allowed Geiger to get an arrest warrant. But Unterweger had fled the country with his new girlfriend, 18-year-old Bianca Mrak (Leake, 2007). He was back in the United States. From there, he had contacted his media associates to claim that the police were framing him. It was a huge story, he said, and he needed their help. Some were willing to oblige. They began to write about Unterweger as a victim of police abuse.

Through an FBI office in Vienna, Geiger spoke with Supervisory Special Agent Gregg McCrary in the BSU at Quantico (McCrary & Ramsland, 2003). He wanted an analysis for his cases. McCrary invited him to Virginia. Geiger invited Thomas Mueller, Chief of the Criminal Psychology Service in the Federal Ministry of the Interior, to accompany him. They took several boxes of files.

At Quantico, McCrary explained the procedures of CIA and case linkage. Before they opened the files, he requested that they withhold all suspect information until after they had done a victimology and crime scene analysis.

Why would McCrary make this request?

    1. He wanted to solve the crimes himself.
    2. He did not want to have suspect information bias him.
    3. He could not work with German crime scenes on a US system.
    4. The information was incomplete.

McCrary did not want to be biased when he placed the information about victimology and the crime scenes into the program. He had no interest in solving the crime himself, and if he could not work with German information, he would not have invited them to Quantico. Incomplete information does not matter, as long as there is enough for an analysis. The answer is number 2.

For the analysis, McCrary used ViCAP. He filled out the painstaking forms for each case and put them into the computer system in the order in which the women were killed to be able to see evidence of linked similarities, change in MO, or escalation. McCrary knew that if these 11 murders came up linked, this serial killer was rare, because he had traveled internationally and overseas.

Once the computer had sifted through 15 cross-referenced search criteria in more than 10,000 homicide cases, it provided the matching data. McCrary, the analyst, spotted a pattern based on victim profession, the killer's MO, body dumpsite characteristics, trauma to the bodies, treatment of the remains, carefulness of the offender, lack of sexual assault, rituals, and lack of trace evidence. A dozen cases were linked, four of them in California, but one had been resolved with a conviction. The other eleven were Geiger's cases and the three suspected cases from the LAPD.

Next, it was time to examine the suspect data. Geiger had plenty to show.

What aspect of the suspect's data might be most helpful for the investigation?

1. The kind of car he drove
2. His current whereabouts
3. His prison writings
4. His timeline

When McCrary placed the timeline that Geiger's team had developed for Unterweger over the timeline for the incidents, it added up. The answer is number 4.

They also compared his MO in the 1974 murder for which he had been convicted to the other 11, adding an analysis from the Los Angeles Crime Lab by criminalist Lynn Herold on the knots used to tie the ligatures on the three victims in Los Angeles. It was a complicated knot and it matched the pantyhose knots used on the Austrian victims. The behavioral analysis, reinforced with a ViCAP selection process, was strong.

Unterweger was caught in Florida and returned to Austria for trial. He had Austrian public opinion on his side, and he knew that the physical evidence against him was flimsy. As Unterweger awaited his trial, the remains of Regina Prem were found in the woods.

Which of the following items could best prepare investigators for a trial?

1. Devote their resources to getting more physical evidence
2. Devote their resources to building a behavioral case
3. Devote their resources to battling the media so the coverage does not prejudice a jury
4. Devote their resources to finding more witnesses

Since the bodies were found in outside locales that had already been searched, and since Unterweger's apartment and cars had been searched, the use of resources to keep going over ground already covered is not as effective as looking for other supporting data. Likewise, the media were on Unterweger's side, so launching a campaign to attempt to negate their support of him could not only backfire but also produce more support. Given the intense media coverage, it was likely that if willing witnesses were to be found, they would probably have already stepped forward, so the best strategy would be to look at how the crime scene behavioral evidence showed unique consistency and to be prepared to explain compulsive serial murder to citizens on a jury who had little experience with such crimes. The correct response is number 2.

The trial began in June 1994 in Graz, Austria. Detective Jim Harper from the LAPD and Lynn Herold from the LA crime lab arrived to testify about their information. The use of a specific type of knot was especially unique ritualistic behavior. McCrary discussed the ViCAP system and the many behavioral patterns that linked the incidents to one another and to behaviors associated with Unterweger's first confirmed murder. The prosecution also had a psychiatric report about Unterweger's sadistic criminal nature; Blanca Bockova's hair recovered from Unterweger's car; numerous red fibers from Brunhilde Masser's body consistent with Unterweger's red scarf; and character witness testimony from former associates whom he had conned.

Unterweger tried to charm the jury and use his allies from the media and the Austrian elite, but the behavioral evidence stacked up against him. It was the first time that an FBI profiler had spoken in an Austrian court. The ViCAP analysis proved to be powerful, as did testimony about the knots. Unterweger was convicted. He quickly committed suicide (Leake, 2007; McCrary & Ramsland, 2003).

DATA VERSUS CLINICAL JUDGMENT

Besides ViCAP, there are other useful databases, and some provide data for a better interpretation of linkage analysis. In the past, experienced clinical judgment was generally accepted as sufficient for the final evaluation. However, information in databases can undermine this notion. An expert's experience, no matter how extensive, is limited by personal circumstances, not to mention their accumulation of mental habits and biases. Former Supervisory Special Agent Mark Safarik was invited to consult on a series of cases from South Carolina. An experienced medical examiner had declared the three cases to be linked, but Safarik used a medical database and came to a different conclusion (Safarik & Ramsland, 2012).

On September 16, 1981, a neighbor found Melva Neill, 82, sexually assaulted, beaten, murdered, and dumped into her bathtub. She had been strangled, and missing items suggested a burglary. Sterling Barnett Spann had done odd chores for the victim. His fingerprints matched items at the scene and a gold coin necklace missing from the home was in his pocket. He said he had received it from someone else. A jury convicted him and he received the death penalty.

Then, a private detective turned up some cases that required another look at the Spann conviction. Two months before Neill was murdered and a few blocks away, 57-year-old Mary Ring had been sexually assaulted, beaten, strangled, and left in her bathtub. The same pathologist had performed both autopsies and had spotted no similarities. Nor had the police, although Spann had once worked for both victims.

Another elderly white female, Bessie Alexander, was murdered 2 months after Neill, just 12 miles away. She had been beaten, sexually assaulted, strangled, and dumped on her dining room floor before her body was drenched with liquids. A psychotic former minister named Johnny Hullett had been convicted.

During a hearing to review the Spann case, a forensic psychiatrist, a former FBI profiler, and an experienced forensic pathologist agreed that the same person had committed all three murders. Since Spann could not have killed Alexander, his attorney stated, someone else had killed Melva Neill.

The forensic pathologist hired to examine the cases as an outside expert testified that, based on his four decades of experience, all three victims had been strangled in a "unique" way. He noted that the absence of neck structure injury (no fracture in the small hyoid bone and the thyroid and cricoid cartilages) indicated that the killer had used a carotid chokehold (*State v. Spann*, 1999).

Spann got a new trial, but now he was a suspect in the first two murders, not just Neill's. DNA analysis could not eliminate Spann as the man who had raped and killed Ring. Should he be convicted based on clinical judgment?

Given what is known about mental limitations and cognitive errors, the answer is no, not if there are better resources. Clinical judgments often rely on a high degree of self-trust in past experience that encourages quick assumptions, especially based on familiarity. As mentioned earlier, cognitive psychology confirms that we develop perceptual habits, known as *cognitive maps*, that limit judgment and encourage confirmation bias.

Data gathered from many cases provide a more objective ground from which to make a statement about linkage. Safarik, an expert on the sexual homicides of elderly women, had created a database of relevant demographic, behavioral, anatomical, and injury-related information (Safarik, Jarvis, & Nussbaum, 2002). Safarik used this to focus on a subset of data about the relationship between neck structure injuries in elderly women and a cause of death identified as either manual or ligature strangulation.

In his study of 128 elderly female victims of sexual homicide, which included databases from earlier medical studies, autopsy protocols in two-thirds of the cases revealed (at least) one cause of death as strangulation. The subjects were at least 60 years of age. In 67 cases that had sufficient data for analysis, 66% involved manual strangulation, 31.5% involved ligature strangulation, and two cases included both. Safarik looked at data on neck injury and bone structure. Relevant to the victims in South Carolina, analysis of the 44 cases involving manual strangulation revealed that 23% had no neck structure injury. Safarik's examination failed to corroborate the clinical judgment of the forensic pathologist. There was an unacceptably large margin for error. It shows the need to look first for a database before using clinical judgment.

In addition to databases that are specific to cases like these, there are others that might offer assistance. The National Institute of Justice's National Missing and Unidentified Persons System (NamUs.gov) is a national centralized repository and resource center for missing persons and unidentified decedents, many of whom are victims of homicide. It offers a free system that can be searched by medical examiners, coroners, law enforcement officials, and the general public from all over the country. Included are a Missing Persons Database, Unidentified Persons Database, and an Unclaimed Persons Database. Whenever new information is added, the system automatically updates and performs cross-matching comparisons. NamUs also provides free DNA services for unidentified human remains.

SUMMARY

From the early days of the BSU, the goal has been to aid investigations with as much expertise and rigor as possible. The agents who became part of the unit set out to learn as much as they could about criminal psychology. They interviewed offenders to create databases from which they could offer the most sophisticated analyses. This led to various programs, including ViCAP, the database that would speedily and effectively match signature and MO behaviors across jurisdictions, even internationally. Numerous cases could be matched to a single offender. However, the ability to predict future behavior was still anchored in subjective analysis, albeit based on experience from past cases. In fact, certain subtypes of offenders began to show sufficiently similar behaviors that made risk prediction possible. The next chapter examines the ability to use behavior from crimes to see the future.

REFERENCES

Busch, A. (1996). *Roadside prey.* New York: Pinnacle.

DeNevi, D., & Campbell, J. H. (2004). *Into the minds of madmen: How the FBI Behavioral Science Unit revolutionized crime investigation.* Amherst, NY: Prometheus.

Krafft-Ebing, R. V. (1879/1928). *Psychopathia sexualis with especial reference to the antipathic sexual instinct: A medico-forensic study.* Revised Edition. Philadelphia: Physicians and Surgeons.

Leake, J. (2007). *Entering Hades: The double life of a serial killer.* New York: Farrar, Straus and Giroux.

Lunde, D. (1976). *Murder and madness.* San Francisco, CA: San Francisco Book Co.

McCrary, G., & Ramsland K. (2003). *The unknown darkness: Profiling the predators among us.* New York: Morrow.

Michaud, S. G., & Hazelwood, R. (1998). *The evil that men do.* New York: St. Martin's.

Morton, R. J., Tillman, J. M., & Gaines, S. J. (2014). *Serial murder: Pathways for investigations.* https://www.fbi.gov/file-repository/serialmurder-pathwaysforinvestigations.pdf/view

Ramsland, K. (2011). *The mind of a murderer: Privileged access to the demons that drive extreme violence.* Santa Barbara, CA: Praeger.

Ressler, R., & Shachtman, T. (1992). *Whoever fights monsters: My twenty years tracking serial killers for the FBI.* New York: St. Martin's Press.

Petherick, W. (2013). *Profiling and serial crime: Theoretical and practical Issues.* 3rd ed. Waltham, MA: Academic Press.

Safarik, M. E., Jarvis, J. J., & Nussbaum, K. E. (2002). Sexual homicide of elderly females: Linking offender characteristics to victim and crime scene attributes. *Journal of Interpersonal Violence, 17*(5), 500–525.

Safarik, M., & Ramsland, K. (2012, Summer). Clinical judgment vs. data analysis. *The Forensic Examiner, 21*(2), 14–19.

State of South Carolina v. Sterling Barnett Spann. (1999). *334 S.C. 618; 513 S.E. 2d 98.*

ViCAP. (n.d.). Retrieved from https://www.fbi.gov/wanted/vicap

CHAPTER 8

Motives and Threat

In 2005, nurse Stephan Letter admitted to killing 16 patients at the Sonthofen hospital clinic in the Bavarian Alps. Most were elderly. It was his presence during each of the events that statistically made him a suspect. Missing medication was found in a search of his home. His mission, he said, was to "liberate" the souls of people who he believed were suffering.

He had mixed a muscle relaxant with the respiratory drug Lysthenon so he could administer fatal injections. Authorities exhumed more than three dozen bodies to check for these drugs. A sophisticated analysis helped to determine that in some cases, just before death, the drugs had been administered in high doses. This added more charges. An investigation showed that Letter began killing just a month after he was employed. At least six patients had been in no danger of dying and two were not elderly.

Letter's trial began in Germany in 2006. As the proceedings opened, he admitted his guilt. He claimed he had wanted only to help. In contrast, the prosecutor compared Letter's spate of killing to an assembly line. He was found guilty of 12 counts of murder, 15 counts of manslaughter, and one mercy killing (Patterson, 2006).

Although the latest FBI analysis on investigating serial murder dispenses with motivational categories, motive is relevant for understanding some series that can be evaluated for future danger. Investigators who engage in behavioral analysis must learn about the variety of driving forces behind repetitive crimes. Motive and MO will show them more specifically the types of crimes in which predictive efforts will more likely pay off.

The following module provides an overview of the variety of motives that show up most often among serial killers. We then focus on those for which we can predict future danger. Some call this approach "prospective profiling," but it is closer to the method of threat assessment.

MOTIVATIONS

A common assumption holds that serial killers are sexually driven, but this is just one of several possible motivators. (Some of the motives below also apply to other types of repeat deviance, such as arson, bombing, rape, and child molestation.) To avoid stereotypical thinking, analysts should become familiar with the differences between compulsion, addiction, and arousal. Any of the conditions listed in Table 8.1 can drive serial crimes, but some are more likely to escalate or follow a predictable ritual.

It helps to understand how rehearsal fantasies, which can be part of many of the above conditions, often drive serial crimes. Hazelwood and Michaud (2001) described what was gleaned from the FBI prison studies on this subject, especially regarding the force of sexual sadism and other coercive paraphilias. These people have a firm narcissistic impression that they can do whatever they want to other people as long as it is self-gratifying. *Their* needs come first. There are no limits to what

TABLE 8.1   Motives for Serial Murder

- Lust: Driven by excitement and arousal; generally calculating and predatory; becomes addictive and often triggers escalation; most lust-driven offenders have one or more paraphilias.
- Psychosis: Involves bizarre and disturbed emotions, behaviors, thoughts, and beliefs that can interfere with a person's ability to function; can make people dangerous when delusions are paranoid.
- Delusion: Not as extreme as a psychosis, but based in a belief system detached from reality; sometimes pressured by an emotion that compels action for relief.
- Power/control: Need to feel dominant, interpreted as control over others; often has a sadistic component.
- Mission: The urge to punish or rid the world of a specific class of people; an obsessive vendetta; the feeling of being chosen or specially endowed.
- Rage/hate/revenge/punishment: Violence as a defiant or punitive act; expresses fear and frustration; might choose symbolic targets; often has violent rehearsal fantasies.
- Glory/attention: Seeking publicity or notoriety through violence; needs to feel important; usually looks to role models.
- Greed/profit: Self-enrichment at the cost of lives; often believe they are owed something.
- Artistry: Using deviance to enhance one's sense of creative superiority; posing and ritual often present.
- No particular purpose: Acts when the mood strikes, rather than with a reason or a target.
- Coercion: In a team, the partner who goes along out of fear or devotion but does not wish to commit the deviant or violent act.

a depraved person can imagine. If the elements of that fantasy involve harm or death to others *and* the individual has the means to carry it out, the chance of the fantasy becoming reality is high. When "BTK" killer Dennis Rader experienced the thrill of stalking, he could not stop, despite being married, having a job, and being engaged in other social obligations. His fantasies since adolescence had involved "girl traps," so stalking women meant imagining them under his control, aware of his mastery over them, and terrified of his power. The pleasure he derived from this fantasy eventually leveled out, so to intensify it he broke into a home to bind and kill one of his stalking targets. It produced such a rush that he added more bondage details to his fantasies and then went looking for other victims (Ramsland, 2016).

From a collection of data (offender interviews, nature of wounds, crime commission items), Hazelwood described how crime originates in the mind. The more situated is the offender's experience with sensory details like hair color, soap fragrance, or taste of blood, the more compelling it becomes. He or she might calculate the risks of gain versus loss, but the evaluation of consequences generally has less weight than the anticipated pleasure. It is but a short step to justifying the act.

The pleasure might be from a sexual or power fantasy, which usually becomes an addiction (Satel & Jaffe, 1998). Alternatively, it might be from the sense of momentum from a having a special mission. Of these types, mission-oriented killers are certain to strike repeatedly until their mission is accomplished. Past cases assist to predict behavior for current investigations with a higher degree of accuracy, especially those in which behaviors are similar enough to group them as a subtype. Lust, power, and profit killers tend to have a diverse range, whereas mission killers (which includes lethal aggression fueled by hate and the need to punish) target certain types of people and tend to use the same MO.

ON A MISSION

Some mission killers are psychotic, which offers an opportunity to identify them at some point in their spree by looking at psychiatric records. A classic case is that of Herbert Mullin. He developed schizophrenia during his teenage years but did not get the treatment he needed, because he lived in California during the movement to clean up the mental health programs and treat people in community centers. Those centers were disorganized at best, and he slipped through the cracks. Still, he had been partially evaluated. There were records (Torrey, 2008).

Mullin had developed a delusional idea that the planet kept a balanced tally of deaths, so that if war did not eliminate people, a natural disaster would occur. He saw signs and predictions for a cataclysmic event in Santa Cruz and believed that he was the designated person to start eliminating people (creating "small disasters"). The number he "heard" was 13, so he set out to accomplish this goal. Starting in October 1972 and ending in February 1973, he shot, stabbed, and bludgeoned 13 people. Although anger and personal vendetta had motivated some of his attacks, they still counted in his mind, contradicting his belief that all 13 would voluntarily sacrifice themselves for the sake of the greater good (Lunde, 1976; Torrey, 2008).

How would this play out for threat assessment? Mullin had been hospitalized several times but released without supervision. Had he described his vision and the necessary deaths it entailed, a threat evaluation for future danger might have kept him in treatment, especially if they knew he had weapons. He claimed he heard voices and he told quite a few people his delusional beliefs. His mission was urgent, because he thought a massive earthquake was imminent. He was armed and he seemed angry and aggressive. These are all red flags for someone who is ready to act and who believes his acts are both justified and necessary. Mullin was a ticking time bomb (Torrey, 2008). He was easy to predict.

In the Seattle, Washington, area during the mid-1980s, Gary Ridgway held a similar belief about prostitutes: they had to die and he was the designated executioner. However, he was not psychotic. He thought he was doing the police a favor by strangling and stabbing women he had hired for sex. In 1983 alone, 27 women disappeared, 9 of whom were found dead. Most of these victims were dumped along the Green River. In 1984, the *Seattle Post Intelligencer* received a note with the heading, "what you need to know about the green river man." The author claimed to be the killer, signing it "callmefred." The BSU profiler who assisted the task force, John Douglas, dismissed it as a hoax. It did not fit what he expected, but in fact, Ridgway had written it. In 2001, DNA linked him to one of the victims and he was arrested. He had been an early suspect but had passed a polygraph. In 2003, Ridgway admitted to 48 murders, although he believed it was more like 60. He had actively hunted for these victims. When he had them under his control, they were his "possessions." He treated them like trash, even having sex with their bodies (Rule, 2004).

The lessons to be learned include: (1) never eliminate a suspect with a polygraph, (2) pay attention to hate-based rants by people who hold elitist or punitive religious views, (3) use a profile only to assist in narrowing a suspect pool, not in identifying *or* entirely eliminating a suspect due to specific behaviors. Often, an offender has had some type of earlier contact with the police.

The "callmefred" letter was behavior that might have yielded productive clues. Despite its rambling appearance, it mentioned the murder methods, deflections at scenes for law enforcement, postmortem sexual contact, details that associated him with specific victims, and his attitude about prostitutes. The letter was certainly a killer attempting to get attention, and many offenders have been identified through errors they made when showing something of themselves.

Similar to hatred over behavior like prostitution, racism can become a violent mission as well. The FBI profiled a series of attacks in New York in 1980. Witnesses saw a white male shoot a black youth in Buffalo, New York, on September 22. Over the next 2 days, three more black males were shot with a 0.22-caliber weapon. Special Agent John Douglas surmised that this killer was organized and was possibly a member of a hate group. He might have a military background, but he would be a discipline problem due to mental instability. Then, a similar murder spree occurred in one day in Manhattan, 380 miles southeast, but with a different weapon. Five black men and one Hispanic man were stabbed. Four died, but the survivor described a slender white male. It was not clear whether the two sprees were linked. Then, a man was killed in Rochester, followed by three more attacks in Buffalo. Now, it seemed more likely that they were all related. There were no leads, not even with a description of the suspect.

An incident in Georgia broke the case. Private Joseph Christopher, 25, attempted to kill a black soldier and he was placed under arrest. He admitted to the 13 murders in Buffalo and Manhattan while he was on leave, claiming he hated Blacks. His gun proved to be the murder weapon. Although a profile in this case had not helped to solve it, there was no doubt that the killer would not have desisted from his racist rampages until caught. Buffalo seemed to be his primary target area (Douglas & Olshaker, 1995).

A number of mission killers have worked in the health-care industry. They tend to have similar MOs and motives, which gathers them into a subcategory, so once the red flags show up for a suspect, it is easier to predict the circumstances of a future murder. It might also link them to past unsolved homicides. For example, a team of females had decided to play a "murder game" in Michigan in 1987. Gwendolyn Graham and Catherine Wood worked together at the Alpine Manor Nursing Home. They were sexually involved and, for kicks, they plotted to kill patients as a way to up their game. They picked victims whose initials, taken all together, would spell out the word "murder" when recorded in a book that listed deaths and discharges. They eventually fatally smothered five. They even openly joked in front of colleagues about what they were doing and showed off victim items they had taken (Cauffiel, 1992).

Could a threat analysis have been any easier for someone who worked at this care facility? Pay attention to what they say and check the discharge book. It would not be difficult to identify the group of potential victims, especially since these killers had also volunteered to wash down the bodies of their victims. Their suffocation MO would have been obvious.

The behavioral patterns from one fatal health-care perpetrator to another are so similar that it is possible to do *prospective* profiling in the presence of certain red flags (Ramsland, 2007). Some are mission killers, but some have other motives.

HEALTH-CARE SERIAL KILLERS

Threat assessment of future danger to others involves making educated predictions from a variety of factors about whether a given offender will repeat the offense (Monahan et al., 2001). The idea of future dangerousness has been a pressing issue in the legal/mental health arena for decades. Earlier, we discussed probability analysis. Threat evaluations face the same issues. Yet improvements have been made to increase accuracy.

Researchers involved with the MacArthur Foundation examined the relationship between mental disorder and violent behavior directed against others (Monahan et al., 2005; Quinsey, Rice, Cormier, Harris, & Cormier 1998). They devised a list of risk factors consistent with existing theories that have been associated with violence. Table 8.2 lists some of them.

The potential for harm must be assessed with several instruments that approach the evaluation from different perspectives, then scaled for degree of seriousness. The database from which threat is predicted must be large, representative, and based on factors that emerge from research.

Some people become killers after they enter the health-care system, while others are already predators looking for an arena of trust that will offer easy prey. Children and the elderly or patients in critical condition are the most vulnerable. The type of killer who chooses a

TABLE 8.2   Risk Factors for Predicting Violence

Mental health issues that involve paranoia or anger
A past history of violence
Lack of quality support systems
Record of repeated substance abuse
Poor stress management abilities
Presence of life stressors
High degree of impulsiveness
Presence of psychopathy
Physical or verbal abuse during childhood
A criminal parent or guardian
A past diagnosis of an adjustment disorder
Violent role models, past or current
Thoughts or fantasies about harming others

health-care occupation often seeks personal power, control, or attention. Sometimes, hospitals cover up such incidents for fear of damage to their reputations, which plays well into a serial killer's hands. Even privacy laws have protected them.

Crossing several jurisdictions in seven counties in New Jersey and Pennsylvania, nurse Charles Cullen was stopped after killing patients at 10 different institutions. Sometimes he was an employee and sometimes a temp. Based on Cullen's review of around 240 files after his arrest, he admitted to 29 murders and 6 attempted murders (Graeber, 2013; Ramsland, 2007).

The case broke soon after two patients at Somerset Medical Center in Somerville, New Jersey, were given the wrong medication, with fatal results. An internal investigation found Cullen to be a common factor in four cases of mismanaged medication. When two more patients barely survived similar overdoses, Cullen was charged with two murders. He was suspected of using a lethal dose of digoxin, a heart medication, which he procured through computer manipulation from hospital supplies. Cullen admitted it, and more. He said he had killed 30–40 patients in Pennsylvania and New Jersey.

The New Jersey State police interrogated Cullen. He talked freely, describing how easy it had been to move from one health-care facility to another when suspicions were raised. No one had stopped him. Although Cullen claimed to be a mercy killer, it was soon apparent that many of his victims had been in no danger and were not near death. Some were not even suffering, and a few were on the mend.

Somerset Medical Center administrators said Cullen's credentials had checked out, with no red flags raised. It was at this facility that Cullen admitted to killing between 12 and 15 patients in just over a year. Placing these events against the timeline of his murders, reporters determined that Cullen was acting out during times of stress and failure (Hepp, 2004). Each time he had faced a particularly stressful period in his life, such as from a divorce, he murdered a patient. It appeared that power over someone else's life made him feel better, perhaps less helpless.

One of his methods of operation was to get medications by opening patients' medication drawers or closets, because he knew that no one tracked the drugs. When he did find electronic drug tracking, he learned how to get around it. He left "tracks," but no one checked.

Cullen even offered to assist authorities in how to prevent others like him ("In his own words," 2004). There should be protocols for accountability of staff, he pointed out, and for drug-handling procedures. Install surveillance cameras, swipe cards, and bar codes and make a daily count of lethal medications. He also said there should be a national database for updating employment history of health-care workers. These precautions, collectively, would have caught him earlier (Assad, 2005).

There were several opportunities prior to 2003 to look closely at Cullen, but each was stymied. In 1999, 4 years before Cullen was caught, coroner Zachary Lysek in Northampton County, Pennsylvania, told officials that there might be an "angel of death" at Easton Hospital (Graeber, 2013; Hepp, 2004). He believed an elderly patient had been murdered with a fatal dose of digoxin. He requested an internal investigation, which took 8 months, but it was inconclusive because Cullen had worked there as a temp. (He eventually admitted that he had killed the patient in question.)

Also, a group of nurses at St. Luke's Hospital collected evidence and warned hospital administrators and the state police about Cullen (Krause, 2005). In June 2002, they had found packages of drugs improperly discarded and had seen Cullen leaving the rooms of patients who soon died. They told Lysek about Cullen, and he contacted the state police. Feeling pressured, Cullen resigned and moved on. Because he had been just a temp at Easton Hospital, he had no employment record there, so the investigation reached a dead end.

In addition, Steven Marcus, a toxicologist and executive director of New Jersey Poison Information and Education System, had warned Somerset Medical Center in July 2003 about a poisoner in the hospital. He had identified four suspicious cases. Hospital officials complained to the state's health department, stating that Marcus had rushed to judgment on too little evidence.

Cullen's problems, known to hospital officials, were never reported to state boards; his poor performance was hidden from future employers; and his theft of drugs went undocumented. Thus, he was able to keep getting hired. The laws at the time protected nurses from false accusations. Since the Cullen case, however, politicians in both states have made it easier for health-care facilities to report suspicious behavior ("Codey signs Healthcare," 2005).

A health-care serial killer might be a physician, nurse, psychiatrist, or any of the key support staff. (A respiratory therapist decided to ease his workload by killing patients on overburdened shifts.) Yorker et al. (2006) published a study that examined 90 cases of health-care killers from 20 countries. Most had used one or more of the following methods: the injection of lethal substances, poisoning, suffocation, or equipment tampering. Nurses comprised 86% of known cases, and the number of suspicious deaths among more than 50 confirmed cases was more than 2,000.

Among the few physicians proven to be a serial killer was Michael Swango. In his case, it was easy to predict his danger to others but difficult to get around laws in order to do so. One official risked his job to warn others. Swango entered medical school in 1980 at Southern Illinois University.

He focused on dying patients. At his internship at the Ohio State University Medical Center, he began to experiment. After he checked on a head injury patient, she died. The nurses immediately suspected that Swango had done something. She was the first of six who unexpectedly died there before he left. An investigation ensued, but it was superficial, so he was cleared. A telling detail is the nickname other students gave him— "Double-O Swango," for his supposed "black thumb" around patients (Stewart, 1999).

Swango returned to Illinois and joined a team of paramedics at the Adams County Ambulance Service. To them he reportedly described his fantasy of a busload of children caught in an explosion. He also enjoyed stories about traffic accidents and mass murder. One day, when his coworkers ate donuts that Swango brought in, they fell ill. Officials found poison in his locker and called the police. In 1985, Swango was convicted of six counts of aggravated battery and received a 5-year sentence.

Yet he rebounded, getting positions in several different states by faking his credentials and forging recommendations. He landed a psychiatric residency at the Northport Veteran's Administration Medical Center at the Stony Brook School of Medicine. However, his employer from South Dakota called the center. The dean fired Swango and alerted teaching hospitals. Undaunted, Swango went to Zimbabwe. At a hospital there, he experimented on patients until an investigation unmasked him. He was charged with five murders. Once again, he managed to get away. In 1997, feeling invulnerable, he entered the United States. The FBI nabbed him.

Swango was finally tried for murder. The FBI estimates that Double-O Swango might have killed 30–50 patients. Arraigned in 2000, Swango pled guilty to fatally poisoning three patients in 1993 at a New York hospital. In addition, he was convicted of another murder in Ohio. He was sentenced to life in prison without the possibility of parole.

Health-care providers such as Swango know how to use subtle means of murder, and they have access to drugs that can poison without being detected. Even when patients complain that someone has injected them, such complaints are often overlooked. Institutions protect their reputations, so "accidental" medication might get ignored, dismissed as part of the job, or even covered up.

Female nurses, too, become serial killers. Their methods and motives are similar to males, but some key differences are important for predictions of future danger. Genene Jones, convicted in Texas of killing a child and attempting to kill another (and suspected in up to 50 deadly assaults on infants) seemed to suffer from a form of Munchausen syndrome by proxy, in which people injure themselves or others for attention.

On her shift, a child under her care was 10 times more likely to die. Jones seemed thrilled at the excitement of a cardiac arrest. She also insisted on sitting in the morgue after a baby's death, holding the corpse in her arms (Elkind, 1983).

Some experts believe that attempting a profile based on a psychological and behavioral "blueprint" is risky, as it can result in selective attention to stereotypical details, but others find sufficient overlap in certain types of cases to devise a threat evaluation. Several studies support the latter position (Ramsland, 2007; Yorker et al., 2006). Serial killers in the health-care industry share many similar behaviors, even when operating from different motives. This makes it possible to create a list of red flags that will assist in identifying key behavioral and personality signals. No single behavior is sufficient to make a person suspicious, but if half a dozen or more behaviors from the list in Table 8.3 below show up consistently, the facility should consider careful scrutiny and documentation (Ramsland, 2007).

Murders in health-care facilities are not easily detected. Stopping them requires an observant person, knowledge about the typical traits and behaviors of such offenders, and a desire to ensure that suspicions about people who work with patients are taken seriously.

TABLE 8.3   Behaviors That Signal a Potential Health-Care Serial Killer

- Has been given macabre nicknames
- Entered rooms where unexpected deaths occurred
- Moved from one facility to another
- Is secretive
- Likes to "predict" patient deaths
- Jokes about killing patients
- Enjoys death discussions with colleagues or shows excitement about a death
- Seems enthused about his or her skills
- Tends to arrive early or stay late and likes to be helpful
- Makes inconsistent statements when asked about the incidents
- Prefers shifts with fewer coworkers
- Is associated with several incidents at different institutions
- Craves attention
- Prevents others from checking on patients
- Hangs around during death investigations
- Has lied about personal information or credentials or falsified reports
- Lies for no apparent reason
- Has a criminal record
- Collects information about poison, murder, or death
- Has had disciplinary problems
- Has a substance abuse problem

ANTICIPATING TROUBLE

Establishing an empirical body of data from which to make accurate predictions has been difficult. Those who make predictions seek to avoid "false positives"—people predicted to be potentially violent who are not—and "false negatives"—people believed to be safe who are not. During the 1980s, studies were undertaken to develop instruments focused on the known risk factors. Those profilers who have experience with the best tools and the latest research on threat assessment have an edge for offering recommendations for an offender's future behavior.

A reliable instrument is the Violence Risk Assessment Guide (VRAG). Researchers tested what they called "predictor variables" with "outcome variable" (new criminal charges for a violent offense). The VRAG includes 12 variables, such as type of violence committed, early school malad-justment, a mental illness diagnosis, and revised Psychopathy Checklist (PCL-R) score. A high score on the PCL-R is well correlated with repeat offenses. In addition, psychopaths tend to be more criminally diverse and more violent than nonpsychopaths (Hare, 1998).

The Historical Clinical Risk Management Scheme combines case analysis details with statistics. This 20-item checklist identifies histori-cal and clinical risk factors in a specific person's life (Conroy & Murnie, 2008; Monahan et al., 2005). Professionals have also devised computer software, the Classification of Violence Risk, to assist the process, which has been validated by the National Institutes of Health.

Different levels of risk are associated with different types of threats. They are categorized as low, medium, and high. In general, when threats are vague, inconsistent, or indirect, with no planned date or target, the risk for imminent violence is low. Risk levels rise when details become more specific, especially if a plan is in place. A medium-level risk threat could be carried out because the person has the means to do it, but the location and date indicators are vague. When preparatory steps are clear, anger or paranoia is intense, and the potentially violent person has access to the weapons he or she wants to use, the threat for violence is high. This person needs immediate intervention.

Those tasked with predicting the likelihood that someone might act out violently or continue with a string of violence already in motion would look for evidence of preoccupation with violence, low frustration tolerance coupled with high stress, and few behaviors that indicate the capacity for resilience. Significant recent stressors such as broken rela-tionships, loss, humiliation, or loss of personal power raise risk levels, as do uncharacteristic social withdrawal and an excessive need for atten-tion. Such people might also express admiration for other violent indi-viduals and enjoy violent media. They express approval of mass murder.

There is no formula for getting a prediction right, but enough is now known about certain types of violence that some prediction strategies are better than others. Knowing the type of motives among certain populations is part of best practices.

SUMMARY

The ability of behavioral analysts to predict what will happen next, where, and to whom depends a lot on knowing the motivation for violence. No one can predict future risk of violence with unerring accuracy, and accuracy decreases rapidly over time or with the person's changing circumstances. Yet with the right tools, fairly solid predictions for some types of violence can be offered to those charged with public safety.

REFERENCES

Assad, M. (2005, May 21). Cullen gives tips for stopping killings: Serial killer nurse outlines flaws in hospital security and hiring practices. *The Morning Call*. http://articles.mcall.com/2005-05-21/news/3740532_1_charles-cullen-serial-killer-nurse

Caulffiel, L. (1992). *Forever and five days*. New York: Zebra.

Codey signs Health Care Professional Responsibility And Reporting Enhancement Act. (2005, May 3). *New Jersey Office of the Governor-Press Release*. Retrieved from www.state.nj.us/cgi—bin/governor

Conroy, M. A., & Murrie, D. C. (2008). *Forensic assessment of violence risk*. Hoboken, NJ: Wiley.

Douglas, J., & Olshaker, M. (1995). *Mindhunter: Inside the FBI's elite serial crime unit*. New York: Scribner.

Elkind, P. (1983). *The death shift: The true story of nurse Genene Jones and the Texas baby murders*. New York: Viking.

Graeber, C. (2013). *The good nurse: A true story of medicine, madness, and murder*. New York: Twelve.

Hare, R. D. (1998) Psychopaths and their nature: Implications for the mental health and criminal justice systems. In Millon, T, et al. (Eds.). *Psychopathy: Antisocial, criminal, and violent behavior* (pp. 188–214). New York: Guilford Press.

Hazelwood, R., & Michaud, S. (2001). *Dark dreams: Sexual violence, homicide and the criminal mind*. New York: St. Martin's Press.

Hepp, R. (2004, October 3). Coroner had gut feeling about an 'angel of death.' *Newark Star Ledger*, p. 1.

In his own words. (2004, September 12). *Newark Star Ledger*.

Kraus, S. (2005, July 10). Seven nurses had warned about killer. *The Morning Call*, p. 11.

Lunde, D. (1976). *Murder and madness*. San Francisco, CA: San Francisco Book Company.

Monahan, J., Steadman, H., Robbins, P., Appelbaum, P., Banks, S., Grisso, T., Heilbrun, K., Mulvey, E., Roth, L., & Silver, E. (2005). An actuarial model of violence risk assessment for persons with mental disorders. *Psychiatric Services, 56*, 810–815.

Monahan, J., Steadman, H., Silver, E., Appelbaum, P., Robbins, P., Mulvey, E., Roth, L., Grisso, T., & Banks, S. (2001). *Rethinking risk assessment: The MacArthur study of mental disorder and violence*. New York: Oxford University Press.

Patterson, T. (2006, February 8). Stephan Letter wanted to 'help' patients. *The Independent*.

Quinsey, V. L., Rice, M. E., Cornier, C. Harris, T. & Cormier, C. A. (1998). *Violent offenders: Appraising and managing risk*. Washington, DC: American Psychological Assn.

Ramsland, K. (2007). *Inside the minds of healthcare serial killers: Why they kill*. Westport, CT: Praeger.

Ramsland, K. (2016). *Confession of a serial killer: The untold story of Dennis Rader, the BTK killer*. Lebanon, NH ForeEdge.

Rule, A. (2004). *Green River, running red: The true story of America's deadliest serial killer*. New York: Simon & Schuster.

Satel, S., & Jaffe, D. J. (1998, July). Violent fantasies. *National Review, 20*, 36–37.

Stewart, J. (1999). *Blind faith: How the medical establishment let a doctor get away with murder*. New York: Simon & Schuster.

Torrey, E. F. (2008). *The insanity offense: How America's failure to treat the seriously mentally ill endangers its citizens*. New York: W. W. Norton.

Yorker, B. C., Kizer, K. W., Lampe, P., Forrest, R., Lannan, J. M., & Russell, D. A. (2006). Serial murder by healthcare professionals. *Journal of Forensic Sciences, 51*(6), 1362–1371.

CHAPTER 9

Psychological Evidence in Court

Christine Burgerhof, 24, was murdered in 1996. Her nude body was dumped behind a truck in a warehouse parking lot in Scranton, PA. Her arms were posed at her sides, palms down, and her hair was carefully fanned out. Her numerous injuries suggested an anger-based assault, and she had been strangled manually and with a ligature. A married receptionist, she seemed to be a low-risk victim, but an investigation turned up evidence that she had lived a double life: she had worked in a massage parlor as a prostitute (Hazelwood & Michaud, 2001).

Colleagues said she had believed she was being stalked and the person was sending flowers. Soon thereafter, her husband reported her missing. Her body was found the next day.

A suspect popped up in a former boyfriend, Christopher DiStefano. He was 27. He knew that Christine had been stalked and had told a mutual acquaintance details about the murder. He was seen near the crime scene while police were processing it. When they questioned him, he said he was a private investigator and offered an ID. DiStefano's roommate told police that he was an extreme introvert who had posted numerous photos of himself with a girl—Christine. The photos were from 16 years earlier, intended as a memorial.

When detectives invited DiStefano in for questioning, he brought a photo album of himself with Christine. He then wrote a detailed chronology of their on-again, off-again relationship. They had become friends and he had even attended her wedding. He asked the officers if they were inviting the FBI to draw up a profile of Christine's killer and then offered his own ideas and motives. He thought her death had occurred by accident when she had angered a man by refusing to go out with him. The man had hit her too hard. DiStefano believed that the suspect had respected Christine and regretted his actions. He had placed her lovingly in the parking lot (Hazelwood & Michaud, 2001).

Detectives questioned DiStefano on three occasions, believing they had their man, and when they pressured him he confessed. He said he had visited Christine that night and asked her to go out with him. She had refused, so they had argued and he had gripped her throat, accidentally killing her. Frightened, he left but had then come back and taken the body, stripped, to where it was found. He took her clothes with him. However, the clothing was not among his possessions, and DiStefano offered several details that were inconsistent with the facts, such as denying the use of a ligature.

DiStefano was arrested. He then recanted, said he had "left holes" in his statement, and refused to talk further.

In 2000, the case went to trial. DiStefano believed the evidence was weak (it was) and that he would be acquitted. Without the victim's clothing and with no direct physical evidence from the scene, the prosecutor asked the FBI for a behavioral analysis. Supervisory Special Agent Roy Hazelwood responded. He thought that DiStefano had done many suspicious things, both pre- and postoffense. "Sexually deviant criminals usually display some, but not all, of the behaviors that profilers look for in particular types of crimes. But DiStefano came as close as any subject I have ever seen to having all the behaviors that we look for" (Hazelwood & Michaud, 2001, p. 242). He was narcissistic, intelligent, obsessive-compulsive, interested in police-related subjects, and troubled. He suffered from panic attacks and for a decade had kept a detailed diary in which there were hundreds of references to Christine. He also possessed handcuffs, bondage photos, duct tape, a gas mask, pieces of rope, texts on aberrant sexual behavior, suspicious Internet searches, and a stash of letters to women that showed an obsession with sexual domination.

His 2,450-page diary also showed his self-absorption, as he recorded every small detail of his life. He included his sexual fantasies. Some were masochistic, some sadistic. His autoerotic activities involved the gas mask and he knew a lot about various forms of bondage. Some of his letters about women were quite aggressive.

Hazelwood was asked to do three tasks: analyze the defendant's sexual deviance, analyze his postmurder behavior, and evaluate whether the crime scene had been staged (Hazelwood & Michaud, 2001). He submitted three separate reports, in case the judge admitted only one area of behavioral analysis. (Judges had grown less tolerant of these psychological evaluations than during the early days of criminal profiling.)

DiStefano requested a bench trial, without a jury. Judge Carlon M. O'Malley presided. The prosecutor requested to use reports from two experts on behavioral analysis, but he was allowed only Hazelwood. In addition, only one of Hazelwood's three reports would be admitted.

Profiling was not generally accepted in the scientific community, Judge O'Malley observed, so it did not meet the *Frye* standard that Pennsylvania used (explained in Chapter 4). "What the Commonwealth seeks to establish through using Mr. Hazelwood's testimony," the judge stated, "is that the defendant exhibited the characteristics and behaviors of how a murderer *may* act. Not only is the testimony profiling, but it is also speculative and expressed in terms of probabilities. ... Furthermore, Mr. Hazelwood's report and related testimony evidences little probative value and is extremely prejudicial to the defendant. Such testimony is akin to an expert eyewitness account that the defendant committed the murder. This court will not allow such an account" (Greziak, 1999).

In addition, O'Malley found Hazelwood's report too tentative. "The language 'not unique' in Mr. Hazelwood's report and 'may' expressed in his testimony is deficient and not supportive of admissibility" (*Commonwealth v. DiSefano*, 2001).

However, O'Malley decided that Hazelwood could testify about a narrow aspect of the behavior. "Based upon Mr. Hazelwood's vast experience in analyzing sexual and homicide crime scenes, Mr. Hazelwood formulated his opinions and drew conclusions related to the physical evidence or lack of physical evidence of the crime scenes," he said. "This court feels this testimony would be helpful to the jury, to the extent that Mr. Hazelwood's report and opinions do not seek to profile, Mr. Hazelwood's testimony will be allowed" (Greziak, 1999).

Essentially, Hazelwood could not discuss any link between his assessed behavioral traits of an unsub associated with this crime scene and specific characteristics of the defendant or his potential guilt. "We remain mindful that an opinion couched in terms of probabilities and/or possibilities is to be excluded as lacking the requisite certainty to be admissible as an expert witness" (Greziak, 1999).

Hazelwood took the stand and testified that the motive for the sexual crime was anger. Christine had been struck at least 12 times in the face and was manually strangled from the front. Transporting the body had increased the killer's risk of being seen. If he had meant only to kill her, then removing her clothing and positioning the body had been unnecessary. Thus, carrying her to the spot had satisfied a gratification ritual. The way she was posed, with her hair arranged, had meaning to him, but leaving her nude, with legs open, next to a dumpster, suggested hostility. He had then taken the clothing and sanitized the scene. This killer was careful, Hazelwood testified, intelligent, and not under the influence of drugs. He had given thought to what he was going to do; it had not been impulsive. Staging the scene as a burglary gone wrong was meant to deflect investigators, but an inexperienced person had done it. In addition, the offender had left no physical evidence behind. Taking the caller ID box suggested that he had called and left his ID on the tape and did not want this to be discovered (Hazelwood & Michaud, 2001).

In his report for the prosecutor (not stated in court), Hazelwood had detailed specific behaviors that matched DiStefano's traits and behaviors: killers often return to the scene, possibly to sanitize it or to relive it. They also want to see if the murder has been discovered because they want to see the press coverage. They might insert themselves into the investigation and even offer police suggestions. They provide third-person accounts. They seek attention. They collect trophies and news items. Often, they will contact the victim's family.

DiStefano was convicted of third-degree murder and given a 15- to 40-year sentence. He reportedly told a friend that he had killed Christine because she was a prostitute (Hazelwood & Michaud, 2001).

On appeal, the Superior Court of Pennsylvania agreed that DiStefano's confession, which he claimed had been coerced, should have been suppressed, because at the time he was questioned, the police did not advise him of his Miranda rights. The sentence was vacated. To avoid another trial, DiStefano agreed to enter a *nolo* plea to a charge of misdemeanor involuntary manslaughter and was released in 2001.

THE KEY ISSUE

As noted in Chapter 4 regarding behavioral analysis in the courtroom, expert testimony based in probability analysis can be introduced into the courtroom in only a qualified manner (if at all). *Frye* and *Daubert* standards, or some version of them, will guide evidence admissibility in all US jurisdictions. How behavioral evidence analysis is viewed has been inconsistent over the years, ranging from admitting completely subjective clinical judgment to barring genuinely scientific research. Cases that have successfully used the procedures of profiling or CIA are described here, especially in light of the 2009 National Academy of Sciences (NAS) report on the current state of the forensic sciences. Behavioral analysis attracted particular scrutiny. Attorneys who hope to use profiling or crime scene analysis as part of the totality of evidence for a case must be aware of the evolving legal climate.

When Congress directed the National Academies to assess the forensic science community in 2006, a distinguished committee from the NAS National Research Council had gathered to hear presentations from the primary forensic organizations. After 2 years, the committee issued a fairly critical report, "Strengthening Forensic Science in the United States: A Path Forward." This report found too much variability across the forensic disciplines in terms of expert qualifications, reliability of findings, and proof of claims—especially the claim to be basing procedures on the scientific method. Disciplines that involved biological or chemical analysis had an edge over fields based on subjective interpretation. The council recommended developing a better foundation in standards for mandatory accreditation and accountability. In view of the many exonerations of innocent people imprisoned for years—even decades—based on faulty or substandard procedures, it was time to hold the forensic sciences accountable (National Research Council, 2009).

For prosecutors, admissible evidence is that which is used to support a point in a case, such as to prove guilt beyond a reasonable doubt. Before it can be used, it must be evaluated according to several factors. Items irrelevant to a case are inadmissible, as are items collected in a manner that violates a law (e.g., no search warrant). The source of the evidence must also be credible. Sometimes, evidence is barred because it would arouse a highly emotional response without adding anything material to the case. Evidence that is considered misleading might be barred, as would most hearsay and any privileged evidence. Experts must prove their expertise with evidence of training, academic credentials, peer-reviewed publications, and/or solid experience, and the judge will decide if their expertise will assist the fact-finders with information they would not ordinarily know. (Judge O'Malley in the DiStefano case decided that Hazelwood's 16 years of experience in the FBI's BSU qualified him to testify about specialized knowledge of crime scene behavior that would assist the jury.) To be able to claim that one is following scientific protocols, that is, approaching facts with a method that can be objectively replicated under controlled conditions by competent practitioners, one must be able to show a testable hypothesis that fits the fullest array of facts, without distortion (Shelton, 2011). This has been challenging for behavioral analysis.

BEHAVIORAL SCIENCE AND THE PROFILER

In 1996, Clarence Simmons was arrested for killing a woman in Alabama. A profiler from the FBI testified in his trial that, based on victimology and the condition of the body, it had been a sexually motivated homicide. Simmons was convicted and he appealed, saying that the profiling testimony did not meet *Frye* criteria. The Court of Appeals stated that the testimony was not profiling, because the agent had not linked the characteristics evaluated from the scene to the defendant. (Note: The court appears to have misunderstood the method's purpose.) There was no doubt that the agent was an expert, but it was not clear that the method of evaluating victimology had a standard. Yet, the agent's expertise and enumeration of theories in support convinced the court that this was an expert assisting jurors with a specialized area of behavioral analysis. "Crime-scene analysis and victimology do not rest on scientific principles like those contemplated in *Frye*," said the court. "These fields constitute specialized knowledge. Specialized knowledge offers subjective observations and comparisons based on the expert's training, skill, or experience that may be helpful to the jury in understanding or determining the facts." The conviction stood (*Simmons v. State*, 1999).

The opposite result occurred in *State v. Stevens* in 2002. The former FBI profiler, hired for the defense, had 25 years of experience, but the Supreme Court of Tennessee decided that CIA did not meet the *Daubert* criteria for scientific reliability. The profiler had cited an FBI study that showed an accuracy rate of 75%–80%, but for several reasons the study was not trustworthy.

> ... [T]here is no testimony regarding how the FBI determined the accuracy rate of this analysis. For example, was accuracy determined by confessions or convictions, or both? Even then, the absence of a confession does not indicate the offender's innocence and thus an inaccuracy in the technique. Clearly, the accuracy rate alone, without any explanation of the methodologies used in the study, is insufficient to serve as the foundation for the admission of this testimony.

Ultimately in this case, expertise was insufficient for allowing the method to be used.

> [N]othing in either *Daubert* or the Federal Rules of Evidence requires a district court to admit opinion evidence which is connected to existing data only by the *ipse dixit* of the expert. A court may conclude that there is simply too great an analytical gap between the data and the opinion proffered ... Indeed, Mr. M___ himself acknowledged that his analysis involves some degree of speculation, and he further negated the sufficiency of his own analysis when he conceded that each case is "unique" and that criminals are often driven by any number of motives. (*State v. Stevens*, 2002)

Further, an appeals court in Ohio viewed profiling testimony as character evidence, which was inadmissible. A court in Maryland refused to allow profilers to use anecdotal cases for predicting the defendant's potential to be violent in the future. They found that it failed most of the *Daubert* criteria (Bosco, Zappala, & Santtila, 2010).

It seems that the *Daubert* criteria have shifted court opinion about behavioral profiling as evidence. The legal system now emphasizes the principles of reliability, regardless of whether the science is hard or soft. The same trend holds for courts in Canada, Australia, and Great Britain. The methods must be standardized within a scientific community (Bosco et al., 2010).

Behavioral science presents hurdles to these goals, due to interpretive ambiguity and shifting error rates with new research. Because clinical opinion derives from observation and subjective analysis, important questions are raised over whether it could meet the *Daubert* definition of reliable science (Brodin, 2004; Goodman, 2010; Shelton, 2011). This category includes profiling. While profiling has not been subjected to scientific analysis or testing that confirms its reliability or validity, some professionals have acted as if a profiler's judgment is unerring (Bosco et al., 2010).

The judge's gatekeeping task applies to profiling, and Judge O'Malley took this role seriously when he decided to prohibit its use in the DiStefano case. He had asked about the existence of a standard or even a textbook to which the relevant scientific community adheres, but none was cited. Through the mid-1990s, profiling was presented as forensic evidence, based on experience (Scherer & Jarvis, 2014a). FBI special agents, as well as other mental health professionals and criminologists, would describe its methods and applications, citing the few studies performed to reinforce its merits. The courts rendered opinions in three areas: motivational analysis, profile evidence, and linkage analysis (Bosco et al., 2010).

Because there had initially been no pressure to show the scientific method for drawing inferences, little research was done in this area. For years, it was accepted that experience was the primary factor for reliability and validity. Variability in application was not evaluated as a factor in accuracy, but this would certainly affect reliability. Although ViCAP analysis appears to minimize bias, in the DiStefano case Judge O'Malley dismissed ViCAP as being merely a sophisticated record-keeping system.

Critics of profiling state that the courtroom must guard against an inappropriate prioritization of a suspect, which can happen at the investigative level if profiling factors are overemphasized (Sherer & Jarvis, 2014a). Rainbow (2008) suggests that investigators use a hybrid approach that involves an evidence-based listing of the most likely suspect traits and behaviors for specific crimes, grounded in empirically confirmed psychological principles.

The FBI did conduct a study of how serial killers treat their victims as a way to standardize specific items for practical investigative purposes (Morton, Tillman, & Gaines, 2014). The agency presented a monograph that represented 5 years of empirical research to assist detectives with understanding criminal motivation and behavior that show correlation between crime scenes and suspects. The 92 offenders and 480 cases seem impressive at first, but (1) most of the specific research areas (travel routes, chosen body dump sites, etc.) used small, unrepresentative numbers; and (2) the claim that the study would be effective for law enforcement was not actually tested. As an overview of cases, the report offers a lot, but as a scientific analysis of CIA or of the study's purpose, it does not.

Even if solid methods were in place, the question could be asked whether those engaged in CIA possess some type of exceptional analytical ability that would support their claim to expertise. Certainly for legal proceedings, they should be more advanced than detectives (Scherer & Jarvis, 2014a). Yet does the research prove that they are? Although the studies thus far have relied on small subject numbers, profilers do perform marginally better in mock profile exercises. Yet this does not confirm expert superiority. In addition, there is no consensus or supportive research that confirms that mental health practitioners without law enforcement experience demonstrate expertise as profilers. Whether or not they should serve as adjunct consultants remains an open question, despite some anecdotal successes (Kocis, Irwin, Hayes, & Nunn, 2002).

USEFUL VERSUS SUCCESSFUL

There are difficulties with defining a success for the various forms of criminal profiling. It does not involve counting how many suggested traits and behaviors prove to be correct. Yet it has been a challenge to analyze the method's practical value to law enforcement, as well as to interpret this value for a *Daubert* hearing.

Most of the studies that evaluated profiling's usefulness were performed pre-*Daubert*, but a 2001 survey of 186 British detectives turned up a low figure of just 14.1% saying that profiling had helped to solve a case, yet nearly 83% said it was nevertheless useful (Scherer & Jarvis, 2014b). Thus, those who thought it was useful but had not used profiling to solve a case must have thought that it assisted in other ways. Often, through brainstorming with a profiler, detectives learned more ways to view a case, especially if the profiler had a lot of experience. Those who understood that profiling is just one tool, not a recipe for resolution, were the most satisfied. In another study with 27 respondents, 67.5% thought the profile had moved the case forward (Scherer & Jarvis, 2014b) and over half said they had gained some new ideas or methods. (It should be noted that ego can influence whether or not detectives will admit that external agents were helpful.)

LINKAGE ANALYSIS

The case of Jack Unterweger from Chapter 7 demonstrates how linkage analysis might be used in court. He was tried in Austria, and Gregg McCrary testified. McCrary described the ViCAP system and showed how the crimes were behaviorally linked. Lynne Herold, from the Los Angeles crime lab, demonstrated the signature knot that the killer had used on most of the victims. The court admitted this testimony and Unterweger was convicted. He did not attempt to appeal; instead he killed himself shortly after his conviction (McCrary & Ramsland, 2003).

We might suppose that a computerized analysis would strip data of bias and offer a more balanced result. This should provide the method of linkage analysis with a more stable foundation and potential claim to meet *Daubert* criteria. With over 100,000 cases on file, and the claim on the FBI's site of "an untold number of leads" and "countless suspects identified," along with increased sophistication in statistical measurements and comparisons, ViCAP-based claims appear more accurate than judgments based on a profiler's experience. Some courts agree; others remain cautious (FBI.gov).

An appeal in a US-based serial murder case resulted in opinions about the use of linkage analysis that had one state's legal officials deciding that another state's officials were in error.

In 1987–1988, several female victims were discovered along the I-40 corridor that runs through Maryland and Delaware. First, a prostitute was found at a construction site. Gouges on her left breast indicated that someone had used a tool on her, and the Delaware medical examiner found marks on her head that suggested being hit several times with a hammer. Duct tape was stuck in her hair (Ramsland, 2016).

It was 7 months before another woman was found in similar condition. On her body were blue trilobal fibers. Investigators visited a carpet store in New Jersey that provided carpeting of this texture and shade for vans and trucks. This did not lead to a suspect but went into the file.

The New Castle Police Department requested assistance from the FBI's BSU. Special Agents John Douglas and Steve Mardigan offered a behavioral profile that suggested that the perpetrator would be a white male between 25 and 35, with a connection to the construction business. He lived in the area and sought victims from prostitute hangouts. He used strangulation and binding to make them helpless before using the hammer to kill them. He would probably take trophies and carry a murder kit, which would contain tools, duct tape, a knife, a hammer, and possibly a gun. He might shift his MO somewhat, but the torture was important to him. He would kill again soon (Douglas & Munn, 1992; Ramsland, 2016).

Two more women soon disappeared. One was seen entering a blue van with round headlights, so investigators decided to set a trap, using a female officer as bait. She observed a medium-blue van with round headlights cruise past her. The driver checked her out, as if looking for a "date." She called in the tag number. It was registered to Steve Brian Pennell, 31, who lived nearby. When he pulled over, she flirted with him while surreptitiously collecting fibers from blue carpeting on the door of his van. Lab analysts said they were the right color and texture.

When another brutalized woman was found dead, the police watched Pennell as he cruised the I-40 corridor. He was pulled over for a traffic violation and his van was searched. Bloodstains allowed police to cut carpet swatches. With search warrants, they seized a buck knife from Pennell, eight pairs of pliers, a bag of flexicuffs, and two rolls of duct tape. Pennell was charged with three counts of first-degree murder.

His trial began on September 26, 1989. The state claimed that the cases were all related to a serial killer, so prosecutor Kathleen Jennings was allowed to introduce evidence from four victims. The fibers from one linked the victim to Pennell's van, and DNA matched her to the blood from the van. The hit kit tools provided strong circumstantial evidence, since the pliers fit her gouge wounds. Hair strands and fibers linked two other victims to Pennell.

From items in Pennell's van, victim wounds, and the undercover officer's description of Pennell's approach, it was easy to reconstruct his disturbing MO. When he saw a woman alone, he'd drive up to coax her into his van. In an isolated spot, he would threaten his companion with a knife and bind her with duct tape or flexicuffs. He might use pliers or a whip to torture her before beating her to death with a hammer.

Special Agent Douglas described pattern similarities of the wounds and the torture signature that linked the cases. The defense challenged by showing that the wounds did not match as well as Douglas had portrayed, but he countered that as the fantasies matured, the violence escalated and sometimes took different forms. (This remark demonstrates the slipperiness of behavioral interpretation: it can go either way, making both potentially right.)

The jury returned two guilty verdicts, giving Pennell life sentences. He appealed. Among his points was that the trial court abused its discretion in allowing expert testimony on linkage analysis.

The Delaware Supreme Court found that Pennell's reasoning regarding the FBI's testimony was misplaced, because Douglas's specialized expertise was necessary for the jury to better grasp the issues. The court said that none of his statements was overreaching. The convictions stood (*Pennell v. State*, 1991).

This decision assisted a case in California in which another convicted serial killer, Cleophus Prince, Jr., had similarly challenged the admissibility of FBI profilers. He claimed that the participation of a profiler was unnecessary and had made an impression on the jury that was unfair.

Prince's six murders had occurred between January and September 1990. All were white woman killed inside their homes early in the day, and five had been stabbed with a knife that was grabbed inside the residence (not brought). They were left face-up on the floor, partially or entirely nude. Five had been repeatedly stabbed in a distinct pattern centered on the chest. Based on DNA evidence on the only victim who was raped, Prince was convicted of that murder. The other five convictions rested on linkage analysis.

The California Supreme Court concluded that the testimony had been proper: the expert had described the FBI's method of linkage analysis but had not identified Prince as the guilty party. The expert testimony had been restricted to methodology, which offered knowledge beyond what a layperson could perform. The agent had not used the word "signature," because the trial court had ruled that it bordered on an analysis of psychological motive. He had made no claim that profiling was a science.

The court also noted that a profiler had testified in Delaware (the aforementioned Pennell case), and on appeal the Delaware Supreme Court had concluded that it was proper.

However, the New Jersey Supreme Court, examining *State v. Fortin*, had raised other issues. This court had concluded that the prosecution should not have used a profiler's testimony to link two murders, because the method did not pass the *Daubert* criteria. Compared to a DNA analysis, it fell short of being scientific. Prince's attorney's included this decision in their appeal. However, the justices in California decided that New Jersey had used an incorrect standard and made an unfair comparison. Thus, the *Fortin* case gave no weight to Prince's appeal. Pennell's case did. Prince's convictions stood (*People v. Prince*, 2007).

ULTIMATE ISSUES

The *Fortin* case presented other issues related to a profiler's testimony. In 1995, Steve Fortin pleaded guilty and received 20 years for a savage attack on a female state trooper in Maine. New Jersey officials investigating an unsolved case from August 1994 heard about the Fortin arrest and noted striking similarities. Both victims had been beaten, robbed, and bitten on the left breast and chin. The New Jersey victim had also been strangled. Investigators discovered that Fortin had lived in the New Jersey area at the time and had been at a restaurant that day near the crime scene. Fortin was indicted and went to trial.

Special Agent Roy Hazelwood testified about the MO and signature that linked the two cases. He explained that linkage analysis was not a science, but the deductive reasoning on which it was based involved training, education, research, and experience in working on thousands of violent crimes over an extended period of time. Providing 15 points of similarity between the Maine and New Jersey attacks, he described the high-risk nature of both incidents, the degree of impulsivity and anger evident, the geographic similarities of the crime scenes, and the nature of the trauma inflicted. Among other behaviors, he said that the bite marks and facial battering were too similar to be coincidence. They comprised a ritualistic signature, done for the perpetrator's emotional gratification. "In my 35 years of experience with a variety of violent crimes," Hazelwood testified, "I have never observed this combination of behaviors in a single crime of violence. The likelihood of different offenders committing two such extremely unique crimes is highly improbable. It is my opinion that the same person is responsible for the two crimes" (*State v. Fortin*, 2000). Fortin was convicted.

In 2000, aside from the lack of scientific credibility, the New Jersey Superior Court decided that Hazelwood had encroached on the ultimate legal issue, which is reserved for a jury. That is, he should have offered the similarities and allowed the jury to deduce the linkage and Fortin's guilt (Bosco et al., 2010). In 2004, Fortin's conviction was set aside. Retried again in 2007 with better physical evidence, Fortin was convicted again.

Whether it is a lack of a standard, a lack of error rate, or a lack of scientific studies, profiling testimony faces increasingly difficult challenges in the future. Some researchers are trying to determine if this method at least has general acceptance in a relevant professional community. More peer-reviewed articles have been published in professional journals, and there is greater sophistication among practitioners about admissibility criteria. Still, consensus among professionals who use profiling (or CIA) in some capacity is still lacking.

Torres, Boccaccini, and Miller (2006) conducted a survey with 161 forensic psychologists and psychiatrists to evaluate attitudes about the scientific nature of profiling and whether it had practical utility. The descriptions included geographic profiling, behavioral evidence analysis, CIA, and profiling methods from "investigative psychology." They noted that the number of different approaches made it difficult to perform standardized research, because they include different methods and supporting theories.

Only 10% of respondents in this study had experience with a profiling method (since forensic psychology and psychiatry are concerned more often with evaluations for the court than with consulting for law enforcement). When renamed "CIA," 40% thought it was scientifically valid and reliable versus less than 25% who evaluated "profiling." In other words, the label conveyed an impression, which is bad news for the scientific nature of such evaluations. It means that the respondents did not quite know what they were evaluating. Despite this lack of scientific support, 86% thought that profiling was useful for law enforcement and 94% thought CIA was useful. Ninety-seven percent affirmed that empirical research should be performed. They found that professionals did have concerns about the scientific merit of profiling, but these same professionals did not view this as a reason to prevent it from being used in court. That is, without clear evidence for either position (it is or is not scientific), these respondents thought that there was insufficient reason to prevent it from being used in court.

One line of research focused on reliability and accuracy, but such studies are rare and often flawed or outdated. A 1985 study involved just six FBI profilers on the question of how to classify crime scenes (organized, disorganized, mixed, or unknown). Not surprisingly, since they had all been trained in this method, there was 74% agreement. However, the participant size was too small to take such results seriously. In general, profilers are disinclined to participate in such studies and no study has replicated actual field conditions. Profilers did perform better than untrained psychologists, students, psychics, and detectives, but there was notable variability within the profiling group (Kocis, 2003).

Even today, there is little standardization. For various reasons, no textbook is accepted as the bible of profiling. An early FBI-generated study that questioned law enforcement agencies on how well a profile had worked was skewed, because it was strictly voluntary and because some agencies might have responded positively to show appreciation to the FBI for its free services. In addition, there might be disagreement among detectives in any given department about whether or not to take the method seriously. Not surprisingly, profiling is well regarded among those who do it and less so among those whose disciplines overlap some of the techniques (Kocis, Irwin, Hayes, & Nunn, 2000). Detectives, for example, often fail to see the need for a profiler because they think it adds nothing to what they can do themselves. Clearly, more information is needed about how to study this method's effectiveness and whether it can achieve the status of a science.

Scherer and Jarvis (2014c) described a survey of 40 practitioners (retired FBI personnel, individuals who had worked with the BAU, and FBI-trained individuals) on various aspects of CIA services and legal proceedings. This included direct testimony and assisting with trial preparation. Just over half gave a qualified "maybe" to the question about whether CIA should be admitted in court, with 87% saying that *profiling* should not be admitted. Crime scene analysis testimony had just 65% naysayers. (Equivocal death investigation, interestingly, had high ratings: 92.5% thought it should be allowed.) Just over half thought that profilers could be "education experts" on such things as staging and sexual homicide. Fifteen percent of respondents thought that experts in CIA should be allowed to assist with trial preparation.

This brings us to the final subject: consulting with attorneys.

OTHER ROLES

Even if profiling methods are not admitted, prosecutors might seek consultation from a profiler on a range of other subjects, because CIA encompasses other activities. The 40 participants in the above-mentioned study listed three distinct areas: behavioral testimony by proxy, jury selection, and case presentation (Scherer & Jarvis, 2014c). Testimony by proxy means that analysts assist prosecutors with how to incorporate keys items into other testimony, so that profiling methods are never raised on appeal. For jury selection, they watch videos to assist with behavioral interpretation and construct juror questionnaires. The third option means that the profiler might teach crime scene analysis to the prosecutor, to show the best strategies for questioning witnesses and for opening or closing arguments. In the Wayne Williams trial in Atlanta, for example, John Douglas instructed the prosecutor to put pressure on Williams, because he had the kind of personality that would eventually react and probably say something that would implicate him. In fact, Williams did get angry while on the stand about the profile that had been done (Douglas & Olshaker, 1995).

As with law enforcement, profilers can offer assistance to court personnel in recognizing personality traits and behaviors that are consistent with certain types of crimes. The profiler can also clarify other aspects of forensic evidence, explain technical angles, and help to reconstruct the crime. They can offer information on typical behaviors before, during, and after a crime to shed light on how offenders might have been thinking when they made certain decisions, and they can instruct on such concepts as "undoing," personation or signature, and staging (Ramsland, 2010).

Profilers should also be familiar with psychological states, because their expertise overlaps that of clinical psychologists and psychiatrists. The legal system relies on the belief that people are generally rational and that they freely make decisions. Thus, they are responsible for their behavior. Mental health professionals can weaken this link by introducing factors that mitigate culpability. The law recognizes that responsibility for committing a crime depends on evidence that the accused did engage in the act and did have the requisite intention or ability to foresee its consequences (*mens rea*). The latter involves areas of competency and defenses for insanity, emotional disturbance, or diminished capacity. When experts in CIA testify about crime scene behavior, they might also address mental state, particularly evidence of psychopathology. Thus, they must be familiar with the psychological literature associated with such things as paraphilias, sexual additions, rage disorders, ritualized behavior, paranoid psychosis, and personality disorders. However, clinicians, not profilers, will generally evaluate these items for legal purposes.

SUMMARY: BEHAVIORAL EVIDENCE IN PERSPECTIVE

Behavioral profiling depends on the same probability analysis technique as psychological autopsy and is correctly scrutinized for admissibility. Database analyses assist with rigor for some items, and recent attempts to standardize methodologies make them increasingly more valuable for investigators today. However, there is still no standard, no known error rate based on solid research, no clarity on the relevant scientific community, and no consensus on specific profiling methods. In jurisdictions that use *Daubert* criteria, admissibility is clearly not met by reference to investigative experience alone. Just as the emphasis on science over the past decade has called other forensic areas into accountability, offender profiling should be among them. If the task proves too difficult, then judges like O'Malley in the DiStefano case are correct to be skeptical. Whether profilers can speak to crime scene analysis more proficiently than case detectives for jury education also remains to be proven. Unlike psychological autopsy, which does require psychological expertise that goes beyond the training detectives receive, it is less clear that criminal profiling enjoys a privileged status.

In the final chapter, we show both methods for analyzing a couple of cases.

REFERENCES

Bosco, D., Zappala, A., & Santtıla, P. (2010). The admissibility of offender profiling in courtroom: A review of legal and court opinions. *International Journal of Law and Psychiatry*, *33*, 184–191.

Brodin, M. S. (2004–05). Behavioral science evidence in the age of *Daubert*: Reflections of a skeptic. *University of Cincinnati Law Review*, *73*, 867–943.

Commonwealth v. DiStefano. *PICS Case No. 99–0640*, 2000.

Douglas, J., & Munn, C. (1992). Modus operandi and the signature aspects of violent crime. In J. E. Douglas, A. W. Burgess, A. G. Burgess, & R. K. Ressler (Eds.). *Crime Classification Manual* (pp. 259–268). New York: Lexington.

Douglas, J., & Olshaker, M. (1995). *Mindhunter: Inside the FBI's elite serial crime unit*. New York: Scribner.

Goodman, M. (2010). A hedgehog on the witness stand – What's the big idea? The challenges of using *Daubert* to assess social science and non-scientific testimony. *American University Law Review*, *59*(6), 35–685.

Greziak, H. (1999, April 12) Profiling testimony inadmissible in murder trial. *Pennsylvania Law Weekly*. Retrieved from http://www.corpus-delicti.com/court_hazelwalter.html

Hazelwood, R., & Michaud, S. G. (2001). *Dark dreams: Sexual violence, homicide, and the criminal mind*. New York: St. Martin's Press.

Kocis, R. N. (2003). Criminal psychological profiling: Validities and abilities. *International Journal of Offender Therapy and Comparative Criminology*, *47*, 126–144.

Kocis, R. N., Irwin, H. J., Hayes, A. F., & Nunn, R. (2000). Expertise in psychological profiling: A comparative assessment. *Journal of Interpersonal Violence*, *15*, 311–331.

Kocis, R. N., Irwin, H. J., Hayes, A. F., & Nunn, R. (2002). Investigative experience and accuracy in psychological profiling of a violent crime. *Journal of Interpersonal Violence*, *17*(8), 811–823.

McCrary, G., & Ramsland K. (2003). *The unknown darkness: Profiling the predators among us.* New York: Morrow.

Morton, R. J., Tillman, J. M., & Gaines, S. J. (2014). *Serial murders: Pathways for investigations.* Retrieved from https://www.fbi.gov/file-repository/serialmurder-pathwaysforinvestigations.pdf/view

National Research Council. (2009). *Strengthening forensic science in the United States: A path forward.* Document No.: 228091. Washington, DC: National Academy of Sciences, National Academic Press.

Pennell v. State. (1991). 602 A2d. 48. Del.

People v. Prince. (2007). SO36105, Supreme Court of California.

Rainbow, L. (2008). Taming the beast: The U.K.'s approach to the managements of behavioral investigative advice. *Journal of Police and Criminal Psychology, 23*(2), 90–97.

Ramsland, K. (2010). *The forensic psychology of criminal minds.* New York: Berkley.

Ramsland, K. (2016). *The corridor killer.* Washington, DC: Crime USA.

Scherer, A., & Jarvis, J. (2014a). Criminal investigative analysis: Practitioner perspectives (Part Two). *FBI Law Enforcement Bulletin.* https://leb.fbi.gov/2014/june/criminal-investigative-analysis-practicioner-perspectives-part-two-of-four

Scherer, A., & Jarvis, J. (2014b). Criminal investigative analysis: Practitioner perspectives (Part Three). *FBI Law Enforcement Bulletin.* https://leb.fbi.gov/2014/june/criminal-investigative-analysis-practicioner-perspectives-part-three-of-four

Scherer, A., & Jarvis, J. (2014c). Criminal investigative analysis: Skills, expertise, and training (Part Four). *FBI Law Enforcement Bulletin.* https://leb.fbi.gov/2014/june/criminal-investigative-analysis-practicioner-perspectives-part-four-of-four

Shelton, D. E. (2011). *Forensic science in court: Challenges in the 21st century.* New York: Rowman & Littlefield.

Simmons v. State. (1999, Sept. 17). CR-97-0768 AL.

State v. Fortin. (2000). 724 A 2d 509 NJ.

State v. Stephens. (2002, May 14). No. M1999-02067-SC-DDT-DD. TN.

Torres, A. N., Boccaccini, M. T., & Miller, H. A. (2006). Perceptions of the validity and utility of criminal profiling among forensic psychologists and psychiatrists. *Professional Psychology Research and Practice, 37*(1), 51–58.

CHAPTER **10**

Behavioral Analyses in Perspective

Intelligence specialist and Navy Petty Officer Amanda Jean Snell failed to report for duty on July 13, 2009, at the Office of the Chief of Naval Operations at the Pentagon. Someone looked for her in her room in Keith Hall. The door was unlocked, but no one was there, and Amanda did not respond to her name. Nothing looked out of place. Then, someone opened her locker door. She was there, wedged into a small space with a pillowcase over her head. She had suffocated.

Yet, her manner of death was unclear. A victimology showed that 20-year-old Amanda had clear plans for her life. She had volunteered as a youth minister, and she hoped to teach in special education. On her social media, she had described her sense of purpose. Although she had a good relationship with her family and several close friendships, she had expressed feeling isolated in her current situation. She had made few friends, but she also had no known enemies.

The Naval Criminal Investigative Service (NCIS) came in to investigate, but a crime scene analysis turned up very little. Amanda's room was undisturbed, so there had been no struggle. No one had broken in. If she were killed, it seemed likely that she knew her killer, perhaps even trusted this person. Other residents of Keith Hall were questioned and cleared. The manner of death remained undetermined.

One suggestion was that this was an accident. Amanda had suffered from migraine headaches and might have crawled into the locker to block out the light. However, her mother refused to accept that anyone would hold a pillow so close that she would inadvertently smother herself. Some investigators wondered if she might have grown depressed and committed suicide. Again, there was no indication of suicide factors, although no one did a full work-up. Suicide seemed like a greater possibility when accident and homicide seemed unlikely and natural causes were ruled out.

However, NCIS missed a crucial clue that a profiler would have noticed. (Recall Hazelwood's comments during the DiStefano case.)

A resident of Keith Hall, Jorje Torrez, approached the investigators and offered to assist. He lived just a few rooms away from Amanda. So he injected himself into the investigation. The officers decided to accept. With the hope of spooking the perpetrator, they asked him to float a rumor that someone had been seen entering her room. Torrez agreed to do it, but nothing came of this strategy and the case went cold. Only later, after other incidents occurred in the area, was there reason to reexamine this scene.

During a snowstorm in the DC area, police noticed a silver Durango cruising around with no apparent purpose but then they left the area. The driver was following a woman. He approached her and used a knife and a gun to try to force her into his Durango. She managed to break away and run. Reporting it, she provided a description to a sketch artist.

Two weeks later near the same area, a man followed two young women on their way home around 3 a.m. With a knife and pistol, he forced them into their house, bound them with whatever cord he could grab, forced one woman into his car, and drove off. The other woman called the police and provided a description.

The kidnapper parked, raped his victim, and drove into an isolated area to dump her. He used a scarf to strangle her before leaving her. She survived. A couple driving by rescued her and she described her assailant as a young man driving a silver SUV.

An officer who had noted the silver SUV during the snowstorm ran the number. It came back to their helpful Marine, Jorge Torrez. The victims who had seen his face positively identified him from the photo. All of them said that he had seemed uncertain, inexperienced, and clumsy.

Questioned, Torrez was cagey but cooperative. There was sufficient evidence in his car to arrest him. On his computer was behavioral evidence of a coercive paraphilia: a collection of rape and suffocation pornography. Despite his gentle, youthful demeanor, this suggested that he was capable of serious acts of violence against women.

As they prepared for Torrez' trial, detectives from Zion, Illinois, showed up with a case file from 2005. Two girls, aged 8 and 9, had been murdered. Both had been stabbed and one was sexually assaulted. The father of one of the girls had been convicted based on his confession, which he claimed had been coerced. He faced the death penalty. Thanks to the Combined DNA Index System (CODIS) database, the Illinois officers realized they had convicted the wrong man. Torrez' DNA turned up in one of the murdered girls and he had lived in Zion at the time. He had been just 16. In addition, a witness had seen him with the girls that day. Police had interviewed him as a witness. He had been helpful.

That is, he had figured out how to deflect attention.

Then, there was Amanda Snell, killed in a way consistent with Torrez' preferred paraphilia. It was time to reinterview him. Her bedding had never been tested, because no one had been sure that her death was a homicide. Had they performed a full victimology and psychological autopsy, with the known indicators of suicide, perhaps it would have been clear that they should get this testing done—especially when Torrez initiated contact with investigators. DNA found in the sheets came back to Torrez as the source. He was not just a rapist; Torrez was a serial killer.

In jail, he bragged about the murders and plotted to have his accusers killed. He did not realize that an informant was recording him. Dishonorably discharged, he went to trial and was convicted on multiple charges, including the Snell murder (Jaffe, 2012). Torrez received a death sentence.

In a case this complicated, where a killer stages a scene to resemble a suicide, psychological autopsy complements criminal profiling. Examining Amanda Snell's life for suicide indicators using IS PATH WARM would have shown nothing except some complaints about feeling isolated. No anger, no ideation, no hopelessness, and just average anxiety. A profiler would have been alert to Torrez' offer of help, especially since he lived close to Amanda's room. Experts on extreme offenders would not have accepted a friendly gesture at face value, since they would know about cases like Dennis Rader, Ted Bundy, and John Joubert. When suicide did not seem likely, profilers would have suggested a more comprehensive investigation. Torrez could have been caught at this point. Although linkage analysis would not have assisted in this case, because the behaviors were different, a database did. However, Torrez' behavior in the Illinois case was similar to the Amanda Snell case. A criminal profile was not needed for court, since physical evidence was sufficient, but a profiler could have assisted the prosecution with strategies based on Torrez' manipulations, paraphilias, and inept criminality. Being a Marine, he would probably have reacted to suggestions that he had lost control and was not as good at his crimes as he believed. In addition, a behavioral analyst could have discussed the staging behavior.

Besides ongoing cases, a combination of psychological autopsy and criminal profiling can assist with cold cases. Following is a complicated case that had behavioral ambiguities that continue to confuse. This one starts with profiling a crime scene and ends with an analysis of a murder–suicide, or suicide pact. Cold case work is also vulnerable to a particular type of cognitive error.

COLD CASE

Among the most glaring problems for cold cases are (1) gaps in information, which can lead to (2) working within an incomplete frame that gradually feels complete. Investigators can come to believe they are working with all of the facts merely because they have mastered the set of facts available. The urge to get closure supports this illusion. In addition, reporting mechanisms from past decades might contain undetected bias or imprecise information that was good enough for investigations at the time, such as in the following case from 1934.

On the morning of November 24, John E. Clark and his nephew Clark Jardine picked up firewood in the woods off Rt. 233 near Pine Grove Furnace on South Mountain in Cumberland County, Pennsylvania. They went along a dirt road and spotted a green blanket about 50 feet away, under bushes. Clark thought it might be a deer carcass. He walked over to look underneath, only to see the corpse of a fully dressed young girl lying on her side. Knowing something about police protocol, he dropped the blanket, but he could see from the outlines that something else was under it.

The state police arrived within an hour, with coroner E.A. Haegele and District Attorney Fred J. Templeton. Under the blanket, they discovered the bodies of three young girls, dressed in coats with fur collars, lying on their right sides next to each other. They looked like sisters. The smallest one lay in the middle. Underneath them was another blanket, damp from released urine. Nothing with the bodies assisted to identify them. Even the manufacturer tags had been removed from their clothing. Based on weather conditions and dampness on the top blanket, it was assumed that they had been placed there during the night before it had rained, or possibly earlier ("Three girls slain," 1934).

Two days later, a hunter heard the news and gave police a black leather Gladstone bag that he had found just over 2 miles from the girls' bodies. It contained clothing for children and adults, as well as a notebook. Inside, in a child's scribble, was the name "Norma."

Police were already wondering about another connection. On the same day that the children were found, around the same time, the bodies of a young couple were discovered inside a deserted railroad flag-stop near Duncansville, 100 miles northwest of Pine Grove Furnace. Both had been shot 8–10 hours earlier, the woman twice. It appeared to have been a suicide pact. The first shot to the woman's heart had not damaged her clothing, which she appeared to have held out of the way. It was a close-range wound. The man was shot in the side of the head. As reports came in from witnesses who had seen them walking on the tracks, an abandoned 1929 blue Pontiac sedan was located at a lovers' lane in Mifflin County. It had a burned tube on the exhaust pipe but no license plate or gas. Were these two decedents related in some way to the children? If so, there were many other questions.

Thanks to widespread press accounts and serial numbers from the car, relatives were located in California. They helped investigators piece together a story. Yet some of it made no sense. The dead man was Elmo Noakes, 32. Two of the girls were his daughters, Dewilla, 10, and Cordelia, 8. Noakes' wife, Mary, had died during a self-administered abortion 2 years earlier. The oldest girl, Norma, who was 12, was Mary's daughter with another man, who had sued after her death to get custody. Noakes had left Utah at this time to move to California. The adult female victim from the Duncansville incident was Noakes' 18-year-old niece, Winifred Pierce, who had dropped out of high school. She had helped him take care of his children but did not live in his house. There were rumors among relatives that their relationship was improper.

Autopsies conducted by two physicians, with blood analysis, ruled out carbon monoxide poisoning or any type of known and testable poison. Dr. Milton Walter Eddy from Dickinson College conducted hair analysis to determine what chemicals the girls might have ingested. The children's brains were turned over to Dr. Moffitt for further examination.

Haegele could not identify a definitive cause of death but concluded that the girls had been smothered. It seemed likely that their father was their killer, although he could not rule out Winnifred. The younger ones had shown evidence of nosebleeds. They had not died from strangulation or blows, although Norma had a nasty bruise on her swollen forehead and a scratch on her cheek. The coroner thought there was evidence of sexual molestation on Dewilla, the middle girl, because there was some genital irritation. It appeared that they had not eaten in 18 hours (although this indicator is deceptive). They had been dead from 12 to 72 hours before being placed in the woods.

A restaurant owner in Philadelphia reported that a family had come in recently. The man was looking for work. He mentioned that his children had become a "burden" and he had been unable to buy meals for them. It seemed possible that Noakes had tried getting work. Failing, he had committed filicide and then suicide.

Noakes' relatives recalled that his mother had recently purchased a 1929 Pontiac sedan for him, the first car he had owned. The next day, the entire family had vanished, with money still due on the car. Noakes had failed to pick up 2 weeks of severance pay owed to him ($50), possibly because the only way to get it was to say he was quitting and, from other behavior, it seemed clear that he did not want anyone to know about his trip east. The reason remains unknown.

As of November 10, Noakes had given no indication to family that he was leaving. The departure was hasty: food was on the table in his home and lights were on. He left California on November 11, covering 3,000 miles in 7 days in an unfamiliar car. He seemed to have failed in his mission, whatever it was, and had begun the trip west, going more slowly. He settled his retinue at a tourist camp in Langhorne on November 18 and remained for two nights. He and Winnifred went to the movies while the girls starved. The girls probably died on November 21. Elmo and Winifred placed the bodies and drove away, possibly trying to use the car to commit suicide. The tube on the tailpipe and the empty gas tank suggested they had tried this method and failed. They had hitch-hiked to Altoona.

They spent the night of November 22 at the Congress Hotel. The next day, Elmo attempted but failed to sell his glasses. Instead, he sold Winifred's coat, whereby he acquired $2.85 to purchase a defective single-shot Stevens .22 rifle. They walked along the railroad track until they reached the station. They were seen here on Friday night, November 23. They were discovered dead the following morning. One of them had set a small fire in the abandoned shed where their bodies were found, as if burning some papers. The autopsy reports were not available for them, but newspaper accounts indicated that Winnifred had never been pregnant. Her virginity was not confirmed.

As detectives identified Noakes and pieced together his route, it seemed that he had used fictitious names: J.C. Gardner, J.C. Malone, and J.C. Cowden. It was possible that he was trying to avoid the court order that had been served in Utah to turn over Norma to her biological father, although it had no weight in California. Yet this would not account for the haste in which he left or drove to his apparent destination, Philadelphia. Noakes had served honorably in the Marine Corps until April 1922. It seemed that he had worked a number of jobs temporarily, sometimes leaving the family for long periods to go work elsewhere. Why he had not sold the clothing in the Gladstone bag to get money, or sold the car, remains a mystery.

Family gossip, picked up by *True Story* magazine, was that Elmo and Winifred were romantically involved. The article had been written by the girls' aunt but possibly revised by staff writers. Accordingly, Elmo became physically abusive every time Mary was pregnant. She had health issues after the birth of Dewilla and had a miscarriage before Cordelia was born. Yet relatives insisted that Elmo had been a good father.

Other theories were suggested for cause of death that would make it an accident. Yet no one could explain why Elmo would have left his children on a blanket by the side of the road rather than take them to a hospital. One idea was that he believed he could marry his niece in Pennsylvania but then discovered he could not. However, he did not need to travel the entire length of the state to learn this. There seemed to be a reason he went to Philadelphia, but no one could discover it. He did not seem to know anyone there and witnesses said he did not ask about anyone or any addresses.

A later family theory, hoping to cast a more benign light, was that Noakes (and potentially his whole family) had lead poisoning from living and working in mining areas of Eureka, Utah. Mining operations during this period used zinc, arsenic, mercury, and lead. However, lead poisoning does not account for some of his actions, and he did not have quite a few of the most common symptoms (Smith, 2014).

Although this cold case was not fully resolved, the manner of death is clear, although with hints of familial abuse from a father with anger issues and an inability to make his life work. Meticulous behavioral analysis assists to dismiss some notions, even if it cannot resolve all of the questions.

A cold case mentioned in Chapter 6, in which child killer John Joubert was linked to an unsolved murder in Maine, also demonstrates the value of behavioral interpretation for linkage analysis. So does the case above involving Torrez.

SUMMARY

Psychological analysis has its challenges when it comes to the type of certainty that the courts desire. However, this does not negate its value. Whether an investigator needs a psychological autopsy or a profile and whether it is for determining manner of death, linking crimes, or detecting staging, behavioral analysis remains an important aspect of evaluating and reconstructing incidents. The more investigators collect and interpret how to learn the finer points of mental state and human behavior, the fewer errors will be made.

REFERENCES

Jaffe, H. (2012, September 11). Predator within the ranks: A real-life NCIS murder case. *Washingtonian*. Retrieved from https://www.washingtonian.com/2012/09/11/predator-in-the-ranks-inside-a-real-life-ncis-murder-case/

Smith, D. (2014). *The three babes in the woods story*. Carlisle, PA: Cumberland County Historical Society.

Three girls slain and left in woods under blankets. (1934, November 25). *New York Times*, p. A-1.

Glossary

Psychological terms and concepts are defined for easy reference.

asphyxiophilia: Sexual arousal from asphyxiation.

assortative relating: Like-minded people tend to form groups, which can be a cause of suicide contagion.

autoerotic fatality (AEF): A death that occurs as the result of a dangerous erotic ritual that goes wrong, such as a safety mechanism not working.

behavioral evidence: Forensic evidence suggestive of certain behaviors, generally used for criminal profiling.

behavioral profiling: See *criminal profiling.*

Behavioral Analysis Unit (BAU): The investigative part of the National Center for the Analysis of Violent Crime, specific to threat, serial crimes, and terrorism; formerly the Behavioral Science Unit.

Behavioral Science Unit (BSU): The first name for BAU, the unit of special agents who learned how to read behavioral evidence at crime scenes to assist in extreme crimes such as serial murder.

burdensomeness: A primary suicide marker.

cause of death: The conditions that led to a death, such as disease or wounds.

coercive suicide: When a suicidal person decides to make others die during his suicidal event.

cognitive errors: Poorly formed opinions from observation and perception due to mental shortcuts that are natural to the human brain, for example, tunnel vision and confirmation bias.

crime reconstruction: Using evidence to determine the sequence and types of actions involved in a crime or series of crimes.

criminal investigative analysis: The FBI's structured approach to identifying whether a crime occurred, what type of crime it is, and how it should be profiled and managed.

criminal profiling: The use of observation of the crime scene and pattern of crimes to determine investigatively relevant characteristics of the perpetrator; it guides police in narrowing the field of suspects and devising a strategy for questioning.

***Daubert* ruling:** A 1993 court decision about the admissibility of scientific evidence. The court decides whether the methodology is scientific and can be applied to the facts at issue.

disorganized offender: A person who commits a crime haphazardly or opportunistically, using weapons at the scene and often leaving clues; usually has a history of mental instability.

echo cluster: After an initial cluster suicide, others occur on an anniversary.

emulation suicide: A copycat suicide that mimics an initial suicide; the Werther effect.

equivocal death analysis: See *psychological autopsy.*

evidence: Documents, statements, and all items that are included in the legal proceedings for the jury's sole consideration in the question of guilt or innocence.

***Frye* standard:** A test that governs the admissibility of scientific evidence, such that evidence entered into a case must be generally accepted by the relevant scientific community.

geographic profiling: Using aspects of a geographical relationship among crime scenes to infer offender characteristics.

high-risk victim: A person continually exposed to danger, such as a prostitute or drug addict.

incident reconstruction: Use of physical and behavioral evidence to figure out the sequence of events at a death scene.

intent: Mental state ranging from purpose to awareness of consequences.

IS PATH WARM: A mnemonic device for quickly evaluating suicidal vulnerability.

lethality: Degree of a person's involvement in his or her suicide, including knowledge about the method used and access to it.

linkage analysis: Using evidence, particularly behavioral, from a series of crime scenes to indicate that they are associated with a specific offender or set of offenders.

linkage blindness: Failing to see the commonalities among crime scenes that associate them with a specific offender or set of offenders.

manner of death: The NASH classification system that labels a death as one of the following: natural, accident, suicide, homicide, or undetermined.

mass cluster: Widespread suicides in response to a highly publicized suicide, such as that of a celebrity.

mass suicide: Cults that elect to commit "groupmind" suicide, as a unified body.

***mens rea*:** The mental state that accompanies a forbidden act, required for conviction.

modus operandi (MO): An offender's method of carrying out the offense.

MSO: Acronym for *mental state at the time of the offense*; usually referring to legal proceedings.

NASH classification: See *manner of death.*

National Center for the Analysis of Violent Crime (NCAVC): The FBI's organizational structure that combines research, operations, training, consulting, and investigation to support local jurisdictions investigating unusual or repetitive crimes.

organized offender: A person committing a crime in a planned, premeditated manner, leaving few or no clues.

paraphilia: Deviant forms of sexual behavior in which people get fixated for sexual arousal on items, activities, or events; necrophilia, cannibalism, and vampirism are common among serial killers.

point cluster: A number of suicides occurring closely in time and place, related to one another.

postmortem: After death.

probability analysis: Calculation of data based on inductive reasoning or the likelihood of something occurring, based on known incidents.

profiler: A mental health professional or law enforcement officer with behavioral science training who helps to determine the traits of an unknown offender from aspects of the victim and crime scene.

prospective profiling: Devising a series of behaviors of a type of offender, prior to a crime being committed, and for use in threat assessment.

pseudocide: The act of faking one's own death, often through a staged suicide or accident.

psychache: Edwin Shneidman's term for a mental pain that is too difficult to bear.

psychological autopsy: Method used to determine the state of mind of a person where the scene of a suicide is ambiguous and therefore questionable; also to make a determination about manner of death.

psychosis: A major mental disorder in which a person's ability to think, respond, communicate, recall, and interpret reality is impaired. They show inappropriate mood, poor impulse control, and delusions. Often confused with *insanity*, which is a legal term for *lack of awareness of wrongfulness*.

qualitative analysis: Collecting narrative data and using methods such as inter-rater reviews for reliability.

risk factors for suicide: The list of factors that are often precursors to a suicidal mentality.

retrospective profiling: Assessing behavior at a crime scene to devise a portrait of the unsub; see also *criminal profiling*.

serial crimes: Any type of crime occurring in a pattern that indicates a single offender or criminal team.

serial killer: According to the FBI's new definition (since 2005), an offender who kills at least two different people in two separate events.

signature: A crime scene that bears a personality stamp of an offender, characteristic of a need for ritual or theme. These acts are not necessary to complete the offense. Also called *personation*.

staged crime scene: A disposal site where an offender has arranged the body and other items to serve a ritual fantasy; also a scene made to look like something other than what it actually is, such as a staged domestic homicide made to look like a suicide.

suicide cluster: After an initiating suicide, others also kill themselves in response.

suicide contagion: Negative impact of a suicide on a vulnerable person, who is in danger of repeating the act; the Werther effect.

suicide hotspot: A specific location that tends to draw people intent on committing suicide, such as a high building or bridge.

suicide markers: Indicators of a person's vulnerability to committing suicide, identified through research.

suicidology: The science of analyzing suicide data for prediction and treatment.

testamentary capacity: Mental state during decisions about one's last will and testament.

threat assessment: The procedure for determining how likely it is that a certain person or group might become violent in the future.

UNSUB: The term used in criminal profiling to refer to an *unknown subject*.

ViCAP (Violent Criminal Apprehension Program): The FBI's nation-wide data information center, designed for collecting, sorting, and analyzing information about crimes.

victimology: A study of victim information to find clues about the offender's opportunity and selection process.

Werther Effect: See *emulation suicide*; *suicide contagion*.

Index